D1394047

ULTIMATE
CAT

ULTIMATE

CAT

DAVID TAYLOR

BVMS, FRCVS

COMMISSIONED PHOTOGRAPHY BY

DAVE KING • JANE BURTON

LONDON, NEW YORK, MELBOURNE,
MUNICH, DELHI

Original edition (1989)
Project Editor: Maria Pal
Project Art Editor: Liz Black
Editors: Elizabeth Eyres, Elizabeth Nicholson
Designers: Martyn Foote, Christian Sevigny
Managing Editor: Vicky Davenport
Managing Art Editor: Colin Walton

This edition
FOR DORLING KINDERSLEY
Senior Editor: Simon Tuite
Senior Art Editor: Joanne Doran
Managing Editor: Deirdre Headon
Managing Art Editor: Lee Griffiths
DTP Designer: Louise Waller
Production Manager: Lauren Britton
Production Controller: Kevin Ward
Picture Researcher: Diana Morris
Picture Library: Claire Bowers

FOR SANDS PUBLISHING SOLUTIONS
Project Editors Sylvia & David Tombesi-Walton
Project Art Editor Simon Murrell

Produced for Dorling Kindersley by
Sands Publishing Solutions
4 Jenner Way, Eccles, Aylesford, Kent ME20 7SQ

Contents

The Essential Cat

One of the most finely designed of hunting carnivores, the cat has been refined over the ages to become the creature we know today. Unlike the gregarious canine, the cat has taken the road to individuality and self-reliance. It hunts alone using its well-honed arts of stealth, ambush, and lightning foray. There is little difference between the domestic feline and its wild relatives, and so we see in our pet cat a character that it shares with the wildcats of the Scottish forests and the tigers of the mangrove forests of Bangladesh.

The cat displays the disdain, nobility, and hauteur of the knight errant or the samurai and, like them, is a polished exponent of the martial arts. The cat is also elegant and neat in all its movements. Whereas the dog is prone to fawning before human friends, the cat gives friendship and love cautiously and on an even-handed basis. A cat's respect and affection must be earned.

Behind the handsome face and piercing gaze of the cat there is always a tantalizing, inscrutable something – the exotic, secret centre that harks back to an ancient connection with sacred cults and the black arts. Cats are truly magic.

A UNIQUE BEING The cat is a fur-wrapped enigma. Self-possessed, independent, and likely to change its mind, yet importuning and beguiling. Owned by no man, but rather lodging with good friends.

Origins and Domestication

Domestic cats are a fairly recent evolutionary development that can be first traced back to Ancient Egypt. However, the history of the cat began several million years ago.

THE EARLY MAMMALS

About 65 to 70 million years ago, the close of the great age of the dinosaurs was witnessed by a new and rather insignificant sort of animal that, to any observer at the time, might have seemed to bear little promise of success in the evolutionary stakes. These were the first mammals: small, tree-climbing, long-nosed, insect-eating, and not very bright.

As the millennia passed, these primitive mammals took different pathways of development. Some became herbivores, whereas others preferred to concentrate on a diet of meat, in the form of other animals. These latter, meat-eating mammals were the earliest ancestors of the cat.

THE EVOLUTION OF CREODONTS

The first carnivorous mammals, called creodonts, had long bodies, short legs, and clawed feet. Their brains were very small, but they were sufficiently developed to have 44 teeth for killing and chewing. The creodonts went on to evolve into a whole spectrum of predators, some as big as a wolf or even a lion. However, their relatively low intelligence led to a gradual decline that ended in their extinction ten million years ago. Before the creodonts died out, one of their forms gave rise to another new kind of animal, the miacid, which, although a small, shy forest-dweller, had that important ace card for survival up its sleeve: a much bigger brain. As time passed, all the modern carnivores, including the canids (dogs, wolves, and foxes) and the viverrids (mongooses, genets, and civets) evolved from the miacids. It is likely that the cat family sprang from the ancient civet species.

Forty million years ago, an animal that was half civet and half cat, called *Proailurus*, made its entrance. It had long legs and a tail, but unlike true modern cats it was a plantigrade (it walked placing all its footbones flat on the ground). Twenty-five million years ago, the first nearly true cat appeared, which walked almost as a digitigrade – that is, on the tips of its toes. This creature, *Pseudoailurus*, possessed the dentition of a true cat, with "stabbing" canine teeth.

A RICH FAMILY HISTORY The family tree of the cat shows how the modern cat family is divided into three branches. The domestic cat is part of the *Felis* group.

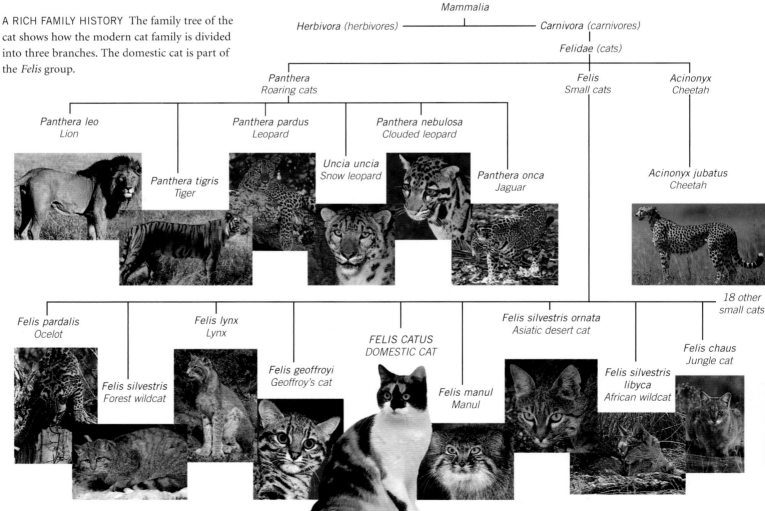

Mammalia

Herbivora (herbivores) ———— Carnivora (carnivores)

Felidae (cats)

Panthera
Roaring cats

Felis
Small cats

Acinonyx
Cheetah

Panthera leo
Lion

Panthera pardus
Leopard

Panthera nebulosa
Clouded leopard

Panthera tigris
Tiger

Uncia uncia
Snow leopard

Panthera onca
Jaguar

Acinonyx jubatus
Cheetah

Felis pardalis
Ocelot

Felis lynx
Lynx

Felis silvestris ornata
Asiatic desert cat

18 other
small cats

FELIS CATUS
DOMESTIC CAT

Felis chaus
Jungle cat

Felis silvestris
Forest wildcat

Felis geoffroyi
Geoffroy's cat

Felis manul
Manul

Felis silvestris
libyca
African wildcat

THE SPREAD OF THE DOMESTIC CAT

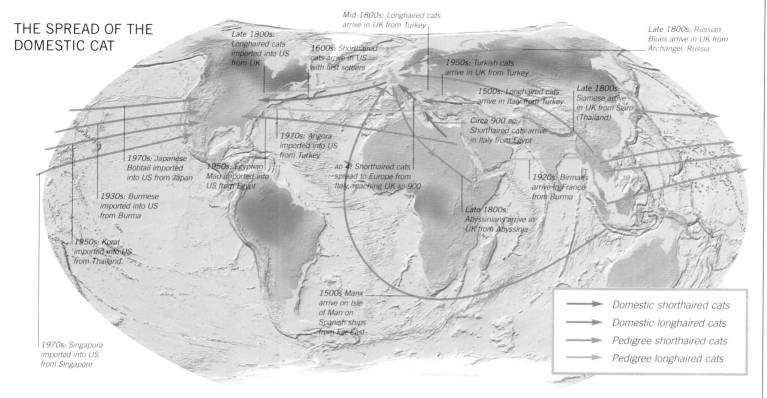

Mid-1800s: Longhaired cats arrive in UK from Turkey

Late 1800s: Longhaired cats imported into US from UK

1600s: Shorthaired cats arrive in US with first settlers

1950s: Turkish cats arrive in UK from Turkey

Late 1800s: Russian Blues arrive in UK from Archangel, Russia

1500s: Longhaired cats arrive in Italy from Turkey

Late 1800s: Siamese arrive in UK from Siam (Thailand)

Circa 900 BC: Shorthaired cats arrive in Italy from Egypt

1970s: Japanese Bobtail imported into US from Japan

1950s: Egyptian Mau imported into US from Egypt

1970s: Angora imported into US from Turkey

AD 4: Shorthaired cats spread to Europe from Italy, reaching UK AD 900

1920s: Birmans arrive in France from Burma

1930s: Burmese imported into US from Burma

Late 1800s: Abyssinians arrive in UK from Abyssinia

1950s: Korat imported into US from Thailand

1500s Manx arrive on Isle of Man on Spanish ships from Far East

1970s: Singapura imported into US from Singapore

→ Domestic shorthaired cats
→ Domestic longhaired cats
→ Pedigree shorthaired cats
→ Pedigree longhaired cats

THE FIRST "REAL" CATS

At last, about 12 million years ago, the first true cats began to stalk the earth, and their fossil remains show that there was soon a wide range of felines. The Tuscany lion, smaller than a modern lion and perhaps more closely related to the leopard, roamed Northern Italy and Central Europe along with lynxes and giant cheetahs. Giant tigers were living in China, and giant jaguars prowled the forests of North America. But there were also smaller species of wildcat, like the manul and Martelli's wildcat. The latter is now extinct, but the manul is still found in parts of Asia.

Martelli's wildcat lived all over Europe and in parts of the Middle East. It faded out perhaps a little less than one million years ago, but it was arguably the direct ancestor of the modern small wildcats from which domesticated cats were later to be developed.

Spreading all over Europe, Asia, and Africa, Martelli's wildcat gave rise to three main types: the Forest wildcat (*Felis silvestris*), which padded into the picture between 600,000 and 900,000 years ago; the African wildcat (*Felis silvestris libyca*); and the Asiatic desert cat (*Felis silvestris ornata*). It is from the African wildcat, with the Asiatic desert cat perhaps contributing something, that the domestic cat is thought principally to be descended.

DOMESTICATION

As with so many other keystones of human civilization, the domestication of the cat appears to have its origins in the Middle East. African wildcat bones have been found in the cave dung heaps of ancient man. Did man hunt cats just to eat them, or did he perhaps also rear and tame wild kittens to be companions and to control the pests that threatened his hard-won grain stores? There is evidence that man the hunter admired and envied the hunting skills of the wildcats and perhaps began to venerate the creatures he would dearly have loved to imitate in the skills of the chase.

Certainly, the Ancient Egyptians both employed cats as guardians of grain stores and worshipped them as gods, and it is to Egypt that we can trace the original source of the non-pedigree domesticated cat as we know it.

The Ancient Egyptians revered their cats and went into mourning when they died. The cats were then mummified and taken to the temple of the cat-god, Bast. Large numbers of these mummies have survived,

THE DOMESTIC CAT'S ORIGINS The map above shows how shorthaired domestic cats travelled from Egypt – long before the birth of Christ – and through Europe. Longhaired cats, on the other hand, came from Iran and Afghanistan.

enabling modern scientists to identify this first domestic species of cat as *Felis libyca*.

From Egypt, Phoenician traders took cats into Italy, and from there they spread slowly across Europe. By the 10th century, domestic cats had arrived in England, although they were still rare. The first colonists in their turn took cats with them to the New World.

Longhaired cats probably have an ancestry stemming from countries even farther to the east. It is likely that modern longhairs descended from the wildcats of Iran and Afghanistan, which in turn may have developed from the longhaired manul of Central Asia.

Although cats have been domesticated for at least 5,000 years, the concept of selectively breeding cats and producing pedigrees did not catch hold until the mid-19th century. This is in strong contrast with domestic dogs, which have been selectively bred for centuries to perform a wide variety of specific and disparate tasks.

The Design of the Cat

Cats – like humans, dogs, and giant pandas – are mammals, and they possess anatomical features common to most mammals, such as mammary glands, which produce milk for their young, and hair.

The basic body pattern of mammals is the same, which means that cats have tissues and organs that are fundamentally no different in structure or function from those of human beings. However, just as humans are upright, omnivorous primates with unique specializations, so the body of the cat displays structural adaptations that suit its role as a quadruped and a carnivorous predator.

The average adult cat weighs 2–5 kg (6–12 lb). The heaviest cat on record was Himmy from Australia, who tipped the scales at just under 21.25 kg (47 lb). He died from respiratory failure in 1986, aged ten. The smallest of the wildcats, the Rusty-Spotted cat of India and Sri Lanka, rarely exceeds 1.5 kg (3 lb) in weight.

FLEXIBILITY

The cat has a most elastic body. Its backbone or spine is held together by muscles (rather than by ligaments, as is the case in humans), and this makes the back very flexible. The cat's shoulder-joint design permits the foreleg to be turned in almost any direction. In fact, looked at in automobile terms, the "suspension" of the feline model gives a near-perfect "ride".

Another factor that enhances flexibility in the cat is that its spine has up to 26 more vertebrae than the human backbone. Also, unlike the human

being, the cat lacks a clavicle (collarbone), having instead just a small scrap of clavicle tissue deep in the breast muscle. A fully developed collarbone would broaden the chest and both reduce the cat's ability to squeeze through restricted spaces and limit the length of its stride. In humans, the collarbone enables the forearm to be lifted outward. Since this movement is not required by the cat, it is unnecessary for it to have this extra bone.

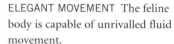

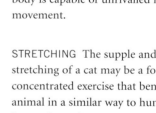

A MINIATURE TIGER Lions and tigers work out in just the same way as the domestic cat.

ELEGANT MOVEMENT The feline body is capable of unrivalled fluid movement.

STRETCHING The supple and luxurious stretching of a cat may be a form of concentrated exercise that benefits the animal in a similar way to human isometric workouts.

FELINE INGENUITY The "cross-hand climb" of a typically athletic and ingenious cat.

THE BRAIN

As you would imagine, the parts of the cat's brain associated with the senses are well developed, as befits a skilled hunter that depends upon its detection mechanisms. On the other hand, the "intelligence" areas in the frontal lobes are much simpler than in primates, such as the ape or human, or other highly intelligent animals, like the dolphin.

THE INTESTINES

The cat is a more highly specialized carnivore than the dog, and it possesses an alimentary tract designed purely for meat eating. Consequently, the cat's intestines are proportionately shorter than those of the omnivorous human or dog. Interestingly, the intestines of domestic cats are somewhat longer than those of wildcats – probably because our pets have become used to, and fond of, more varied and to some extent less meaty food.

FELINE DENTITION The most conspicuous features of the mouths of many carnivorous animals, including the cat, are the canine (or fang) teeth.

instrument. To give strength to the feline bite, the cat has short, sturdy jaws worked by powerful muscles that are anchored on reinforced arches of bone placed strategically on the skull.

The skull is notable also for its well-developed bone structures, which include large auditory bullae (echo chambers). These contribute to the cat's sensitivity in hearing such delicate sounds as the scurrying of a mouse or the rustling of a bird among the leaves.

BODY SHAPES

Although domestic dogs come in all shapes and sizes, domestic cats have not yet been produced with much in the way of anatomical extremes. There are three main body shapes: the cobby, the muscular, and the lithe. The cobby cat is a solidly built individual with short, thick legs, broad shoulders and rump, and a short, rounded head with a flattish face. The muscular body type has medium-length legs, with shoulders and rump that are neither wide nor narrow, and a medium-length, slightly rounded head. The lithe cat is lightly built with long, elegant, slim legs, narrow shoulders and rump, and a long, narrow, wedge-shaped head.

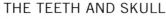

THE TEETH AND SKULL

The cat has 24 milk teeth and 30 permanent teeth, 16 in the upper jaw and 14 in the lower. These include canine, or fang, teeth for biting, and specialized blade-like carnassial molar teeth for shearing flesh. The canines in the wild animal are the main killing

Balancing Acts

Cats, as we all know from watching the tom next door effortlessly negotiate the length of the garden fence, have a wonderful, innate sense of balance.

The main reason behind feline balance is the speed of the cat's muscle reaction to remarkably fast messages sent from the eyes and balancing organs in the inner ear by way of the brain. The animal is ultrasensitive to changes in its position, and communicates any alteration to the muscles and joints far faster than a human being.

THE USE OF THE TAIL

It is generally thought that the cat's tail acts as a counterbalance to its weight in much the same way that a tightrope walker uses a long pole. The principle is simple: for example, if a cat is walking along a narrow wall or fence and decides to peer over in one direction, thereby shifting its centre of gravity, it will automatically move its tail in the opposite direction, re-establishing its body's centre of gravity and keeping itself from falling off.

The tail also acts as a counter-weight when the cat is making quick turns while running at high speed. Watch a cheetah going flat out after a zig-zagging gazelle, for example. At each turn, the cheetah's tail is swung away from the direction of its body to give the predator split-second stability on the "cornering". It seems logical that the cheetah, the champion sprinter among cats, should have such a long tail.

When jumping, a cat's tail is often said to act as a sort of rudder. However, it is nevertheless true that cats with very short tails, like lynxes or Manx cats, still jump exceedingly well.

A FINE BALANCING ACT The domestic cat has all the balancing skills of its wild cousin, the leopard.

THE ART OF FALLING

When a cat falls through the air, its eyes and specialized structures within the inner ear transmit information to the brain on the position of the head in relation to the ground. As the head changes position or is subjected to changes in acceleration, crystals and liquid inside the inner ear are affected, and this movement is detected by sensitive hairs. In milliseconds, the brain receives the signal and sends ultra-fast nerve commands to the head to put it "square" with the ground. The rest of the

USING THE TAIL A cat can be perfectly at ease on a narrow perch. The tail is used as a counter-weight as the cat begins to lean forwards.

body aligns with the head, and the cat ends up in a position perfectly prepared for landing. A newborn kitten is born with the inner-ear mechanism fully developed, but since its eyes have not yet opened, it cannot see. Because perfect balance requires a combination of eye and inner-ear messages, a kitten's righting reflex is not operational until its eyes open.

THE RIGHTING REFLEX These serial photographs of a cat falling a short distance on to a soft cushion show the change in the cat's body position and preparation for landing initiated by the eyes and inner ear.

Recently it has been found that cats that fall from tall buildings do not suffer injuries in the way you might expect. As you would predict, the rate of cat injuries increases steadily the higher the storey from which the animal falls – up to seven storeys in height. But above that height, the rate of fractures actually decreases! The reason for this appears to be that, after falling for a distance of about five storeys, the average-sized cat reaches maximum speed, the so-called terminal velocity of a falling body. At this point the cat's inner-ear system is no longer stimulated by acceleration and the speed is constant. The cat therefore relaxes and spreads its legs so that its body and limbs take advantage of maximum air resistance – much in the same way that a free-fall parachutist stabilizes his descent. Relaxed limbs are less likely to fracture, so, strange as it may seem, a cat falling from a ten-storey-high window ledge may well fare better than one tumbling a mere three storeys. (Please do *not* try to prove what I say by experimenting with your pet!)

I well recall incidents of this kind happening when I was a student. In the summer, cats would bask on the narrow window ledges of tenements (apartment blocks), until the owners closed the windows and unwittingly launched the cats into space. They would fall distances of two to five storeys, and many of them survived the descent and landed in the correct position. However, because cats have relatively weak neck muscles, they could not hold back their heads, so their chins hit the ground with some force. One of my commonest accident cases in those summer days was to treat the midline fractures of the lower jaw that resulted from such a fall.

A QUICK LEARNER An older kitten begins to show the characteristic, superb co-ordination of its species.

SLOW BEGINNINGS Still a wobbly walker, this 15-day-old kitten has not yet attained the balancing abilities of its parents.

The Cat in Motion

A cat in the wild survives by excelling as a hunter, often of fast-moving and agile prey. Its skills and movements must match this role.

In order for a cat to be a successful predator, its body must provide rapid acceleration, a burst of high speed, and great nimbleness. These skills allow a cat to change course smoothly and to cope with variations in the terrain. The cat's body must be silent and allow for attacks with paws or bites with jaws while the cat is still in motion. It must also permit athletic leaps and jumps. The cat's particular build is perfectly designed to achieve all this.

AN ACCOMPLISHED JUMPER The cat first crouches, tipping back its pelvis and bending the three joints of the hip, knee, and ankle.

WALKING

Because the feline predator must save its strength for the brief dash of the final charge, it has learned how to conserve energy at other times.

The cat therefore walks with minimum expenditure of energy. It places its feet in a diagonal pattern, left hindfoot followed by right forefoot, followed by right hindfoot and finally left forefoot. The forelimbs and hindlimbs do not move simultaneously, but slightly out of phase, with the hind one moving slightly in advance of the fore.

The animal's centre of gravity is set towards the head, with the forelimbs supporting the frame and actually exerting a slightly retarding effect. The push forward comes from the hindlegs.

True cats have digitigrade feet; they walk on the tips of their toes. Such an arrangement, comparable to the human athlete who sprints along on the tips of his or her toes, is ideal for running.

RUNNING

The cat is a sprint specialist, a 100-m champion rather than a marathon winner. When it runs, its limbs are totally extended in the air. While the forefeet are on the ground, the highly flexible spine bends like a spring, allowing the rear end to continue moving forwards in an uninterrupted fluid fashion. This system enables a cat to increase its speed by stretching its trunk fully and lengthening its stride, rather than increasing the number of times the feet hit the ground. At the gallop the retardation forces exerted by the contact of limbs with the ground completely disappear.

HIP, KNEE, AND ANKLE These joints have little or no lateral mobility and are designed to take strong forces acting in one direction only – down the body.

LEAPING FORWARDS When the muscles contract, the hip, knee, and ankle joints are rapidly extended, propelling the body sharply forwards.

KITTEN ATHLETICISM All cats qualify for the finals in athletics, especially in jumping. The gold medal goes to the wild caracal or desert lynx, which often catches birds by leaping into the air to a height of several feet and knocking them down with its paws. These kittens, while not in quite the same league, display similar general abilities.

While domestic cats can cover about three times their own body length per cycle at full speed (around 50 km/h, or 30 mph) the cheetah can briefly attain 112 km/h (70 mph) and perhaps a little more. It is interesting that the cheetah has unique grooves on the pads of its feet that act like the tread of a tyre in giving the animal grip when sprinting, and particularly when changing direction at high speed. Other cats, including domestic ones, have tough, but "treadless" pads.

The arrangement of the limbs of the cat shows adaptations for running, with long feet and relatively short bones near to the chest. The absence of a collarbone and the narrow chest are features that facilitate twisting and turning and give the animal a longer stride.

CLIMBING

The powerful back and hindleg muscles of the cat make it an efficient climber. The forelimbs, stretched forward with their hooked and extended claws, act like a mountaineer's crampons. If they can get a grip, the clawed hindfeet will power the body swiftly upwards to another hold. Most climbs begin with an initial leap to gain height.

Good as they are at going up, cats are not any great shakes at coming down! The muscles of the hindlimbs cannot be employed to hold the weight of the body back, and the claws curve the wrong way. That is why cats frequently find themselves stuck up trees or are seen letting themselves slither down, rear end first, in rather ungainly and haphazard fashion, relying on their claws to stop them making too undignified a landing.

EXERCISE

Curiously, cats stay in trim without having to spend any time working out in a gymnasium or jogging round the park. The luxurious stretching that all cats indulge in may somehow provide all the exercise necessary to keep the animals in tip-top condition.

A complete lack of conventional exercise, combined with gross overfeeding by doting humans, eventually produces obesity, but this generally does not bring with it the ill-health and curtailed life one would expect in dogs and their owners. Cats seem to have mastered the secret of a life of leisure.

CLIMBING SKILLS Going up looks easy and elegant, but coming down can be positively awkward.

SOFT TOUCHDOWN The spongy pads of the feet, covered in tough skin, also act as shock absorbers when the cat lands.

PREPARING FOR LANDING When landing, the shock is withstood by the feet, wrist, and ankle bones, which are arranged so that there is little possibility of sideways "wobble".

The Senses

Hunting animals depend on their acute senses for the detection of prey, and the domestic cat retains all the perceptual abilities used by the tiger that prowls the jungle at night.

SIGHT

The cat's eye is constructed in much the same way as that of a human being, but there are important modifications that enable the animal to do things we cannot.

Night vision

It is often said that "cats can see in the dark". Not so. In a totally blacked-out room, a cat can see no better than you or me. What it *can* do is gather the faintest quantities of light in its surroundings. Even on a moonless night the sky is never completely empty of light. Faint starlight or the pale reflections of high cloud are always present, and the cat's eye is designed to collect and use such minute scraps of luminosity.

It uses an ingenious though logical method in the form of a "mirror" placed behind the light-sensitive retina. This "mirror" is composed of up to 15 layers of glittering cells and is called the *tapetum*

TAPETUM LUCIDUM This picture shows the typical flash of the special "mirror" (*tapetum lucidum*) in cats' eyes that improves night vision. The odd-eyed cat on the right emits two different-coloured flashes.

lucidum. Faint light beams enter the eye and pass through to hit and stimulate the light receptor cells of the retina (rods and cones). They then carry on past to be reflected by the "mirror" so that they contact the rods and cones for a second time. This "double dose" multiplies the effect of the light and increases the feline night vision immensely.

We know that domestic cats can make clear visual discrimination at one sixth of the light levels required by human beings, but the "mirror" cannot work where there is zero light.

The shining of the mirror is what produces the characteristic golden or green gleam of a cat's eye in the dark. ("Tiger! Tiger! burning bright, in the forests of the night", William Blake's famous lines, were perhaps inspired by this phenomenon.) Human eyes do not gleam in the dark: the red glow of our pupils that is occasionally seen in flash photographs is produced by blood vessels behind the human retina.

Visual field

Another advantage for cats is that they have a wider angle of view than we possess. We have a visual field of about 210 degrees, of which 120 degrees is binocular. Cats have a total visual field of 285 degrees, 130 degrees of which is binocular.

The cat's 130-degree binocular vision is another hunting adaptation that allows the animal to judge depth and distance with accuracy. In practice, there is more to judging distance than merely binocular vision, and cats can be shown to be not quite as good as humans at estimating range. Humans make up for a somewhat narrower field by far more extensive eye movements, permitted by the larger area of white surrounding the cornea and iris.

FELINE VISION

BRIGHT LIGHT In very bright light, the pupil is a vertical slit with a pinhole at either end.

APPROACHING DARKNESS As illumination decreases, the pupil dilates until, at its widest, it can gather every scrap of available light.

High noon　　A cloudy day　　Midnight

THE CHANGING PUPIL This artwork shows the cat's pupils at three stages of dilation, in different light conditions.

How the eye works

The pupil of a cat's eye, like that of other mammals, constricts in bright light and dilates in dim conditions, but the actual shape of the pupil varies among different feline species. Bigger wild cats possess broadly oval pupils, the puma has a round pupil, and only members of the genus *Felis* (including the domestic cat) have a vertical slit pupil. The virtue of having a slit pupil lies in its ability to close more efficiently and more completely than a circular pupil. This serves to protect the ultrasensitive retina. Total closure never in fact occurs – a minute pinhole remains open at each end of the slit.

The rods on the cat's retina give good night vision and are sensitive to low light levels. The cones provide resolving power. The feline eye contains relatively more rods and fewer cones than a human's. It can, therefore, see better in dim light but is not able to discern fine detail quite as well as we can.

Cats focus like we do, by changing the shape of the lens through the involuntary control of tiny muscles. This process, which is known as "accommodation", can either bow the lens to bring close

THE EFFECT OF CATNIP A cat revelling in a bed of catnip is enjoying its scent, which (surprisingly) stimulates a sexual reaction.

objects into focus, or flatten it to concentrate on objects further away. Man and cat share equally good powers of focusing.

Colour vision

Does your cat quietly admire the new lavender-shaded curtains or grit its teeth at the first showing of your youngster's psychedelic T-shirt? In short, do cats see in colour? They do possess cones of at least two and possibly three kinds, and in human beings, cones undoubtedly play a major part in colour vision.

Scientists believe that although cats can see colour it means absolutely nothing to them! The eyes distinguish colours but the brain does not interpret them. This almost philosophical distinction between seeing and perceiving is important, for it has been demonstrated that cats can, with difficulty, be trained to understand colour. In general, however, cats do not use colour perception – it is not an essential part of their normal life, and it plays no part in hunting a mouse or approving a bowl of favourite food, for example.

SMELL

Smell is another very important feline sense. Cats have in the region of 19 million specialized "smelling" nerve endings in the membrane lining their noses, as compared with only five million in humans (although a long-nosed dog, such as a fox terrier, has about 147 million). On the other hand, tigers are supposed to have little or no sense of smell – which is surprising in an animal that is well known for its hunting abilities.

A cat's nose is particularly sensitive to odours containing nitrogen compounds. This permits the animal to reject food that is going "off" or rancid, when it gives off chemicals rich in nitrogen.

One particular olfactory delight of cats, of course, is the plant catnip (*Nepeta cataria*). The reason why your cat is attracted to this garden herb, in which it may well roll and sprawl ecstatically, is that it happens to contain an essential oil that is chemically closely related to a substance excreted by a queen in her urine. As you might guess, toms are "turned on" by catnip more than queens or neutered toms. Catnip, to a cat, is very sexy vegetation! Another plant, valerian, can produce a similar response.

SCENT IS KEY Recognition by smell is more important in the feline than it is in humans.

Flehmen response

Many carnivores, including some cat species, make a curious, lip-curling, nose-wrinkling grimace known as the flehmen. This is believed to bring some odours into contact with a little-understood organ that lies at the front of the roof of the mouth and that consists of a tiny pouch lined with receptor cells similar to the "smell" receptors of the nose.

This structure, called Jacobson's organ, seems to be involved with both smell and taste. It exists in a rudimentary and non-functional state in man but is functional in cats, although only weakly so in the domestic cat. It can be observed at its best in the mouth of a snake, where it analyzes "smell molecules" delivered by the flicking forked tongue. In cats, the Jacobson's organ seems to come into play mainly in connection with odours of a sexual nature.

FLEHMEN The characteristic flehmen response of the cat is believed to be a way of enhancing the senses of both smell and taste.

TASTE

Cats, as we know, tend to be fussy eaters and are more gourmets than gourmands. Whereas dogs quite readily share a human diet and often adore the odd biscuit or chocolate bar, cats do not generally have much of a sweet tooth. As pure carnivores, why should they? Many cats cannot digest sugar and get diarrhoea if they consume much of it.

Perhaps the fact that they do not have a sweet tooth is a natural aid to avoiding sugar. The reason for the difference between canines and felines appears to be that while dogs have "sweet" receptors in the taste buds of their mouth, cats do not. It was once thought that, whereas dogs definitely did have nerve links between tongue and brain that can carry "sweet" messages, cats did not. Now we know that a few "sweet"-bearing nerves do exist in domestic cats, and the numbers seem to be on the increase! I suppose that the breeding of cats that share the homes and habits of their human companions is reinforcing the persistence of such structures, and perhaps one day all pet cats will be toffee addicts!

Moving on from theorizing to the reality of some of the strange things that cats eat, as discussed later in the chapter on diet, the flat-headed cat (*Felis planiceps*) has a liking for sweet potatoes. One assumes it must be able to taste the sweetness. I know that tigers in Manchuria love to eat sweet nuts (shells and all), berries, and fruit in the autumn, and in Malaysia they are keen on durian fruit. Many domestic cats I have known, particularly Siamese and Burmese, have had a sweet tooth. One of mine adored raisins, and another regularly went crazy for slices of juicy tangerine.

Day-old kittens have a well-developed sense of taste but, as with humans, the acuity fades gradually with age.

EARLY SENSES A newborn cat is blind and rather deaf. At this stage, it depends mainly on its sense of touch.

A temporary loss of the ability to taste, with accompanying loss of appetite, can occur in cats with respiratory disease, just as our taste buds are affected by a bad head cold.

A MATTER OF TASTE Fastidious feeders, cats have a well-developed sense of taste, but one that is not as wide-ranging as that of humans.

HEARING

The cat's second most important sense is its hearing, and with 30 muscles working each external ear, as compared with six in man, it can turn its ears precisely to locate sound. This ear-turning is done far quicker by a cat than by a dog.

The outer ear is more than just a funnel for collecting sound waves and channelling them down to the eardrum. Its shape is not as simple as the round Victorian ear trumpet but is irregular and asymmetrical. This shape, combined with the ear movements, produces variations in the quality of received sound that allow the cat to localize its source with precision. A cat has the ability to discriminate between two sounds separated by an angle of five degrees with an accuracy of around 75 per cent.

Range

At high frequencies, the cat's hearing (and the dog's) is far more acute than ours.

A cat can hear sounds up to two octaves higher than the highest note we can hear, and that is half an octave higher than the best a dog can do! In the high-frequency range, where one may expect to find the high-pitch noises produced by small prey animals, the cat exhibits particular sensitivity. It has great powers of discrimination between notes in this range, being able to distinguish one fifth to one tenth of a tone in difference between two notes. The large echo chambers in the skull play an essential part in magnifying sounds for the purpose of analysis by the feline ear and brain. Most cats learn to recognize, without any training, words uttered by the human voice. They will respond to their name, a call to dine, and so on, but their vocabulary never grows as large as that that can be learned by dogs.

HUNTING MACHINE This cat's intent gaze and pricked ears are indicative of a hunter that relies on keen senses.

Hearing loss

As in human beings, age takes its toll upon the hearing of cats. Their sensitivity to high notes reduces quite quickly with the passing of the years, often beginning to decline as early as three years of age, and usually showing marked loss by the time that the cat reaches four and a half.

Senility and diseases of some kind may result in a cat becoming completely deaf.

Ragdoll

Ear infections and blockage with wax generally respond well to prompt veterinary treatment. White cats, particularly those with blue eyes, have a tendency to deafness induced by a rogue gene in their make-up that causes shrivelling of the inner-ear structure. This type of deafness is not amenable to therapy. In general, cats cope extremely well when deafness occurs.

TOUCH

The sense of touch is highly developed in our fireside friend. The function of cats' whiskers, however, is not fully understood. They obviously have something to do with touch, and removing them can distinctly

THE IMPORTANCE OF TOUCH Possessing a skin rich in touch-sensitive nerve endings, the cat is a supremely tactile individual.

disturb a cat for some time. There is no substance in the belief that a cat's whiskers protrude on each side to a distance equal to that of the animal's maximum width, so enabling it to gauge whether or not it can pass through a given space without touching anything or making a give-away noise when stalking prey.

But in the dark, a cat's whiskers are immensely sensitive, rapid-acting antennae used to identify things that the cat cannot see. Scientists have suggested that if a cat's whiskers touch a mouse in the dark, the cat reacts with the speed and precision of a mouse-trap. Other scientists speculate that the cat may bend some or all of its whiskers downwards when jumping or bounding over the ground at night.

Certainly the little desert jerboa uses two of its whiskers to do this – its downward-pointing whiskers are used to detect stones, holes, or other irregularities in its path. Even when moving at full speed, the jerboa can take avoiding action, in the air or on the ground, by changing the direction of its body in a split second. Maybe cats use their whiskers in a similar way.

Reaction to tremors

Apart from touch, cats are highly sensitive to vibrations. Like some other species, they may give warning of a coming earthquake. There were widespread reports of strange behaviour by housecats in the 10–15 minutes preceding the disasters at Agadir, Skopje, Chile, and Alaska in the 1960s.

Similarly, cats showed signs of apprehension and alarm for no apparent reason for up to half an hour before the Mount St Helens volcano in the US erupted in 1980. Many cats in Manchester, England, reacted the same way to pre-tremors of the minor earthquakes in the city in 2002. It seems the animals can detect the first tremors, which are imperceptible to human beings. People living on the slopes of Mount Etna, Italy, keep cats as early-warning devices. When a drowsing tom suddenly wakes and runs for the door, the humans quickly follow.

This hypersensitivity to vibration may be allied to the belief that cats are capable of extrasensory perception and that they pick up "vibrations" of a kind not detected by the five senses. It is impossible to say whether cats are "psychic" in this way, but it is easy to see why they have this reputation.

The acuteness of the cat's senses allows it to react to occurrences of which the relatively blunt-edged human brain is unaware. This, coupled with the inscrutable "knowing" look of its features, no doubt played a large part in the growth of the belief that a cat possesses a supernatural dimension and communicates with strange forces, which many still believe is so today.

Devon Rex

Black-and-White Bicolour Longhair

Red Self Longhair

WHISKERS AND TOUCH The whiskers of pedigree cats, like those of fashionable young men, are nowadays mere vanities. These specialized hairs do, however, have a function in enhancing the cat's sense of touch, although how they do so is not fully understood.

Behaviour

"The Cat he walked by himself, and all places were alike to him."

Just So Stories,
Rudyard Kipling

The cat is a less sociable animal than the dog, and only the lion among wild cats shows much gregarious activity. However, cats are not totally self-sufficient or indeed antisocial creatures. Proud and aloof they may be, but they possess the ability to form close friendships with humans. This is true not only of the domestic cat but also of some of its wild relatives, such as the African wildcat. Tigers, lions, leopards, and pumas that are reared in circuses often dote on their trainers and handlers with as much apparent affection as any pedigree Siamese. Between cats there is very often much affection and what must pass for love.

LOVE CATS Close affection between cats is often demonstrated.

SLEEP

Cats do a wide variety of things in their daily lives, but, as befits specialist hunters that must conserve their energy for brief, high-performance bursts of activity, they delight in rest and relaxation. Taking catnaps of a few minutes at a time, they total about 16 hours of sleep out of 24 and are the greatest sleepers among mammals. They out-drowse even the rather dozy giant panda which is active for about 14 hours per day. Why the cat requires so much sleep, we do not know.

It goes without saying that cats enjoy their naps and are masters in selecting the warmest and most sheltered spot in the garden or the cosiest nook indoors.

While they sleep their brains continue to work at a basic level, recording and analyzing stimuli coming in from their surroundings. In deep sleep, surprisingly, the brain remains as active as it is when awake, and the senses continue to scan for the first signs of danger. At the first alarm, the cat's nervous system, which is ever-alert, rouses the body muscles instantaneously. Experiments have been done in which external stimuli are completely removed and the cat is put into a darkened, soundproof, odour-free room. When its brain-wave activity is recorded, it is found that the mental processes gradually wind down to a minimal, body-maintenance level. There is apparently no spontaneous thought; as the cat lies there it does not compose poetry, recall with relish past dinners, or fantasize about the young queen in the house next door. This is quite different to what is found in human beings placed under similar conditions. They proceed from trains of spontaneous thought to suffering hallucinations and other mental aberrations.

Like ours, the cat's sleep pattern embraces periods of both deep and light sleep. Seventy per cent is light and 30 per cent is deep. The phases alternate, with evidence of dreaming during the deep phases. You can tell that your cat is

FAMILY TIES Although not as social an animal as the dog, the cat does form close and affectionate relationships with human beings.

dreaming when, in a similar way to dogs, its paws and claws may move, its whiskers twitch, its ears flick, and, in some cases, it actually makes noises.

HUNTING

The cat is a natural carnivorous predator, but it is not a completely instinctive hunter. The urge to hunt successfully is induced and honed by competition and demonstration; the skills are learned by observation and trial and error. Cats are not born good bird-catchers, for example – in fact, until they have thoroughly practised the art over and over again, they are downright bad at it.

GREAT SLEEPERS Naturally cats are experts at catnapping.

FELINE ATTACK PATTERN Just like a tiger, the domestic cat displays the phases of the feline hunter's attack: the slink-run, the final charge, and the pounce.

Learning from mother and other cats is essential, and a good teacher makes a good pupil. The offspring of non-hunting cats rarely make good hunters themselves. There may also be a genetic factor. The cat's hunting technique is inherited originally from its forest-dwelling ancestors, for whom ambush was more rewarding than the chase.

HUNTING TECHNIQUE

Once the cat has located a suitable victim by means of its senses, it begins to approach slowly and cautiously, using every bit of available cover. Next, to cross any open space, it travels forward rapidly in a movement known as the "slink-run", its body pressed close to the ground to reduce its outline. The slink-run is broken by pauses when the cat stops and stares intently at the prey.

After several such runs and pauses, the cat reaches a patch of cover nearest to the prey from where the final attack can be launched over a relatively short distance. Here it "ambushes": lying crouched, eyes glued to the prey, hindfeet making treading movements as if revving up for the charge, and the tail's tip twitching in feverish anticipation.

Suddenly the final attack is mounted. The cat breaks cover and shoots forward, body still held fairly close to the ground. When it is within striking distance, it raises its foreparts and leaps on to its prey. While the forepaws pin down the victim, the hindfeet act as anchors planted solidly on the ground.

MINIATURE WILD CAT The lynx and the leopard lurk close beneath the skin of our domestic cat, even in play.

THE KILL

Now comes the kill. If the prey starts to struggle, the cat may release it briefly and then repeat the final attack in order to get a better grip. Alternatively, it may throw itself on to its side, keeping hold with the forepaws but releasing the hindpaws in order that they can rake powerfully, claws extended, at the victim.

The killing bite of a cat – domestic tabby or jungle tiger – is a remarkably well-organized affair. All felines tend to use a neck bite. The prey is usually killed by dislocation of the vertebrae in the neck.

It is fascinating to note that the distance between the left and right fang teeth of a cat is the same as the distance between the neck joints of its usual prey. A domestic cat has its fang teeth aligned for dislocating the neck of a mouse, and the tiger is designed to do the same to its favourite meals, deer and wild pig.

There are special nerves linked to the fang teeth of the cat that sense in the twinkling of an eye when the points of the teeth are positioned over the neck joints of the prey. These nerves then send ultra-fast messages to the brain, which responds in turn by sending messages to the jaw muscles, instructing them to close at an unusually high speed and thereby perform the dislocation. The neck bite of a cat is a brilliant, "computer-controlled" process.

LEARNING TO HUNT

Domestic queens, like the females of other feline species, teach their kittens how to perfect their killing techniques in a graduated series of lessons. First, the queen carries home prey that she has killed and eats it in the presence of her offspring. A little later, she leaves killed prey for the kittens to eat, and then finally, when they are

STARTING YOUNG This growing kitten begins to practise its hunting skills on a toy bird.

two and a half to three months old, she brings home live prey, presents it to her young, and lets them kill it. She does not help them to make the kill, but if the prey escapes from them, she will catch it and re-present it so they can try again. Similar behaviour has been recorded in, for example, cheetahs and tigers.

It is competition among the littermates that, by raising their excitement and enthusiasm, stimulates kittens to make their first neck-bite kills. The learning process is delicate; if no kills are made during the developmental period, the cat finds it difficult if not impossible to learn how to do it later. A hand-reared kitten denied the opportunity to make its first kill at the right time in its development will grow into a non-killer that shows little interest in mice or other small prey.

Domestic cats will swipe at anything that moves, but the hunt proper is reserved for small creatures such as mice, birds, and (worth remembering) pets such as hamsters.

I do not know whether the story of a ginger tom hunting down, killing, and eating a tiny Chihuahua dog that lived in the house next door is apocryphal or not. It is not true to say that cats are better hunters if they are kept hungry, nor that neutered cats are worse mousers than unneutered ones. Plump and well-fed cats are often the best guardians of granaries and food stores. What makes a good, rather than a merely competent, mouser is what makes one human a champion athlete – inborn and probably inherited

talent. The instinct of the domestic cat is to hunt, almost for hunting's sake, unlike the bigger wild cats that tend only to hunt in order to fill their stomachs.

COPING WITH A HUNTING CAT

The successful hunter bears the spoils proudly to his home, and the cat is frequently no exception. Brimming with satisfaction, it delivers a dead mouse or young rabbit to your door, or actually deposits it on the carpet at your feet. Do not scold or try to punish your pet; it is just showing affection towards someone "in the family" by giving a present. Wild cats do it as a social gesture, and you should feel honoured to be thought of so highly. Try to dispose of the gift as promptly and hygienically as possible – though your cat will find it difficult to understand why you dash out to the rubbish bin with the mouse held by its tail between finger and thumb, instead of settling down to eat it!

Those cats that do learn through practice how to catch wild birds can cause havoc among your garden's feathered visitors. Site all birdfeeding devices that you may have in the open so that your cat is denied cover for stalking. Fitting a bell to the cat's collar can be useful as a warning to birds, but I have known cats that still manage to catch birds despite having been "belled". One in particular actually scooted along on three legs holding the bell pressed silently to its throat by a forepaw.

Do not be alarmed if your cat insists on catching and eating flies. It's just another form of the hunt and it will not, as is sometimes claimed, "make the cat grow thin". Flies can carry disease bacteria or parasite eggs, but the risk is low and not worth worrying about.

Domestic cats exhibit great skill in hooking fish out of shallow ponds, as my goldfish and I know to our cost. Some wild species, such as the fishing cat, flat-headed cat, and jaguar, are even better fish

poachers. Big cats such as the lion and tiger tend to eat their meals while lying crouched down, probably to hide their meal from predators, but domestic cats prefer to sit neatly on their haunches or remain standing.

The feral cat (a domestic cat returned to the wild) eats a diet similar to that of its small wildcat relatives – small rodents, other mammals up to the size of a hare, birds up to the size of a hen, insects, and, when available, lizards.

PLAY

Play is a most notable feline activity, and wild cats play with as much eager enthusiasm as their domestic relatives. Because play is generally most pronounced in animal species in which the young pass through a relatively prolonged period of "childhood", carnivores, including cats, are among the most playful of mammals. Naturally, the young play more than the adults.

It is impossible to define *purely* playful activity – that is, behaviour that is only to be observed as a form of recreation. For the cat, play blends naturally into rehearsal of the serious skills and behaviour patterns involved with hunting, killing, fighting, and escaping. When kittens chase one another, the roles of pursuer and pursued switch frequently as the youngsters learn the essentials of a predator's life. With no prey available, somebody has to take on the part of the

THE THRILL OF THE HUNT This cat proudly returning with its trophy is interested in hunting for its own sake.

PLAY-FIGHTING Reminiscent of
two young lions in ritual combat,
these domestic kittens practise
their ancient arts.

mouse – just as happens in children's
games such as cops and robbers or
cowboys and Indians.

Although the games may be played with
much verve and excitement, the essential
principle of play is never lost – bites and
scratches are never carried out at full
force, and injuries are very rare. Because
the end point of a real hunt – the kill –
does not happen in kittens' play, the
various pre-kill phases of hunting and
combat tend to be repeated over and over
again with an animal playing, in quick
succession, the roles of aggressor or
defender, rival or prey.

However, there is never any component
of fear or distress in any of the players.
Indeed, one notable feature of feline play
is the exuberant exaggeration of many of
the movements in the playing. It is
impossible to escape the conclusion
that the animals, apart from learning,
derive real fun and enjoyment from
their sporting.

Play relieves the frustrations of
not being able, for some reason or
another, to hunt. This is why cats
sometimes play "cruelly" with live
prey for some time before killing it.
In the wild, cats hunt often and kill
sometimes, whereas in the domestic

LEARNING VITAL SKILLS This little
kitten is completing a mock attack in
identical fashion to the real thing, as
practised by a tiger.

situation, food (the kill) is readily available
and hunting opportunities are scarce. So,
to satisfy the age-old urge and in-built
adaptations to hunt, the cat will stretch
the "hunting phase" when it does
come across a suitable victim.

The cubs of some cat
species rehearse in play
certain features of adult
behaviour that are specific to
their kind. The youngsters of both
the black-footed cat and the leopard, for
instance, love to somersault as they play.
This is a way of practising the technique,
needed by relatively light predators
attacking much heavier prey, of clutching

with forepaws, raking with hindclaws, and
rolling over with their victim without losing
their grip. Even more striking (literally) is
the way cheetah cubs rehearse on one
another the typical paw slap with which
they will later fell a Thomson's gazelle.

BENEFITS OF PLAYING

All this practice, practice, practice in play
develops the young cats' experience of
the external world and its physical laws.
Through play, they learn how to time
a punch; how far to jump to land on a
moving object; how fast they must run in
order to intercept their prey; and other
useful lessons of this kind.

NEVER TOO OLD TO PLAY Even
very mature cats may play from
time to time.

For adult domestic cats, as well as for
wild cats kept in zoos, play time also
relieves frustration and can increase
their contentment and interest in life.
For these cats, food is regularly provided
without the need for a thrilling (and,
in the wild, often fruitless) chase, so
their powerful hunting instincts surface
instead in the form of play. Such playing
actually makes the animal more keen
to eat, and makes what might otherwise
be a monotonous and predictable
meal more fun.

The moral of this is that you should
play with your cat regularly. The
playing of the domestic cat is not
only a demonstration of hunting
rituals, it is also useful in exercising
and strengthening the growing cat.

Intelligence and Communication

A cat is a very intelligent creature – as a usually solitary, self-reliant hunter, it has to be. It has to learn to calculate, to solve problems, and to be versatile.

DECEPTIVE PERSPECTIVE Just as the human eye and brain can be deceived by tricks of perspective, so can those of the cat. This little kitten, on a glass sheet covering a design that makes it look like a table edge, is peering down and hesitating prudently at the apparent corner.

It is rather a waste of time discussing the intelligence levels of various animal species. People often do it, but they have no reliable yardstick with which to measure "intelligence". Cultural differences, even between the various groups or races in a single species, *Homo sapiens*, are notorious for distorting the results of "intelligence tests". And this is the only species with which we can truly communicate by means of a common language!

An imperfect but objective method is to compare brain weight with length of spinal cord. This gives a ratio that roughly indicates how much brain controls how much body. The human ratio is 50:1, a monkey's 18:1, and a cat's 4:1. But does this mean that a human being is over ten times more intelligent than a cat?

LEARNING AND MEMORY

Cats do learn well, and for many of life's activities they must learn rather than rely solely on their instinct. Hunting, for example, is not an instinctive activity, but it is learned from observation, as is the use of a litter tray. In the latter case, the teacher is either the mother cat or a human companion.

Such learning by example merges with the ability to be positively trained. Cats can be trained to perform tricks, though they do not respond well to coercion (even though I admit that some circus big cats in the old days were "tamed" by unacceptably cruel methods). They are easier to train by rewards, but even so, cats do not show the eagerness to be trained that we see in dogs. Despite a plentiful source of attractive rewards in the form of tasty titbits, they will only co-operate if they feel in the mood. You cannot buy cats – that is part of their independent nature.

The feline memory is well developed and most domestic cats learn such useful knacks as tapping on window panes to gain entrance, opening a door by jumping for the latch, finding their way home, or coming to the call of a familiar voice.

HONING HUNTING SKILLS This cat has learned enough to know both where prey might be found and how to get it.

Essentially cats live for themselves. They have no "work ethic" like some dogs, rodents, or birds, and they will only work to attain a definite end – finding food, for example. That apart, they adopt a rather aristocratic view of life and learn early on to expend energy only as necessary.

SIXTH SENSE

Do cats possess a sixth sense? It has often been claimed that they do. There certainly is an air of mystery about the cat's personality and demeanour. Do cats perhaps know things hidden from us, sense things we cannot?

I firmly believe that the cat has super-efficient natural senses that can detect things we humans cannot. When a cat suddenly raises its hackles when you are alone with it in the house, it is not because it has seen a ghost, but because it is reacting to sounds or vibrations you cannot pick up. This ability evolved primarily as a means of survival, by providing an early-warning system. The world must reveal far more to the highly sensitive cat than to less well-endowed creatures like ourselves.

SOCIAL BEHAVIOUR

Although cats are lone hunters, they are not by any means antisocial. Indeed, they have intricate social interactions with their own kind. Furthermore, there is a complex feline society that, in the case of the domestic cat, forms an infrastructure to human civilization.

Inscrutable it may be, but the cat can communicate with its fellow felines in a variety of ways, such as those illustrated on the facing page. There are four principal methods:

- **Vocalization:** The cat's repertoire is plaintive miaows, seductive purrs, incensed wails, and irate screeches.
- **Body language:** Facial expressions are emphasized by the markings that "make up" the features. Body postures or tail positions are also enhanced by coat markings.
- **Touch:** Cats communicate by rubbing noses with, pressing bodies against, or grooming others.
- **Scent:** Using their sensitive noses, they identify other cats by their scents, sniffing one another's heads and beneath tails, where odour-making glands are situated. They also mark out territory with scent "markers".

VOCALIZATION This little kitten is saying that it feels short of attention. Some cats are more "polite" in their demands than others.

BODY LANGUAGE A pose that speaks louder than words of this cat's desire for its dinner – something its owner can ignore at his or her peril.

RUBBING One of the most attractive feline methods of communication is sensuous rubbing to indicate love and affection.

FRIEND OR FOE? The sense of smell is just one of the senses that is aroused when two cats meet. The complicated process of determining if a new "introduction" is friendly or not involves all of the cat's methods of appraisal.

DEFENSIVE CAT This cat stands with an arched back, usually with its body turned at an angle to the aggressor. The pupils are wide open, the ears are flattened to the head, the mouth is open with the teeth showing, the fur of its back is bristling, and the tail, also bristling, is arched. It makes hissing, spitting sounds.

AGGRESSIVE CAT This cat is poised to strike, with its ears pricked and furled back, the pupils of its eyes closed to a slit, the whiskers bristling forwards, the mouth wide open with the lips curled back into a snarl, and the tail low, bristling, and swishing to and fro. Its fur is smooth and the cat makes growling and spitting noises.

SUBMISSIVE CAT This cat is communicating its submission and pacific intentions by means of its posture. It cringes close to the ground with enlarged pupils, flattened whiskers and ears, and a mouth that may be open and silent or half open and emitting a pitiful distress call. The body fur is flattened to the skin and the tail is thumping the ground.

Look at the map of your town. Depicted there is the framework of civilized society – humble homes, great houses, meeting places, common land, and a network of thoroughfares. But that map is also the plan of the town's feline society, superimposed invisibly upon the man-made geography. The feline citizens also have an ordered division of the land for various purposes, and, much like our own, their society has its social strata, with top cats in feline Beverly Hills and proletarian pussies on the other side of the tracks.

Your cat, unless of course it is kept permanently indoors, is part of the cat

FIGHTING FOR LAND This tense meeting concerns ownership of the tree trunk, which is clearly part of one cat's territory.

BEARING BATTLE SCARS "Top Cat" he may be, but this battered tom shows the scars of his constant battles for supremacy.

community in your local neighbourhood with a precise, though not necessarily unchanging, position in the hierarchy. Like all other members of the community, it must abide by rules and rituals that are laid down in a very precise way. All the cats in the neighbourhood community know one another and their positions in society. A newcomer taking up residence is only allotted a position and territory after fighting for it.

THE CAT HIERARCHY

Cat society is essentially organized as a matriarchy. The unneutered queen with the most kittens reigns at the top of the pecking order. When she is neutered, however, her social status slumps. Males

take their place in the community in macho fashion, by using brawn over brains. The meanest, toughest toms battle for power and prestige. Success in combat determines a tom's social niche. The organization is rigid, and a cat only occasionally loses its place by being vanquished by an up-and-coming young blade.

Unlike monkeys, deer, or seals, toms do not necessarily obtain large harems of queens with the acquisition of a dominant position. Queens seem to be very civilized and do not automatically give courtship rights to the all-conquering thug. Often queens will prefer as suitors toms situated well down the pyramid of power – shades of Lady Chatterley! Interestingly enough, top tom cats do, however, rule the biggest chunks of territory, and it seems that, as with the landed gentry of days gone by, land rather than sex is the key to social status in feline society.

Neutered toms are always at the bottom of the social ladder, the feline equivalent of Skid Row. An entire tom begins to lose his position in the community as soon as he is castrated. After the operation, the amount of male sex hormone, testosterone, declines in the blood and the pungent masculine odour of his urine fades. As this process continues, he descends rung by rung down the social ladder.

It is not that neutered toms cannot fight, but rather that they lose their aggression. To his peers, the neutered tom's weakening scent is a potent signal, which is interpreted, I suppose, as effeminacy. In the world of tom-cat *mafiosi*, you have to smell butch to be "one of the boys"!

TERRITORIAL AREAS

Cats are territorial – they "own" patches of land. Even an indoor cat has its territory – a particular part of the room or a favourite chair. Where several cats live in a household, indoor territorial rights gradually merge until all the cats jointly possess the house and mutually defend it against feline outsiders.

Outdoors, all cats, no matter how lowly they may rank in society, have some territory. Females and neuters hold fairly small properties, but ones that they nevertheless fight harder to defend than any grandee tom with a vast estate. The problem for the top toms is that the large areas of territory that they own are difficult to defend around the clock, if they are to be able to grab forty winks. A dominant tom in a country area with

SOCIAL LADDER This punch to the jaw is the opening move in a fight to determine which cat comes top in the "pecking order".

SCRATCHING As a way of marking territory, scratching is done by many feline species, including the domestic cat and the tiger.

SPRAYING This cat is marking a tree trunk with urine. Such "visiting cards" can sometimes also be left on furniture or even people's legs (to their embarrassment).

SCENT GLANDS Leaving scent by rubbing against a solid object is yet another way of staking a claim to it.

a sparse cat population may rule 50 or more acres, while in the city a "property" may be as small as a backyard. Within a property, the cat, like a human landowner, has its favourite spots for catching the sun, sleeping, or keeping a lookout.

The territory is marked as belonging to its owner in three main ways. The cat may spray the boundaries with urine (sometimes a tom may spray you – in which case you should be flattered that he sees you as a fixture in his estate). The second method is scratching (to leave visible and sweat-scented marks). Another way of territory marking is to rub a solid object with the head, which transfers scent from sebaceous glands in the skin.

If you move house, help your cat establish its new territory by discouraging other cats and breaking up fights. Soon the "locals" will yield up the piece of land considered by the community to be appropriate to your pet's agreed social standing within the feline society.

PUBLIC TERRITORIES

Outside the private territories, land is organized on a "municipal" basis. There are hunting grounds, meeting places, and no-man's lands; the latter might typically be places occupied by dogs. There is a formal network of walkways or roads that link all these places, skirting privately owned feline territories and non-cat areas. Some pathways are private to a particular cat. Others are communal. Some can be used at certain hours of the day by cat A and at other times by cat B, C, and so on. This system avoids conflict. "Main roads" have their traffic rules. For example, any cat moving along a main pathway has automatic and undisputed right of way over any other cat, whatever its social standing, approaching on an intersecting sidepath.

Meeting grounds are used for what can only be described as "cat clubs". Toms and queens gather from time to time to sit in these places in peaceful groups 1–6 m (3–20 ft) apart. Although meetings may involve the mating of a queen in season, normally the gatherings have no sexual overtones. We do not really know why cats assemble like this. It seems to be an important part of their social life and perhaps they exchange information, news, and gossip by some means. Or maybe, like the best of human friends, they just simply and silently enjoy one another's company.

Cat clubs are one of the things that are missing in the life of a cat kept permanently indoors. A solitary indoor cat may become lonely and bored and turn to bad behaviour, like chewing carpets and urinating in forbidden spots. In such cases veterinary advice should be sought.

PEACEFUL FELINE GATHERING This is a group of feral cats in their "clubhouse". Such conclaves, usually very peaceful, are not understood by biologists.

Breeds

The blue-blooded pedigree cat is an aristocrat, but one with a family tree that goes back little more than a century and that has its roots in much humbler soil. Over 100 different breeds and varieties of *Felis catus* are officially recognized worldwide. Although some are "natural" breeds that were originally indigenous to a particular country, the large majority are the result of carefully designed breeding programmes that began with the selection of the best examples of run-of-the-mill *mongrel* cats.

Some breeds are descended from mere chance, genetic mutations that suddenly appeared among otherwise "orthodox" litters and would, by the evolutionary rules of natural selection, have perished because of the disadvantages bestowed by the mutation, had man not nurtured the off-beat line for aesthetic reasons. That it should have taken no more than a century to develop the spectrum of feline aristocracy is due to the relatively short gestation period, rapid maturing, and often generous litter sizes of the cat. Today, national associations in each country – the Governing Council of the Cat Fancy in Great Britain, the Cat Fanciers Association in the US, and, as an international body comprising 40 cat federations worldwide, the Fédération Internationale Féline (FIFé) – lay down the standards by which pedigree cats are judged and also register kittens.

A BREED APART Unlike in many dog breeds, which man developed by artificial selection to perform a variety of tasks, the spectrum of cat shapes, colours, and patterns were selected purely for aesthetic appeal.

Coat Types

A cat's fur is its crowning glory and a source of insulation. In the wild, coat colour serves as camouflage and is related to habitat. Chance colour mutations and selective breeding led to the variety of coats seen today. Coat types also adapted to habitats – the more rugged the climate, the thicker the coat.

TYPES OF TIPPING

Tipping may be very light or extend down the hair almost to the root. A ticked coat has hairs that are banded.

1. Untipped
2. Shell
3. Shaded
4. Smoke
5. Ticking

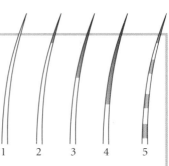

1   2   3   4   5

COAT VARIETIES

The three types of hair in a cat's coat are the topcoat or guard hairs (grey), the bristly awn hairs (blue), and the soft, curly down hairs (pink).

Cornish Rex: Very short, curly awn and down hairs, all of a similar length.

Devon Rex: Guard, down, and awn hairs are all very short and curly.

American Wirehair: This coat has guard, awn, and down hairs, all very curly, even coiled.

Longhair: A dense coat with very long guard hairs (up to 12.5 cm, or 5 in) and thick down hairs.

Maine Coon: Long guard and down hairs like the Longhair, but shaggy and uneven.

Angora: Guard and down hairs are very long, but finer and less profuse than the Longhair.

British Shorthair: The guard hairs are about 4.5 cm (2 in) long, the awn hairs are sparse.

Sphynx: Almost hairless, no guard or awn hairs, but a few down hairs on the face, tail, and legs.

LONGHAIRED COATS The length of longhair coats gives luxuriance, more varieties of shape and texture, and is wonderfully soft to the touch. However, it does require daily brushing and grooming.

WIRY COAT Every hair of the American Wirehair's coat – including the whiskers – is crimped and wiry. This gives an overall somewhat coarse and springy feel.

PATTERNS The domestic cat (like the wildcat) is basically tabby in marking, but selective breeding has produced a wide array of "self", or solid, colours as well as new patterns – from black, lilac, and blue, to tortoiseshell, smoke, or cameo, and many more. Here are just some of the possibilities.

Chartreux

Angora

Russian Blue

Lilac-point Siamese

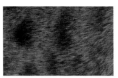
Ocicat

Abyssinian (Usual)

Foreign Lilac Shorthair

Abyssinian (Sorrel)

Tonkinese

Pewter Longhair

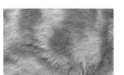
British Red Tabby Shorthair

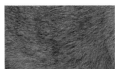
Korat

Bombay

Nebelung

Exotic Colourpoint Shorthair

Somali

British Silver Spotted Shorthair

Black Smoke Longhair

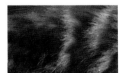
Maine Coon

Cornish Rex

Blue Longhair

British Black-and-White Bicolour Shorthair

British Tortoiseshell-and-White Shorthair

Blue-Cream Longhair

SHORTHAIRED COATS The coats of shorthaired cats are made up of hairs that tend to cast less, seldom become matted or tangled, and need much less grooming than those of longhaired breeds.

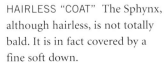

HAIRLESS "COAT" The Sphynx, although hairless, is not totally bald. It is in fact covered by a fine soft down.

Eye Types

The colour of a cat's eyes is controlled genetically and is produced by the iris, which has pigment cells that carry particles of black, brown, or yellowish colouring matter. Where no pigment exists, as in albino cats, the iris is red-pink because all the colour comes from the blood vessels. Blue eyes are due to reflected light being "scattered" from a faintly black-pigmented layer of the iris. Green eyes achieve their appearance by scattering reflected blue light, which then passes through a layer of yellowish pigment.

EYE COLOURS The wide range of eye colours found in the cat depends on the amount of pigment and the degree of light-scattering. Some of the many possible variations are illustrated below.

EYE SHAPES There are three main types of feline eye shape, which is determined by the line and set of the borders of the eyelids. They are round, almond, and slanted.

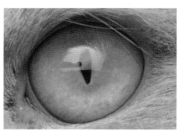

Round

Almond

Slanted

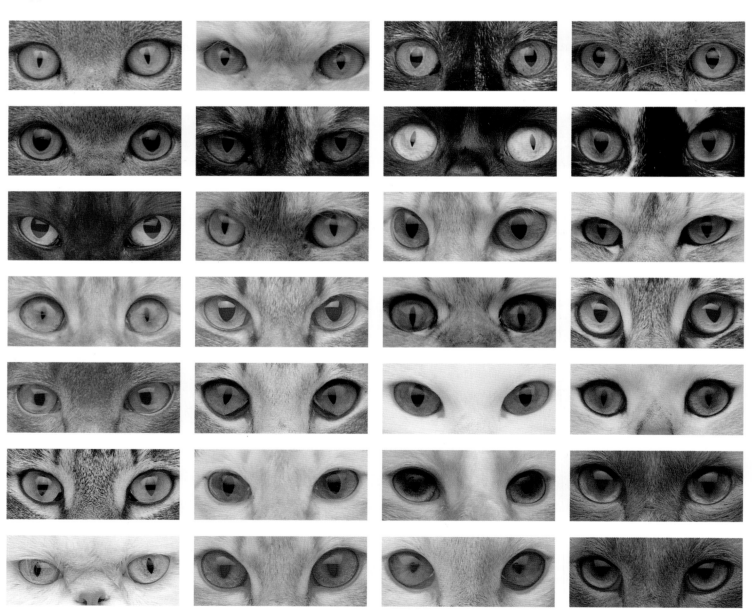

NIGHT VISION Despite the popular myth, cats cannot, of course, see in the dark.
They can, however, gather and use much of the available light in their surroundings.

Longhaired Cats

Most wildcats are equipped with fur of short or medium length (Pallas's cat, or manul, is the longest-haired among the wild felines), and all domestic cats in Europe were originally shorthaired. Longhaired cats may have developed in cold countries such as Russia, where there was need for a long coat, but it seems likely that they arose from spontaneous mutations that were then perpetuated through interbreeding.

By the late 16th century, longhaired cats had arrived in Europe. According to some historical accounts, they were brought back from Asia Minor by the Italian traveller Pietro della Valle, but most of today's longhaired pedigree cats are descended from cats brought to Britain from Turkey and Persia (now Iran) in the late 19th century.

Most longhaired cats are of the exotic-looking Longhair type, popularly known as Persian. In the US these cats are formally grouped in seven divisions: Solid Colour, Silver and Golden, Shaded and Smoke, Tabby, Particolour, Bicolour, and Himalayan. In Australia and New Zealand, these cats are formally classified as Persians, with the colours listed as varieties. However, in Britain they are called Longhairs, and each colour is classified as a separate breed.

All longhaired cats of Persian type have a cobby (sturdy and rounded) body with a round face and head, short, thick legs, a short nose, and large, round eyes. They also possess an exceptionally full, luxuriant coat. This is known as a double coat because it consists of two types of hair: long, soft, woolly undercoat hairs and slightly longer, coarser guard hairs, which can be as much as 12 cm (5 in) long in some show specimens.

There are several longhaired cats that are not of the Persian type. These cats have various origins, but the majority of them come from cold climates where a long coat is useful. On the whole, these cats' coats are not as woolly or as full as those of Longhairs, which makes them easier to groom. They differ from Longhairs in other ways too: they tend to be slimmer, longer in the body and leg, and have narrower, wedge-shaped faces. Examples of these cats are the Balinese, Angora, Norwegian Forest Cat, and Maine Coon.

Although the coat of a longhaired cat is its pride and joy and is often extra-long around the head, where it forms an attractive ruff, there is one major disadvantage to this glamorous upholstery – most longhaired cats moult all year round and, therefore, demand regular daily grooming to prevent matting and fur balls.

MAINE COON (Top right) Big and beautiful with long, lustrous, waterproof fur and a winter neck ruff, the Maine Coon is the oldest feline breed in North America.

RAGDOLL (Below right) Looking rather like a Birman that has mislaid its white socks, the Ragdoll is a fairly new but increasingly popular breed that has a medium-length coat and is renowned for its gentle temperament.

A BEAUTIFUL COAT (Left) The texture and style of the longhaired cat's coat adds an extra dimension of attraction to both pattern and colour. However, it brings with it the risk of tangling and matting, with skin disease as a possible consequence if grooming is neglected.

Black Longhair

Although this breed has a distinguished history stretching back to the 16th century and was one of the first to be given official recognition, the Black Longhair is a relatively rare animal. The difficulties of producing a pure black, unadulterated by any rustiness or smokiness, has made good specimens much prized. The coat needs particular care and attention: damp may lend the fur a brownish tinge, and overexposure to the sun is likely to give a bleached appearance.

HISTORY
Early Blacks frequently exhibited Angora traits *(see p.72)*, which have now been successfully bred out. World War II interrupted breeding programmes in Europe, but not in the US, where a Black Longhair has been voted Cat of the Year a record three times.

TEMPERAMENT
The Black Longhair makes a loyal and affectionate companion, although it can be suspicious of strangers. It is said to be more lively than its white counterpart.

VARIETIES
There are no varieties of Black Longhair.

EYES Large, round, and deep orange or brilliant copper in colour.

EARS Small and round-tipped, with tufts.

FACIAL CHARACTERISTICS

BODY Solid and stocky, with a low carriage, good breadth across shoulders, and a deep chest.

TAIL Short and fluffy, carried straight and low.

LEGS Short, thick, and well covered with fur.

REGULAR GROOMING
Keeping the coat of the Black Longhair in this sort of immaculate condition requires an owner dedicated to grooming.

LONG-STANDING BREED
A true original, this natural
breed is one of the oldest.

HEAD Round and broad,
with full cheeks and a
snub nose that should
have a black nose pad.

COAT Has long guard hairs
and must be a gleaming coal-
black without a single white
hair, rustiness, or any kind of
marking. Kittens may legitimately
have temporary shading or
white speckles; these should
disappear after eight months
or so. Full neck ruff.

FEET Paws should be large
and round, with black paw
pads in Australia and Britain,
and black or brown in the US.

White Longhair

To its devoted followers, the White Longhair combines all the virtues of its type: glamour, a noble expression, fur that is silky to the touch, and a sweet, tranquil nature. Apart from daily grooming, it does not need any special care.

EARS Neat and small with rounded tips and tufts, set far apart and low on the head.

EYES Large, round, and full. Colour should be brilliant blue, orange, or copper, with both eyes having an equal depth of colour.

FACIAL CHARACTERISTICS

HISTORY
Although pure white cats of the Angora type *(see p.72)* were the first Longhairs to be introduced into Europe as long ago as the 16th century, the modern White Longhair is of Victorian origin. It was developed by crossing Angoras with Persians. The breed was first shown in London in 1903, and has increased in popularity since, particularly in the US.

TEMPERAMENT
White Longhairs are fastidious cats that take great pride in their appearance, regularly cleaning themselves. They are calm and affectionate, and make a superb pet for those confined indoors – a classic salon cat.

VARIETIES
Varieties are defined by the eye colour: these cats can be blue-eyed, orange-eyed, or odd-eyed (one blue, one orange). The blue-eyed variety is genetically predisposed to deafness. In odd-eyed cats, deafness may be apparent on the blue-eyed side.

TAIL Short and bushy, carried uncurved and generally at an angle lower than the line of the back.

HEAD Round and broad, with a snub nose and a pink nose pad.

COAT Fur should be lush and silky, forming an immense neck ruff. Colour needs to be a pure, glistening white.

BODY A typical, sturdy, cobby type.

FEET Paws should be large and round with pink pads.

LEGS Sturdy, short, and thick.

BLUE-EYED AND ORANGE-EYED WHITE LONGHAIRS
Both longhaired and shorthaired white cats have varieties that are categorized by eye colour.

Cream Longhair

Before the standard was modified, this luxurious animal was required to be the colour of rich cream, a description that suits perfectly the glamorous good looks of the breed.

HISTORY

The first Cream Longhair probably originated from an off-white variety of the early Angoras *(see p.72)*. Later, accidental matings between Blue Longhairs *(see pp.40–41)* and Red Longhairs *(see p.42)*, or else Tortoiseshells *(see pp.52–3)* and Red Tabbies *(see pp.50–51)*, produced some pale cats that were not taken seriously by British breeders, who nicknamed them "spoiled Oranges", a reference to the fact that Red Longhairs were known as Oranges. American breeders were not so dismissive of the cream-coloured cats, and began to develop the variety. Breeding in Great Britain did not begin in earnest until the 1920s.

TEMPERAMENT

An even-tempered and friendly cat.

VARIETIES

There are no varieties of Cream Longhair.

EARS Small and round-tipped.

EYES Large and round; rich copper in colour

HEAD Broad and round with a snub nose that should have a pink nose pad. Full cheeks.

FACIAL CHARACTERISTICS

AN UNCOMMON LONGHAIR

Probably because they tend to have small litters, Creams are less numerous than most other breeds of Longhairs.

COAT Colour must be sound to the roots. US standard stipulates a colour of buff cream; in Australia and Britain, shades range from buttermilk through rich cream to pale honey. Fur is dense and silky.

TAIL Short and bushy.

BODY A sturdy, cobby type.

LEGS Sturdy and short.

FEET Large and round, the paws should have pink pads.

Blue Longhair

LARGER MALES The male Blue Longhair tends to be larger than the female.

Of all the Longhairs, the Blue's popularity has been the most enduring. One hundred examples of the breed were entered in the 1899 London Cat Show, and today there are special shows in Britain devoted solely to Blues. Carefully controlled breeding has ensured that the Blue most closely represents the standard laid down for Longhairs, and as a result it is frequently used to improve the type of other varieties.

HISTORY

Although longhaired blue cats have featured in artists' impressions for several centuries, and were well known in Renaissance Italy, the modern variety did not come into its own until the late 19th century. The breed probably originated from crossbreeding between Black Longhairs *(see pp.36–7)* and White Longhairs *(see p.38)*, and early examples showed tabby markings. The foundation of the Blue Persian Society in 1901 gave the breed considerable prestige, which was further enhanced by the patronage of Queen Victoria.

TEMPERAMENT

The Blue Longhair has a well-deserved reputation for being calm, considered, and, above all, gentle.

VARIETIES

There are no varieties of Blue Longhair.

TAIL Short and fluffy, usually carried straight and low.

NOT TRUE BLUE The "blue" that gives the breed its name is, in fact, a diluted form of black that may more accurately be described as blue-grey.

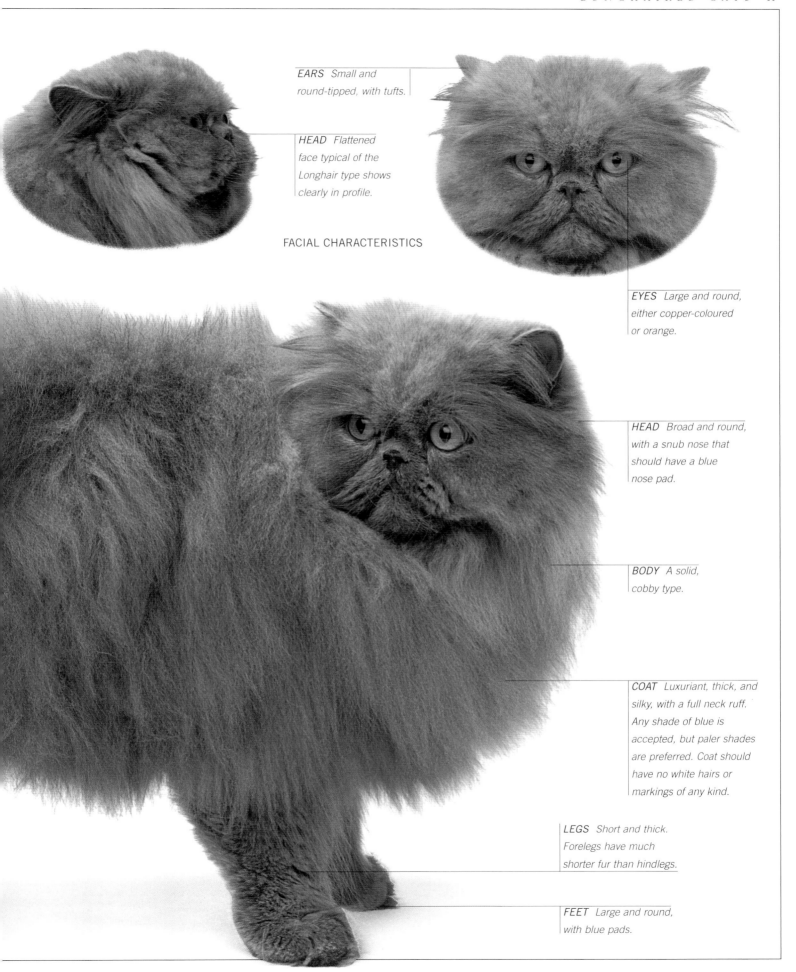

EARS Small and
round-tipped, with tufts.

HEAD Flattened
face typical of the
Longhair type shows
clearly in profile.

FACIAL CHARACTERISTICS

EYES Large and round,
either copper-coloured
or orange.

HEAD Broad and round,
with a snub nose that
should have a blue
nose pad.

BODY A solid,
cobby type.

COAT Luxuriant, thick, and
silky, with a full neck ruff.
Any shade of blue is
accepted, but paler shades
are preferred. Coat should
have no white hairs or
markings of any kind.

LEGS Short and thick.
Forelegs have much
shorter fur than hindlegs.

FEET Large and round,
with blue pads.

Red Self Longhair

It is rare to come across a perfect example of this striking, flame-coloured cat. In practice, most have some tabby markings, particularly on the face, legs, and tail. Elsewhere, the long coat helps to make the markings less evident. Within a litter there may be some kittens that are Red Self and others that are Red Tabby.

HISTORY

Oranges, as Red Longhairs were originally known, were being shown in Britain as early as 1895. In the early 1930s, a German breeder produced some excellent examples of the breed, but unfortunately his stock was destroyed during World War II. The breed remained rare in Britain in the 1940s, but a revival of interest and selective breeding have ensured the Red Self's presence on show benches in Australia and Britain.

TEMPERAMENT

Polite and friendly, the Red Self is a decorative and pleasant companion.

VARIETIES

Peke-faced Reds and Red Tabbies sometimes appear as spontaneous mutations in otherwise normal litters of Red Self kittens. These varieties are controversial because the extreme, squashed facial features may cause breathing difficulties as well as skin problems.

FACIAL CHARACTERISTICS

EARS Small and round-tipped, with fine ear tufts.

EYES Large, round, and brilliant copper in colour.

HEAD Broad and round with a snub nose. The nose pad should be brick-red. Lips and chin should be the same colour as the coat.

RARE EXCELLENCE One of the hardest types to breed for exhibition, good examples of Red Selfs are few.

BODY A solid, cobby type.

COAT Fur is silky and lush, and should be a deep orange-red colour with no shading or tabby markings.

FEET Large and round, with pads that are brick-red in colour.

LEGS Short and thick-set.

TAIL Short and fluffy, usually carried straight and low.

Blue-Cream Longhair

A coat that is a pleasing mixture of mottled cream and pale blue-grey has ensured this breed's enormous popularity. The way in which colour genes are inherited means that male Blue-Cream Longhairs are rare, and almost invariably sterile.

HISTORY
The result of mating Blues *(see pp.40–41)* and Creams *(see p.39)*, longhaired blue-cream cats appeared in litters in the early days of pedigree breeding. They were not accorded official recognition in Great Britain, however, until as late as 1930.

TEMPERAMENT
The Blue-Cream is considered more outgoing than many Longhairs, but it is equally affectionate and amenable.

VARIETIES
There are no varieties of Blue-Cream Longhair, but standards differ. Whereas in Australia and Great Britain a gentle intermingling of the two colours is desired, in the US the blue and creams should form distinct patches.

EARS Small and round-tipped, with ear tufts.

EYES Large and round; should be deep, brilliant copper or orange in colour.

FACIAL CHARACTERISTICS

TAIL Short and bushy, usually carried uncurved and lower than the line of the back.

BODY Very solid and cobby.

HEAD Broad and round, with a snub nose. Nose pad should be blue.

COAT Silky, dense fur. Colour should be a soft mixture of pastel shades of blue and cream.

LEGS Short and thick.

COBBY PERFECTION The best specimens of this breed have a build that is a near-perfect example of the cobby Longhair type.

FEET Large and round, with toe tufts; pads should be blue.

Chinchilla Longhair

Unlike the rodent chinchilla, which has a dark undercoat tipped with white, this cat sports the reverse coloration, giving it a distinctly sparkling appearance. Its luxurious coat requires meticulous grooming to show it to best advantage.

HISTORY

The Chinchilla is one of the earliest man-made varieties, and it was given its own class at Crystal Palace in 1894. It is thought to have evolved from crossbreeding a range of Longhairs, most notably Silver Tabbies *(see pp.50–51)*, and was at first much darker, frequently lavender-tinted, and more heavily marked than the modern form. The pursuit of a paler coloration weakened European stock, which was further depleted during World War II. American types were imported to improve the breed, which is now strong and healthy.

TEMPERAMENT

Chinchillas are sometimes said to be more temperamental than other Longhairs, but they generally have the same affectionate, calm disposition.

VARIETIES

There is one variety, the Shaded Silver.

EYES Large and round; colour should be emerald green or blue-green, outlined in black or dark brown.

EARS Small and round-tipped, with ear tufts.

HEAD Round and broad with a brick-red snub nose outlined in black or dark brown.

FACIAL CHARACTERISTICS

ALSO KNOWN AS... A coat that has the sheen of precious metal has earned this breed the popular name of Silver Persian in the US.

TAIL Short and bushy, normally carried uncurved below the line of the back.

COAT Fur is dense and silky. Colour should be snow white, with black tipping.

BODY Less cobby than usual for a Longhair, with a finer bone structure.

LEGS *Short, thick, and furry.*

FEET *Large and round paws with paw pads that are either black or dark brown.*

DECEPTIVE APPEARANCE More delicate in appearance than the typical Longhair, the Chinchilla is nonetheless a robust, hardy, individual – as this typically playful pose illustrates.

SHADED SILVER LONGHAIR It is more difficult to breed this variety than the Chinchilla because the standard requires heavier, darker tipping to form a mantle shading down the face, sides, and tail.

Cameo Longhair

Like that of the Chinchilla *(see pp.44–5)*, the Cameo's beauty stems from the contrast between its white undercoat and its tipped guard hairs, which can be red, cream, tabby, or tortie.

HISTORY

A breeding programme for Cameos was established in the United States during the 1950s. Originally produced from Smoke *(see p.48)* and Tortoiseshell *(see pp.52–3)* pairings, Cameos can now count other colours in their lineage.

TEMPERAMENT

Languorous and amenable.

VARIETIES

The extent to which the tipping is distributed along the length of the Cameo's hair shaft varies to produce different and dramatic coats. Shell varieties have short coloured tips that give a subtle misty effect; Shaded Cameos have longer coloured tips that glint against the white; and Smoke varieties have such long tips that the white undercoat cannot be seen until the cat moves.

COAT Fur is silky, thick, and dense. Must be white with medium-long cream tips.

BODY A typical cobby type.

TAIL Short and bushy, carried uncurved, usually lower than the line of the back.

LEGS Short and firm.

VARIETIES	MARKINGS	EYES
Red Shell Cameo	Short red tips	Copper
Red Shaded Cameo	Longer red tips	Copper
Red Smoke Cameo	Longest red tips	Copper
Cream Shell Cameo	Short cream tips	Copper
Cream Shaded Cameo	Longer cream tips	Copper
Cream Smoke Cameo	Longest cream tips	Copper
Blue-Cream Cameo	Intermingled tipping in two colours	Copper
Tortie Cameo	Black, red, cream tips	Copper
Tabby Cameo	Cream, red tips	Copper

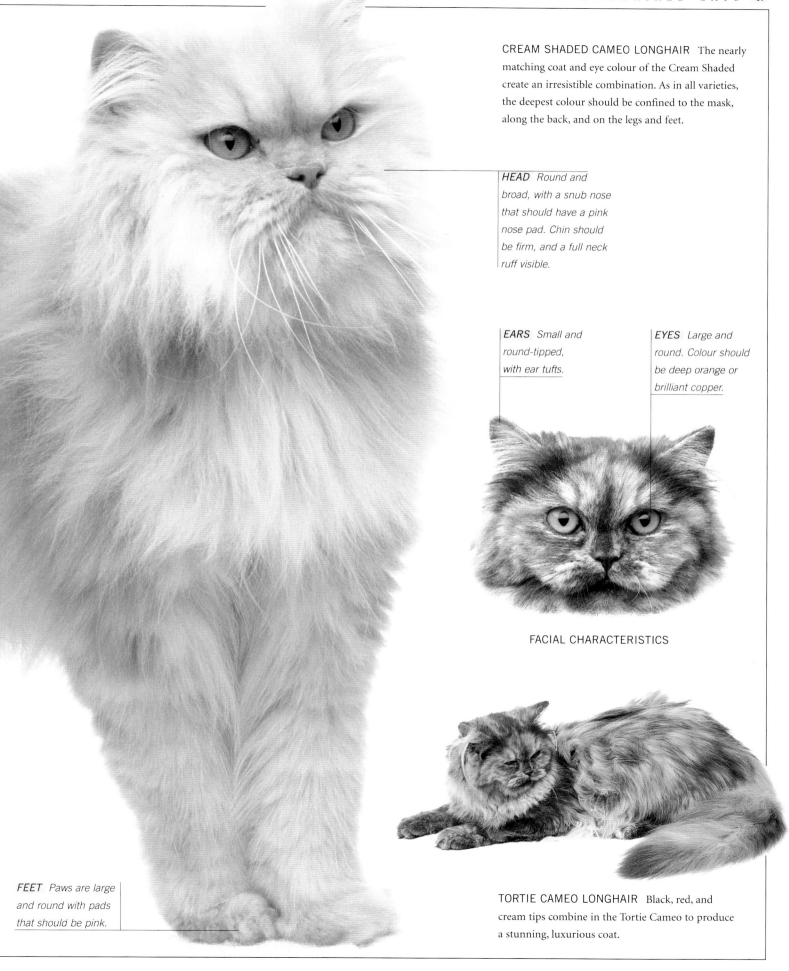

CREAM SHADED CAMEO LONGHAIR The nearly matching coat and eye colour of the Cream Shaded create an irresistible combination. As in all varieties, the deepest colour should be confined to the mask, along the back, and on the legs and feet.

HEAD Round and broad, with a snub nose that should have a pink nose pad. Chin should be firm, and a full neck ruff visible.

EARS Small and round-tipped, with ear tufts.

EYES Large and round. Colour should be deep orange or brilliant copper.

FACIAL CHARACTERISTICS

FEET Paws are large and round with pads that should be pink.

TORTIE CAMEO LONGHAIR Black, red, and cream tips combine in the Tortie Cameo to produce a stunning, luxurious coat.

Smoke Longhair

As the British standard describes it, this is a beautiful "cat of contrasts". Deep tipping gives the appearance of a solid colour, but when the cat moves, the pale undercoat shows through momentarily to produce a delightful shimmer. Keeping the coat in optimum condition is a time-consuming task, and preparation for a show may take weeks. Showing is generally best left for the winter months, because bright sunlight can cause the coat to fade.

HISTORY

Thought to have originated from chance matings between Blacks, Blues, Whites, and Chinchillas, the Smoke Longhair is mentioned in the record books as early as 1860 and appeared in the first cat shows. Numbers quickly declined, however: only 18 were registered in 1912, with the breed becoming almost extinct by the end of World War II. The 1960s saw a revival of interest and, although still uncommon, the breed's future is undoubtedly assured.

TEMPERAMENT

"Smokey" has the relaxed, good-natured, and gentle character typical of most Longhairs.

VARIETIES

Varieties include black, blue, tortoiseshell, chocolate, lilac, and blue-cream tipped types. All varieties have orange or copper eyes.

FACIAL CHARACTERISTICS

EARS *Small and round-tipped, with silver ear tufts.*

EYES *Large, round, and copper or orange in colour.*

HEAD *Round and broad black mask, with a short black nose.*

BLACK SMOKE LONGHAIR Only when a kitten is some months old is it possible to tell whether it will mature into as fine an example as this. Until then, solid-coloured Blacks and Smokes in the same litter may be indistinguishable. One of the most attractive features of the Black Smoke is the contrast between the silver neck ruff and the dark head. If preparing for a show, it is advisable to keep the Smoke out of bright sunlight to prevent the coat becoming bleached.

BODY *A solid, cobby type that tends to be slightly lighter than is usual for Longhairs.*

COAT *Fur is silky, thick, and dense. Undercoat should be milk-white, with black tipping that is solid to the roots in Australia and Great Britain, and white at the roots in the US.*

TAIL *Short and bushy.*

LEGS *Short and thick. They should be solid black in colour.*

FEET *Paws are large and round; paw pads should be black in colour.*

Bicolour Longhair

White plus another colour is a classic combination and, despite the numerous bicoloured street cats, this breed can be thought of as very much a "designer" cat.

HISTORY

Bicolour Longhairs were given their own class only in the late 1960s. The original standard stipulated that the patching should be exactly symmetrical; this proved so difficult that requirements were eased to allow any even distribution of colour.

TEMPERAMENT

The Bicolour Longhair is a placid, affectionate, charming cat.

VARIETIES

These beautiful cats can be any solid colour plus white, the most widely accepted being Black-and-White, Blue-and-White, Red-and-White, and Cream-and-White. The Persian Van Bicolour has head and tail patching resembling that of the Turkish Van (see pp.70–71).

EARS Small and round-tipped, with ear tufts.

EYES Large, round, and orange or copper in colour.

HEAD Round and broad, with a snub nose. Nose pad should either be pink or match the coloured patches of the coat.

FACIAL CHARACTERISTICS

BLACK-AND-WHITE BICOLOUR LONGHAIR The original form of the Bicolour, the Black-and-White was at first meant to imitate the symmetrical markings of a Dutch rabbit. The standard was eventually altered, however, when this proved virtually impossible to achieve.

COAT Fur is dense, silky, and lush; coloured patches should be solid and evenly distributed.

BODY A solid cobby type.

CREAM-AND-WHITE BICOLOUR LONGHAIR
As with all Bicolours, the white of this fairly new variety's coat should cover a maximum of half of the cat, and the coloured patches up to two thirds.

TAIL Short and bushy.

FEET Paws are large and round with pink paw pads.

LEGS Short and thick.

Tabby Longhair

Much rarer than the corresponding shorthaired breed, the Tabby Longhair is nonetheless an old-timer, making its first appearance in Europe by the end of the 17th century.

HISTORY
The Modern Tabby Longhair emerged during the latter half of the 19th century.

TEMPERAMENT
Some owners consider that the Tabby is more independent than is typical for a Longhair, but it still has the same equable nature.

VARIETIES
The Classic should have a butterfly shape on the shoulders, three stripes running down the spine to the base of the tail, an oyster-shaped spiral on each flank, and narrow "necklaces" across the chest. Both the tail and the legs should be evenly ringed, the abdomen spotted, and a characteristic "M" should decorate the forehead. The Mackerel pattern is less blotchy, more striped, and lacks the spirals on the flanks. A "Torbie", or Patched Tabby, also occurs. As well as the original tabby colours of brown, red, and silver, there are also newer varieties (see chart, below).

COAT Fur is dense and silky. Classic tabby markings should be slate-blue over a bluish-ivory base colour. Side markings should be symmetrical.

BROWN CLASSIC TABBY LONGHAIR "Brownies" may be the oldest variety of the Tabby Longhair, but they are still the most rare.

TAIL Short and bushy. Ring markings on the tail are obscured by the long, fine hair.

VARIETIES	COAT	EYES
Red Tabby	Rich copper marked in red	Copper or orange
Brown Tabby	Tawny brown marked in black	Copper or orange
Silver Tabby	Silver-grey marked in black	Copper, green, or hazel
Blue Tabby	Bluish-ivory marked in slate-blue	Copper
Cream Tabby	Pale cream marked in rich cream	Copper
Cameo Tabby	Off-white marked in red	Copper
Patched Tabby	Silver, brown, or blue marked with extra red and/or cream patches	Copper or hazel
Chocolate Tabby	Bronze marked in chocolate	Copper or hazel
Lilac Tabby	Beige marked in lilac	Copper or hazel

EARS Small and round-tipped, with ear tufts.

EYES Large, round, and orange or copper in colour.

HEAD Round and broad, with a short, deep rose-pink padded nose.

FACIAL CHARACTERISTICS
Blue Classic Tabby Longhair

FEET Paws are large and round, with pads that should be rose-pink in colour.

BODY A solid, cobby type.

LEGS Short and thick.

SILVER CLASSIC TABBY LONGHAIR
Considered by many to be the most difficult cat to breed to the required standard, the Silver Tabby is also one of the most stunning.

BLUE CLASSIC TABBY LONGHAIR The deep slate-blue markings of this variety may, to the uninitiated, make it hard to distinguish from a Brown Tabby – until the fur is parted to reveal the bluish-grey base colour.

Tortoiseshell Longhair

A virtually female-only breed, the Tortoiseshell is the centre of some debate on how difficult it is to breed: American breeders do not regard it as especially problematic, whereas in Australia and Britain the desired mixture of red, cream, and black patches has proved more elusive, with good specimens quite rare.

HISTORY
Longhaired cats with tortoiseshell markings were first recorded towards the end of the 19th century, and they appeared in the early cat shows of the 1900s. They probably originated from accidental matings between longhaired black cats and shorthaired tortoiseshells.

TEMPERAMENT
The Tortoiseshell Longhair is affectionate, gentle, and placid, with a reputation for being a good mother to its kittens.

VARIETIES
Shell and Shaded Tortoiseshell Longhairs fall within the Shaded Division in the US; in Australia and Britain they are known as Cameos (see pp.46–7).

MIXED PEDIGREE Because it is impossible to breed like with like, the Tortoiseshell includes numerous other breeds in its pedigree. This has resulted in a cobby build that is a fine example of the Longhair type.

AMERICAN TORTOISESHELL LONGHAIR
The US standard stipulates a black cat with unbrindled patches of red and cream. A desirable feature on both sides of the Atlantic is a red or cream blaze on the face, running from the nose to the forehead.

FEET Paws are large and round, with toe tufts. Pads should be pink or black in colour.

LEGS Short and thick.

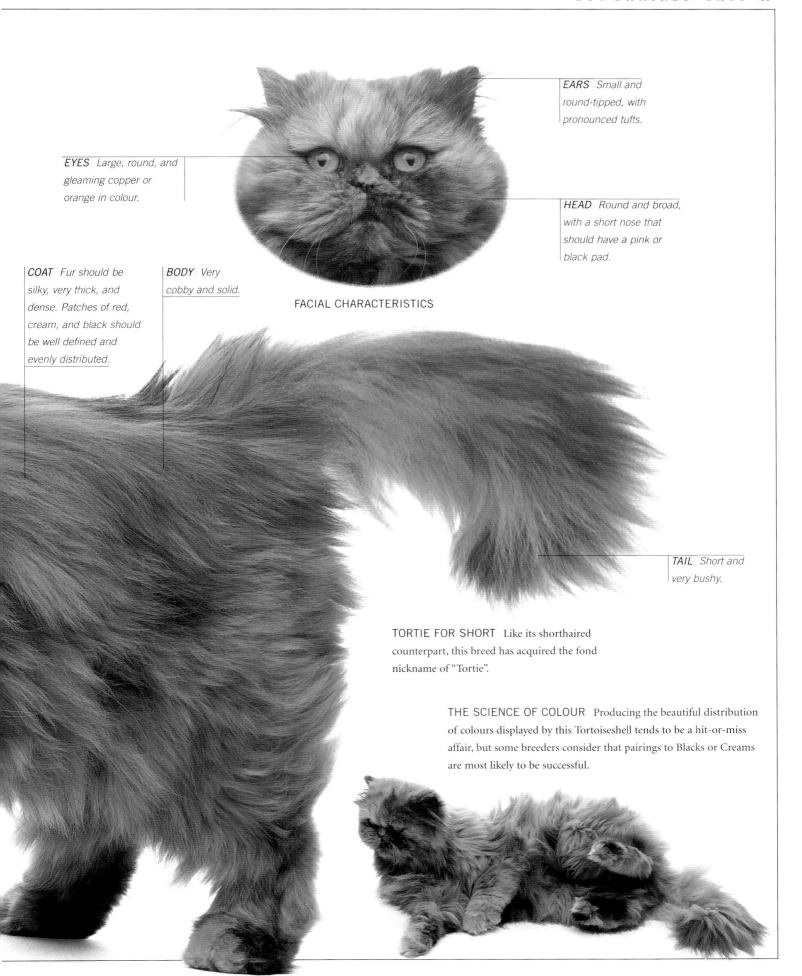

EARS Small and round-tipped, with pronounced tufts.

EYES Large, round, and gleaming copper or orange in colour.

HEAD Round and broad, with a short nose that should have a pink or black pad.

COAT Fur should be silky, very thick, and dense. Patches of red, cream, and black should be well defined and evenly distributed.

BODY Very cobby and solid.

FACIAL CHARACTERISTICS

TAIL Short and very bushy.

TORTIE FOR SHORT Like its shorthaired counterpart, this breed has acquired the fond nickname of "Tortie".

THE SCIENCE OF COLOUR Producing the beautiful distribution of colours displayed by this Tortoiseshell tends to be a hit-or-miss affair, but some breeders consider that pairings to Blacks or Creams are most likely to be successful.

Tortoiseshell-and-White Longhair

Known as a Calico in the US because its bold splashes of colour resemble the popular printed cotton, the Tortoiseshell-and-White is a Tortoiseshell cat with white patches in addition to those of black, red, and cream. Another female-only breed, the Tortoiseshell-and-White is not easy to produce true to type. The kittens are always appealing, however, and there is never a shortage of prospective owners.

HISTORY

Although the Tortoiseshell-and-White's origins are obscure, it probably developed, like the Tortoiseshell *(see pp.52–3)*, from matings between longhaired cats and non-pedigree shorthaired tortoiseshells. It was accepted for championship in the mid-1950s. More recently, consistently good types have been bred by mating queens with Bicolour studs *(see p.49)* produced from Tortoiseshell-and-Whites.

TEMPERAMENT

This is a calm, sweet-natured, and extremely friendly cat.

VARIETIES

The US standard for the Tortoiseshell-and-White differs from that of Australia and Britain, calling for a white cat with coloured patches, the white to be concentrated on the underparts. The Australian and British cats have less white in their coats and more evenly distributed patches of colour. In all three countries, a very popular variety is the Blue Tortoiseshell-and-White, or Dilute Calico. The standard for this most attractive cat is the same as for the Tortie-and-White, but with blue and cream patches instead of black and red.

HEAD A cream or white blaze on the face is a desirable feature.

LEGS Short and thick.

COLOUR DISTRIBUTION
Two views of the same Blue Tortoiseshell-and-White Longhair reveal clearly the random, but still more or less even, distribution of coloured patches.

EARS Small and round-tipped, with tufts.

EYES Large and round, either deep orange or copper in colour.

HEAD Round and broad, with full cheeks. Short nose should have a pink nose pad.

FACIAL CHARACTERISTICS

BODY Solid and cobby.

TAIL Short and bushy.

COAT Dense and silky; said not to mat as easily as that of other Longhairs. Colour is a mixture of blue, cream, and white patches. There should be no brindling or tabby markings.

FEET Large and round, with pink pads.

TORTOISESHELL-AND-WHITE LONGHAIR

It is not hard to understand the enormous popularity of this breed: bright splashes of red, cream, and black contrasted against white create instant appeal. As with the Blue Tortoiseshell-and-White, a facial blaze is desirable. All other features are the same, apart from the paw and nose pads, which are of broken colour.

BLUE TORTOISESHELL-AND-WHITE LONGHAIR

A dilute Tortoiseshell-and-White Longhair, this variety often appears in the same litter.

Colourpoint Longhair

The Colourpoint Longhairs, known as Himalayans in the US, combine the luxurious sophistication of the Longhair family with the poise, good looks, and markings of the shorthaired Siamese (*see pp.114–15*). Like the Siamese, a Colourpoint has bright, sapphire-blue eyes and its mask, ears, legs, feet, and tail (the points) are a different colour to the rest of the body.

HISTORY

Experimental breeding programmes in Sweden and the US during the 1920s produced the first Colourpoints, but it was not until the late 1940s, after a succession of carefully planned crossbreedings between Longhairs and Siamese, that the modern cat emerged.

TEMPERAMENT

To their owners, Colourpoints combine the best of two worlds: they have the gentle nature of a Longhair, but they can also be as spirited as a Siamese, without being so demonstrative.

VARIETIES

All point colours are possible, giving a large number of varieties. The most popular are shown in the chart below.

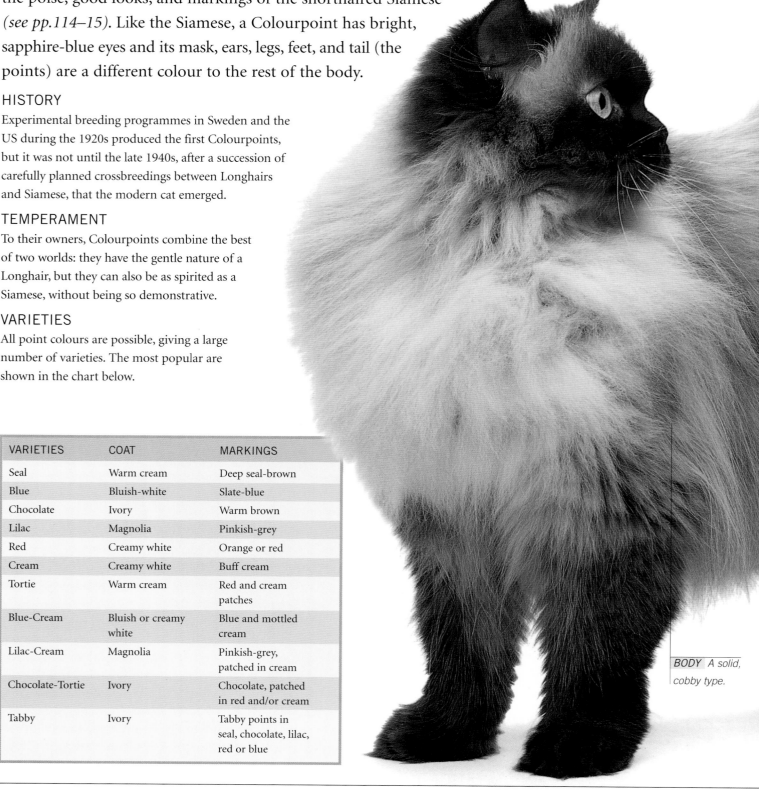

SEAL-POINT COLOURPOINT LONGHAIR
The Seal-point was one of the first varieties of Colourpoint to be developed.

BODY A solid, cobby type.

VARIETIES	COAT	MARKINGS
Seal	Warm cream	Deep seal-brown
Blue	Bluish-white	Slate-blue
Chocolate	Ivory	Warm brown
Lilac	Magnolia	Pinkish-grey
Red	Creamy white	Orange or red
Cream	Creamy white	Buff cream
Tortie	Warm cream	Red and cream patches
Blue-Cream	Bluish or creamy white	Blue and mottled cream
Lilac-Cream	Magnolia	Pinkish-grey, patched in cream
Chocolate-Tortie	Ivory	Chocolate, patched in red and/or cream
Tabby	Ivory	Tabby points in seal, chocolate, lilac, red or blue

EARS Small and round-tipped, with a good width between them.

EYES Large, round, and bright; sapphire-blue in colour.

HEAD Round and broad, with full cheeks and a short nose. Colour of the nose pad should match that of the points.

FACIAL CHARACTERISTICS
Seal-point Colourpoint Longhair

TAIL Short and very full.

COAT Dense, lush, and silky to the touch. Colour should be warm cream with deep seal-brown points.

BLUE-POINT COLOURPOINT LONGHAIR
Slate-blue markings set off to perfection the cold, bluish-white coat of this variety.

LEGS Short, thick, and strong.

FEET Large and round with seal-brown pads and long toe tufts.

SEAL TABBY-POINT COLOURPOINT LONGHAIR
One of the newer varieties, this cat is the result of crossing Brown Tabby Longhairs with Seal-point Colourpoints.

Pewter Longhair

The colouring of this exquisite cat resembles that of the Shaded Silver variety of Chinchilla *(see pp.44–5)*, with which it is sometimes confused. It has a similar handsome white coat, subtly shaded with black over the head, back, flanks, legs, and tail to give the effect of a pewter mantle. Its eye colour is different, however, being bright orange or brilliant copper.

HISTORY
The Pewter Longhair was produced as a result of crossing Chinchillas, Blues *(see pp.40–41)*, and Blacks *(see pp.36–7)*.

TEMPERAMENT
This is an exceptionally affectionate and even-tempered cat.

VARIETIES
There are no varieties of Pewter Longhair.

APTLY NAMED BREED "Pewter" describes perfectly the colour of the breed's tipped mantle.

EARS *Small, round-tipped, and tufted, with a good width between them.*

EYES *Very large and round, with black rims. Either orange or copper in colour.*

HEAD *Round and broad, with a snub nose that gives it a flat profile. The nose pad should be brick-red.*

FACIAL CHARACTERISTICS

COAT *Silky, thick, dense, with long guard hairs. Colour is white with subtle black tipping.*

BODY *A chunky, cobby type.*

STRIKING ADDITION New Longhairs are being developed all the time, among which the Pewter must rank as one of the most attractive. On first inspection it may look like a Shaded Silver Chinchilla, but orange or copper-coloured eyes are a distinguishing feature that firmly identifies the breed.

LEGS *Short and thick. Hair is shorter on the forelegs.*

HIDDEN SHAPE When the Pewter is lying down, its thick, luxurious coat and full frill make it virtually impossible to discern the cat's cobby build.

TAIL Short with a full brush. Guard hairs are delicately tipped in black.

SHOW STANDARDS A Pewter that is destined for the show ring ideally should have a full neck ruff that extends into a deep frill between the front legs.

FEET Large and round with brick-red pads.

Chocolate and Lilac Longhairs

This stunning pair represents a triumph of selective breeding, and might be considered the ultimate "designer" cats: the warm brown tones of the Chocolate and the pinkish dove-grey coat of the Lilac would make a charming decorative addition to any interior colour scheme.

CHOCOLATE LONGHAIR A by-product of the Colourpoint breeding programme, this cat should have a rich, medium to dark chocolate-brown coat, brown nose and paw pads, and orange or copper-coloured eyes.

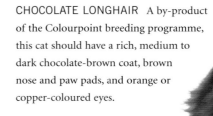

HISTORY

Breeders did not seriously consider developing a chocolate-coloured Longhair until breeding programmes for Colourpoints *(see pp.56–7)* produced solid-coloured kittens in the same litter. Early examples had fur that was prone to fade and bleach, weak eye colour, noses that tended to be too long, and ears that were too tall. It took several years before the colour was made more stable, the type improved, and a standard was able to be laid down. If anything, the Lilac Longhair, which was produced by introducing Blue genes *(see pp.40–41)* into breeding lines, proved even more elusive, and it is still relatively rare. At one stage, these cats were categorized in the US as solid-coloured Himalayans or Kashmirs, but these descriptions have now been dropped by most associations.

TEMPERAMENT

Having inherited some of the Siamese blood carried by their Colourpoint relations, Chocolates and Lilacs tend to be more outgoing and inquisitive than is usual for Longhairs.

VARIETIES

There are no varieties of the Chocolate or the Lilac Longhair.

FEET Large and round, with pink pads.

EARS *Small, round-tipped, with tufts, and set wide apart.*

EYES *Large and round; colour should be orange or copper.*

HEAD *Round and broad, with full cheeks; snub nose should have a pink pad.*

FACIAL CHARACTERISTICS

BREEDING FOR BUILD

Although breeders experienced early difficulties in achieving the desired cobby build for the Chocolate, once those problems were overcome, producing a Lilac of good type, if not of good colour, was comparatively straightforward.

COAT *Fur should be silky, lush, and thick; colour should be a pinkish dove-grey or lavender, sound to the roots, with no sign of a pale undercoat. Full frill.*

LILAC LONGHAIR The Lilac is an example of a recently developed Longhair and illustrates beautifully the aesthetic possibilities of "man-made" varieties.

TAIL *Short and bushy.*

BODY *A cobby, chunky, solid type.*

LEGS *Short and thick.*

Golden Longhair

In their endeavours to create yet more beautiful variations on the longhaired theme, cat breeders created the Golden Longhair in the late 20th century. The hairs on this cat's coat are evenly sprinkled with black or brown tipping to give a beautiful golden effect.

HISTORY

The Chinchilla Golden and Shaded Golden were by-products of the Chinchilla breeding programme *(see pp.44–5)*. Often referred to as "Brownies", they appeared regularly in litters of Silvers, but were most often sold as pets. They eventually achieved show status in the 1980s.

TEMPERAMENT

These new varieties of Longhair usually display the gentle, affectionate disposition typical of the type.

VARIETIES

There are two varieties of the Golden Longhair: the Chinchilla and the Shaded.

CHINCHILLA GOLDEN LONGHAIR As with all varieties of Chinchilla, the Golden requires a great deal of preparation if the coat is to be shown to best advantage.

HEAD Round and broad, with a snub nose that has a rose-coloured pad.

BODY A cobby, solid type.

LEGS Short, thick, and furry.

FEET Paws are large and round, with seal-brown paw pads.

EARS Small and round-tipped, with ear tufts.

EYES Large and round, green or blue-green in colour, and outlined in brown.

FACIAL CHARACTERISTICS

CHINCHILLA SILVER LONGHAIR KITTENS This cat has a white, rather than cream, ground colour, again with delicate black tipping, making its appearance one of the most sublimely ethereal of all Longhairs.

TAIL Short and bushy.

COAT Fur is silky, thick, and dense. Colour should be rich cream, with seal-brown or black tipping.

SHADED GOLDEN LONGHAIRS Long, silky fur and a mantle of black tipping over a warm-cream undercoat makes for a rich combination that is bringing these cats increasingly before the public eye.

Birman

The "sacred cat of Burma", as the Birman is popularly known, has a longer body and narrower face than a typical Longhair, with markings reminiscent of a Siamese, giving it as oriental an aura as the legends that shroud its past.

HISTORY

Said to have originated in the temples of Burma (now Myanmar), the Birman has a more recent history that is almost as colourful. In 1919 two of these cats were sent to Major Gordon Russell in France as a token of gratitude from the priests he had helped to escape from Tibet. The female of the pair subsequently gave birth and may have helped found the breed in the West. Birmans were recognized for showing in France in 1925, in Britain in 1966, and in the US a year later, followed closely by Australia.

TEMPERAMENT

Amenable, civilized, and gentle, Birmans enjoy family life and adapt well to other animals. I can vouch for this; I have five of my own.

VARIETIES

Varieties include the original, "sacred", Seal-point and Blue-, Chocolate-, Lilac-, Cream-, Red-, Tortie-, and Tabby-points.

TAIL *Medium in length and bushy, but longer and finer than in most longhaired cats.*

BLUE-POINT BIRMAN

Tradition has its own story to tell of the development of the Birman. Before the birth of the Lord Buddha, a sacred Burmese temple containing pure white cats was attacked, which led to the high priest collapsing and dying. His favourite cat jumped on to the old man's head and was suddenly transformed: its coat became golden, with points the colour of the Burmese soil, and its eyes turned blue. Where the cat's paws touched the priest, the fur remained white – a symbol of goodness. Encouraged by the miracle, the remaining priests were able to successfully fend off the invaders. However true the tale, the development of this variety was definitely the result of modern selective breeding.

FEET *Paws are large and round, gloved in white, with pink pads. The rear pair should have white gauntlets, extending into "laces" up the back legs.*

LEGS *Medium in length and thick-set.*

SEAL-POINT BIRMAN A characteristic soft, golden hue to the coat, especially over the back, lends the Seal-point Birman a rather distinguished appearance.

LONGHAIRED SIAMESE? The coloration and markings of the Birman give it the look of a long-coated Siamese.

COAT Non-matting, medium in length, and silky in texture. The stomach fur has a tendency to curl. In Australia and Britain, the colour is beige-gold with blue-grey points; in the US, these cats are bluish-white with deep-blue points.

BLUE-POINT AND SEAL-POINT KITTENS A more appealing group than this would be hard to picture.

BODY Strongly built, elongated but still stocky; neither svelte nor cobby.

EARS Should be medium in size, round-tipped and almost as wide at the base as they are tall.

EYES Almost round, set well apart, and slightly slanted. Colour should be sapphire-blue.

FACIAL CHARACTERISTICS

HEAD Fairly round and broad, with a medium-length nose, the pad of which is slate-grey. Australian standard requires the nose to be "Roman" and the forehead slightly convexed and backward-sloping, with a small, flat area just in front of the ears.

VARIETY	BODY	POINTS
Seal-point	Beige-gold	Seal-brown
Chocolate-point	Ivory	Chocolate
Blue-point	Beige-gold	Blue-grey
Lilac-point	Milk-white	Pink-tinged grey

Ragdoll

The Ragdoll is a cat of contrasts: it has the large, imposing physique of a Birman, but when picked up it relaxes all its muscles to become as weak as a kitten and as floppy as the doll from which it takes its name. It was once commonly believed that Ragdolls had a high tolerance to pain, a characteristic inherited, it was said, from the original Ragdolls born to a longhaired queen that had been injured in an automobile accident. However, both vets and breeders are adamant that, in their experience, the Ragdoll's pain threshold is no different to that of any other breed and that to believe otherwise is likely to be detrimental to individual cats.

HISTORY
California in the 1960s was the birthplace of the Ragdoll. The breed has since become increasingly popular outside the US and is recognized by international cat associations.

TEMPERAMENT
The Ragdoll is a cat that is extremely tolerant of the foibles and whims of others, and it quickly becomes devoted to its owner.

VARIETIES
There are three recognized coat patterns for the Ragdoll: the Bicolour has a pale body, a white chest, underbelly, and legs, with a dark mask, ears, and tail; the Colourpoint has a pale body with darker points; and the Mitted has a white chest, bib, chin, and front paw "mittens", but is otherwise the same as the Colourpoint. The established colours are Seal-point, Chocolate-point, Blue-point, and Lilac-point.

EARS Medium in size, round-tipped, and tilted forwards.

EYES Large and oval, set far apart. Colour should be blue.

FACIAL CHARACTERISTICS

TAIL Long and fluffy.

BODY Similar to the Birman; a long, muscular, solid type with a deep chest and heavy hindquarters.

BICOLOUR RAGDOLL KITTEN
Ragdoll kittens are slow to mature, and it may be three years before the shading of the coat and the point colours are fully developed.

SEAL-POINT COLOURPOINT RAGDOLL Despite the origins of its name, physiological tests have detected no difference between the Ragdoll and other breeds.

HEAD Wedge-shaped, with a short nose, full cheeks, and a full, round chin. The mask is a dense seal-brown, providing a distinct contrast with the body colour.

CHOCOLATE-POINT MITTED RAGDOLL KITTEN The white "mittens" and boots are clearly visible even at this early age.

COAT Long, full, and silky. Body colour should be pale fawn, with dark, seal-brown points, although the colour shades to pale cream on underparts. Fur is extra-long on the chest and stomach and is claimed to mat less than is usual for longhairs; it breaks when the cat moves.

LEGS Medium in length, although the forelegs are slightly shorter than the hindlegs.

FEET Large and round, with pads that are either dark brown or black.

SEAL-POINT BICOLOUR RAGDOLL Dense, seal-brown ears, tail, and mask are contrasted against the fawn and pale cream of the rest of the coat in this variety. The inverted white "V" on the face is characteristic of Bicolours.

Balinese

When this cat walks with its tail held erect, its graceful tail plume sways from side to side in a manner not unlike that of a Balinese dancer – hence its name. The natural elegance of the Balinese stems from its Siamese origins: it has the same long, svelte body, wedge-shaped head, and entrancing blue eyes. It can, in fact, be thought of as a longhaired Siamese, although its ermine-like coat is shorter than most longhairs and does not form a ruff.

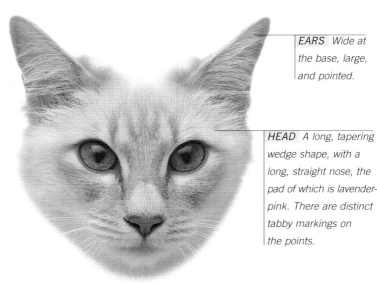

EARS *Wide at the base, large, and pointed.*

HEAD *A long, tapering wedge shape, with a long, straight nose, the pad of which is lavender-pink. There are distinct tabby markings on the points.*

FACIAL CHARACTERISTICS

HISTORY

Most probably, the Balinese derived from Siamese parents carrying a mutant gene for long hair. It appeared first in the US during the late 1940s or early 1950s, and was accepted for championship by all US associations by 1970. The Balinese has keen fan clubs in Britain, Australia, and some other parts of the world.

TEMPERAMENT

The Balinese has the reputation for being less loud and boisterous than a Siamese, but with a tendency to be very playful with its offspring. It usually adores human company.

VARIETIES

All the Siamese colours are recognized for the Balinese. Varieties other than Seal-point, Chocolate-point, Blue-point, and Lilac-point are known as Javanese by some US associations.

LILAC TABBY-POINT BALINESE
This variety is known as a Frost Lynx-point in the US, a name that perhaps more accurately describes its delicate markings.

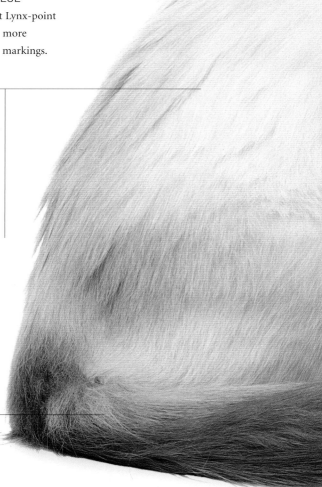

COAT *The relatively non-matting fur is fine and silky, with a tendency to wave where it is longest. There is no soft undercoat. The mask, ears, legs, tail, and feet should be pinkish-grey in colour, contrasting with an even, milk-white body colour.*

TAIL *Long and thin, with a fine point. The tail fur should spread out like a plume.*

BLUE-POINT BALINESE Slate-blue paw and nose pads and blue points provide striking contrast against a blue-white body in this variety.

EYES Medium in size
and almond-shaped.
Colour should be
sapphire-blue.

BODY Medium in size,
and lithe; strong and
muscular, with long,
tapering lines.

FEET Paws are neat, small, and oval,
and the pads are lavender-pink.

LEGS Long and slim,
with the forelegs shorter
than the hindlegs.

CHOCOLATE TABBY-POINT BALINESE KITTENS This is a
popular variety of a popular breed.

Turkish Van

Often referred to as the "Turkish Swimming Cat", this naturally evolved breed is said to be particularly fond of playing in water. It takes its name from the geographically isolated area around Lake Van in south-eastern Turkey, where it has been domesticated for several hundred years. In some ways, it resembles its compatriot, the Angora, or Oriental Longhair *(see p.72)*, but it is sturdier in build and immediately recognizable for its distinctive coat pattern.

HISTORY

Two Turkish Vans were imported into Britain in the 1950s by a couple who had been struck by the unusual markings of the cats they saw while on holiday in Turkey. The pair was found to breed true, and after a slow start, and the introduction of more Turkish stock, recognition was granted in 1969. The popularity of the breed has grown in recent years, especially in the US and Australia, and Turkish Vans are now widely recognized.

TEMPERAMENT

Affectionate, lively, and highly intelligent, the Turkish Van makes an excellent companion.

VARIETIES

Apart from the original Auburn-and-White variety, Cream-and-White, Black-and-White, Tortoiseshell-and-White, Brown/Ebony, Tabby-and-White, and Black Tortie Agouti-and-White Turkish Vans have also been developed.

UNIQUE MARKINGS No other cat has markings quite like those of the Turkish Van. The white, thumb-like, patch on the forehead is said by the Turkish people to symbolize the mark of Allah.

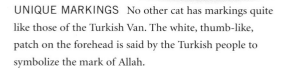

BODY Medium in size, long and muscular.

COAT Fur is silky and long, and should be chalk-white in colour with auburn markings on the face and tail. There is no woolly undercoat.

TAIL Long and feathery.

ODD-EYED AUBURN-AND-WHITE TURKISH VAN Usually amber-eyed, Turkish Vans with odd eyes occasionally appear in litters. They may be prone to the same problems of deafness that afflict other blue- or odd-eyed white cats.

CREAM-AND-WHITE TURKISH VAN Still fairly uncommon, this is a new variety that will no doubt increase in numbers once its delicately shaded markings are more widely appreciated by cat fanciers.

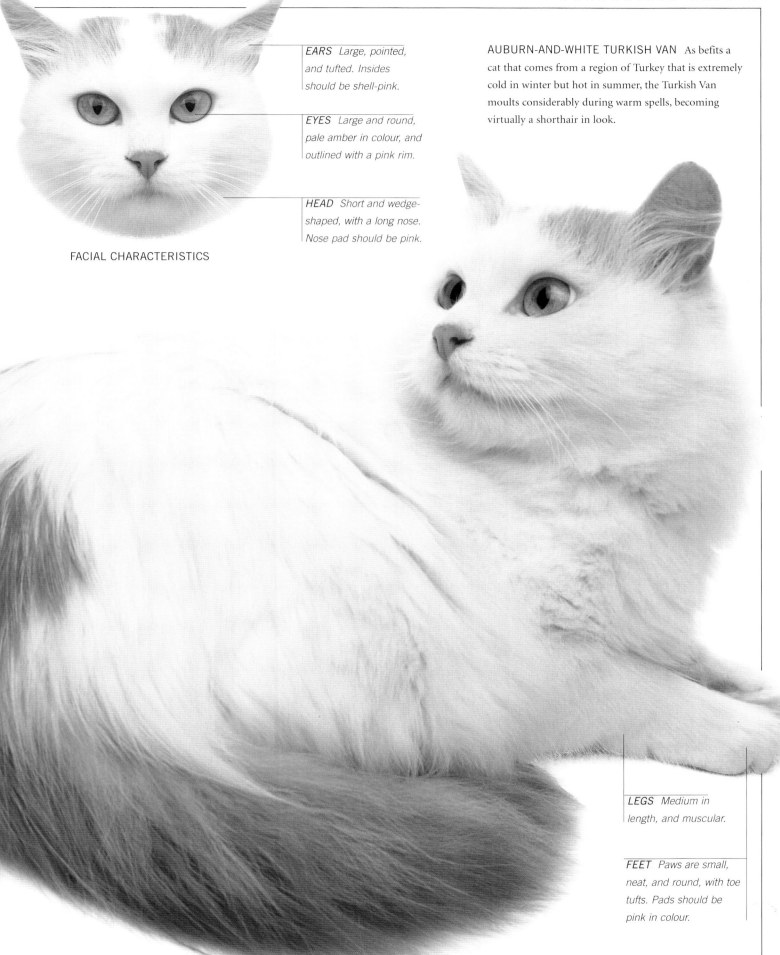

EARS   Large, pointed, and tufted. Insides should be shell-pink.

EYES   Large and round, pale amber in colour, and outlined with a pink rim.

HEAD   Short and wedge-shaped, with a long nose. Nose pad should be pink.

FACIAL CHARACTERISTICS

AUBURN-AND-WHITE TURKISH VAN   As befits a cat that comes from a region of Turkey that is extremely cold in winter but hot in summer, the Turkish Van moults considerably during warm spells, becoming virtually a shorthair in look.

LEGS   Medium in length, and muscular.

FEET   Paws are small, neat, and round, with toe tufts. Pads should be pink in colour.

Oriental Longhair

Since June 2003 the Angora has been known in the UK as the Oriental Longhair (Angora). It is called Oriental Longhair in the US; Javanese by FIFé; and Mandarin by some other cat organizations. This attractive cat has a venerable background.

HISTORY

These cats were sent as gifts from Turkish sultans to the nobles of France and England during the 16th century, but by the end of the 19th century they had fallen out of fashion, being ousted by the new Longhairs and original Persians. Happily, the Ankara Zoo came to the rescue, and the Angora became something of a protected species. In the early 1960s, an American couple purchased two of the cats and re-established the breed in the US. It is not yet recognized in Australia.

TEMPERAMENT

Gentle, friendly, and intelligent, the Oriental Longhair is a fun-loving cat that enjoys playing games.

VARIETIES

The first American Oriental Longhairs were pure white (and prone to deafness). Now, most Longhair coat colours are accepted, some of the most common of which are shown in the chart (*see right*).

EARS Large, wide at the base, and pointed, with tufts.

EYES Medium to large, almond-shaped, and slanted. In Chocolate Tabbies, colour should be green or hazel.

HEAD Small to medium in size and wedge-shaped. Long nose with a red pad.

FACIAL CHARACTERISTICS

VARIETY	COAT	EYES
White	Pure white	Orange, blue, or odd-eyed
Black	Jet-black	Orange
Blue	Blue-grey	Orange
Black Smoke	White, black tips	Orange
Blue Smoke	White, blue tips	Orange
Silver Tabby	Silver, black markings	Orange or green
Red Tabby	Red, rich red markings	Orange
Brown Tabby	Brown, black markings	Orange
Blue Tabby	Bluish-ivory, blue markings	Orange
Calico	White, black, and red patches	Orange
Bicolour	Black, blue, red, or cream with white	Orange

COAT Medium-long, very fine, and silky, with a tendency to wave. No thick woolly undercoat. There should be a well-developed, lush ruff. The cat moults in the winter months.

BODY Medium in size, lithe, and athletic.

CHOCOLATE TABBY ORIENTAL LONGHAIR Angoras in the UK were developed using Siamese blood rather than Turkish stock, producing a cat that looks the same as the original and American Angoras but has a more querulous voice. The Chocolate Tabby is a British variety.

LEGS Long and slim; forelegs are shorter than hindlegs.

TAIL Long and tapering, frequently carried proudly curled, with a full brush.

FEET Small, dainty, and round, with toe tufts.

Tiffany/Chantilly

A cat that is essentially a longhaired Burmese *(see p.122–3)*, the Tiffany has the elegant combination of a modified Foreign or Oriental body type with a luxuriously long, silky coat.

HISTORY

Produced by North American breeders and fanciers from a pair of chocolate-coloured cats of unknown ancestry, the Tiffany is still quite rare and not widely recognized. It is distinct from the Tiffanie, a semi-longhaired breed descended from Burmese/Asian crosses with Longhairs that comes in the Burmese range of colours.

TEMPERAMENT

The Tiffany combines the gentleness typical of a Longhair with the more outgoing and inquisitive personality associated with shorthaired cats.

VARIETIES

A range of coat colour is recognized, including Chocolate, Blue, Cinnamon, Fawn, and Lilac, in solid forms and tabby patterns. The best known Tiffany/Chantilly colour, however, is chocolate.

EARS Medium in size; slightly rounded at the tips and set well apart; tilted forwards.

EYES Rounded to slightly slanted, set wide apart; should be golden in colour.

HEAD Round, with a round chin and a shortish nose with a brown pad.

FACIAL CHARACTERISTICS

BROWN TIFFANY Apart from the length of the coat, all the other features of the breed should be the same as the Burmese.

DEVELOPING COAT COLOUR Tiffany kittens are born a colour that has been described as "café au lait". The darker, mature coat develops gradually, but is usually still slightly lighter in tone than for a Burmese.

COAT Long and silky, the fur should be a warm sable brown in colour.

BODY Medium in size; more muscular and rounded than a Siamese.

TAIL Medium in length and bushy.

LEGS Long and slim in proportion to the body.

FEET Oval to round, with brown paw pads.

Somali

A wild-looking cat that might, to the imagination, have just walked out of an ancient forest, the Somali is a longhaired version of the Abyssinian *(see pp.118–19)*. The fur is lush and slightly shaggy, without any tendency to woolliness. While Abyssinian coat hairs have two to three bands of colour that form the ticking, the longer Somali hairs carry ten or even more bands, giving a very rich colour density.

HISTORY

The longhaired gene may have been introduced into Abyssinian lines during the 1930s, or even before, but Somalis were not systematically developed by North American breeders until the 1960s. A breed club was founded in 1972, and by 1978 the Somali was recognized by all American governing bodies. The breed is now widely distributed throughout Europe and is particularly successful in Australia, where Somalis are bred almost to the exclusion of Abyssinians.

TEMPERAMENT

Somalis are highly intelligent, good-tempered, and playful. They may be slightly more shy than Abyssinians, but are similarly unsuited to a life spent entirely indoors.

VARIETIES

The two most commonly seen varieties are the Usual, or Ruddy, which has a golden-brown coat ticked with darker brown or black, and the Sorrel, or Red, which has a warm-copper coat ticked with chocolate. A recent addition to the show bench is the Silver Sorrel, which should have a sorrel topcoat and a pale undercoat.

SILVER SORREL SOMALI A very new, and still unusual, variety, the Silver Sorrel has already attracted much attention.

USUAL SOMALI Also known as a Ruddy, this variety has a rich, golden-brown coat ticked with black. Darker shading should form a line along the spine and tail, which ends in a black tip. The two short, vertical lines above each eye are another characteristic feature.

COAT Medium-long, dense, silky, and fine-textured, but non-matting. Undercoat should be pale, ticked with chocolate to give a silvery-peach effect. Fur should be longer on the stomach.

FEET Small and oval, with toe tufts; pads should be pink.

TAIL Long, thick at the base, and slightly tapering, with a full brush.

EYES Large, almond-shaped, with dark lid-skin. Colour can be amber, hazel, or green.

EARS Large, set well apart, and pointed, with tufts.

HEAD A moderate wedge-shape. Nose is medium-sized and should have a pink pad.

FACIAL CHARACTERISTICS

BODY An Oriental type, medium in length and elegant; slightly larger than an Abyssinian, and not as fine-boned as a Siamese.

SORREL SOMALI The body colour of the Sorrel, or Red, should be as deep as possible, with chocolate-brown ticking.

DEVELOPING COAT Like all varieties of Somali, the Silver Sorrel's coat may take up to two years to develop its mature, ticked appearance.

LEGS Long and slender; chocolate ticking should extend up the back legs.

Maine Coon

The Maine Coon is the oldest American breed. During the early days of its history it may have roamed free in the state of Maine, drawing comparisons to the racoon, which looks similar to tabby-type Maine Coons and has similar hunting habits. The severe New England climate contributed to the development of the Maine Coon's thick coat. The world's longest cat is a Maine Coon. Owned by Frieda Ireland of Chicago, Leo measures 122 cm (48 in) from tip of nose to tip of tail and weighs just under 16 kg (35 lb).

HISTORY

Robust American farm cats and longhaired cats brought back to Maine by traders and sailors from Europe make up the Maine Coon's probable early forebears. The breed was shown at the 1860 New York Cat Show, was registered in 1861, and won the Madison Square Garden Show of 1895. However, its popularity diminished once Persians were introduced into the US, and did not revive again until the 1950s. The Central Maine Coon Cat Club, established in 1953, contributed directly to the breed's resurgence, which was given further impetus by the setting up of the Maine Coon Breeders and Fanciers Association in 1976, the same year as the breed was given official recognition in the US.

TEMPERAMENT

Two characteristics are unique to the Maine Coon: perhaps because of its humble origins, it is used to "sleeping rough" and is found curled up in the oddest positions, in the oddest places; it is also notable for the delightful, quiet chirping sound that it produces. Maine Coons make affectionate, companionable pets.

VARIETIES

Apart from Chocolate, Lilac, or Siamese-type patterns, the Maine Coon is bred in every colour and combination of colours. For show purposes, the Siamese-pointed (and, in the UK, also the Chocolate and Lavender varieties) are not allowed.

BROWN TABBY MAINE COON
A colourful tradition holds that the Maine Coon is the result of a mating between a cat and a racoon; however, such an ancestry is a genetic impossibility.

HEAD Fairly large, but small in proportion to the body. Should be wedge-shaped, with high cheekbones, a firm chin, and a medium-long nose with a pink pad.

FEET Large and round. Colour of the pads should match that of the coat.

LEGS Medium in length and strong.

EARS Large, set well apart and high on the head. Ears taper to a point and have tufts.

EYES Should be large and slightly slanted, set well apart; green, gold, or copper in colour.

FACIAL CHARACTERISTICS

TORTOISESHELL-AND-WHITE MAINE COON This attractive example is only one of the 30 or so varieties of the breed.

COAT Thick and shaggy, with a silkiness that belies its appearance and a moderate neck ruff. Fur is not as long as that of other longhairs, is more uneven, and relatively easy to groom. Colour should be coppery brown, marked in black.

BODY Very large, long, and well-muscled, with a broad chest. Weight ranges between 3–6 kg (8–14 lb), although larger individuals have been recorded. In silhouette, the Maine Coon's shape is almost rectangular.

WHITE MAINE COON Gold, blue, and odd eyes are all permitted in this variety.

TAIL As long as the body, with a wide base and a blunt end. Fur on the tail should be long and flowing, with a plume-like end.

Norwegian Forest Cat

Norse legend describes the Norwegian Forest Cat as a mysterious, enchanted animal, and perhaps no other breed looks quite so wild or so much like a temporary visitor to the domestic hearth. Although it is, in fact, no more wild than the Maine Coon (*see pp.76–7*), which it resembles, it is still a natural breed that is rugged, hardy, and well-adapted to the cold Scandinavian winters. Most distinctive of these adaptive features is the Norwegian Forest Cat's double coat, which keeps out the wind and the snow, keeps in the warmth, and dries in about 15 minutes after a drenching.

TABBY NORWEGIAN FOREST CAT Tabbies tend to have heavier coats than other varieties of the breed, but as in all Norwegian Forest Cats, the fur is surprisingly resistant to tangles.

HISTORY

All that is certain about the Norwegian Forest Cat is that it is an old breed. Its ancestors may include shorthairs brought from Great Britain by the Vikings and longhaired cats brought by the Crusaders, which then mated with farm and feral stock. Alternatively, the Norsk Skaukatt, as it is known in its native land, may be none other than the troll cat of Scandinavian fairy tales. It was recognized in Norway in 1930 and first shown in 1938. For a while, no cats were allowed to be exported and the breed was largely unknown outside its own country. Since the 1980s, however, it has achieved a higher international profile, and pedigree breeding lines have been established.

TEMPERAMENT

"Wegies" love people and can be very demanding of affection; in exchange they offer intelligent, friendly, playful company. Used to the outdoor life, where they make fine, swift hunters, they can nonetheless adapt happily to staying indoors, as long as they are given plenty of space.

VARIETIES

All coat colours and patterns are acceptable for the Norwegian Forest Cat, with or without white.

BODY *Muscular and robust, medium in length, and square in appearance, with a long neck.*

FEET *Wide, with heavy paws. Pads match the colour of the coat. Special claws allow for rock, as well as tree, climbing.*

LEGS *Powerful and long. Hindlegs are slightly longer than forelegs.*

EARS Long, set high on the head, and pointed, with tufts.

HEAD Triangular in shape, with a heavy chin and full cheeks. Long, wide, straight nose. Nose pad matches the colour of the coat. Long, prominent whiskers.

EYES Large, almond-shaped, and set wide apart.

FACIAL CHARACTERISTICS

COAT Double type, with long, water-resistant guard hairs covering woolly, thick underfur. Profuse neck ruff is usually shed in summer. Colour is blue with white showing through.

BLUE SMOKE NORWEGIAN FOREST CAT
A curious characteristic of this breed is that it tends to come down from trees spirally, head first.

TAIL Flowing, and as long as the body.

Siberian

Forget gulags, salt mines, and frozen tundra, something really beautiful has come out of Siberia – namely this exciting breed of cat. It is a big, powerfully built, and very handsome semi-longhair, similar in some ways to the Maine Coon (*see pp.76–7*) and Norwegian Forest Cat (*see pp.78–9*).

HISTORY
An indigenous Russian breed of cat, the Siberian was first imported into the US in the early 1990s. Though still quite rare, it is increasing in popularity with cat lovers there but is seldom seen in Great Britain or other Commonwealth countries. It is recognized by a number of cat associations, including the CFA, TICA, and FIFé, but not, as yet, by the British GCCF.

TEMPERAMENT
Affectionate and fun-loving, Siberians like to "talk", not by yowling Siamese-style, but in chirps of the kind associated with young puma cubs.

VARIETIES
The Siberian comes in a range of colours with brown tabby being the most common.

BROWN-SPOTTED TABBY-AND-WHITE SIBERIAN The Siberian is a semi-longhair and the national cat of Russia. Its rich, full winter coat is appropriate for life on the steppes.

HEAD A modified wedge with rounded contours. Long, substantial whiskers.

TAIL Medium length, wide at the base, blunt at the tip, and thickly furred.

LEGS Medium length and covered with thick, rather dense fur.

FEET Big and round with tufts of toe hair.

BROWN TABBY-AND-WHITE SIBERIAN It is said that these cats once lived in Russian Orthodox monasteries, patrolling the roof beams and looking out for unwelcome visitors. They would raise the alarm by emitting loud calls.

RED SHADED TABBY-AND-WHITE SIBERIAN Siberians are very slow in maturing and may take up to five years to reach their final medium-large size and magnificent appearance.

EARS Medium sized, set towards the sides of the skull, and with a wide base. Tips are rounded and slightly tipped forwards; ideally they are lynx-tipped.

EYES Large, round, and wide-set; green, gold, hazel, or copper. White cats should be blue- or odd-eyed; in other pointed cats the eyes should be blue.

FACIAL CHARACTERISTICS
Brown-Spotted Tabby-and-White Siberian

COAT Semi-long, with longer hair around the buttocks, tail, and neck ruff. Feels pleasantly smooth due to the hairs carrying a little more oil than is usual in other cats. It does not easily mat.

BODY Medium-large to large; strong and muscular.

Nebelung

In German, the word *Nebel* means fog or mist, and *Nebelung* is an obsolete name for "the misty one", that is, the month of November. Misty is indeed an apt description of this cat's hazy, blue-grey coat colour that in certain lights seems to shimmer with faint phosphorescence.

HISTORY

A rare breed, the Nebelung is a modern re-creation of longhaired Russian cats, some of which were presented at the first Crystal Palace Cat Show in London in 1871. It is, as yet, seldom seen outside Russia, the US, Germany, and Holland. The breed's renaissance began in the US in the 1980s by the accidental mating of a black domestic shorthair queen with a Russian Blue tom *(see pp.116–17)*. Some of the kittens from the first and subsequent litters grew exquisite, long, silky blue coats. Within a few years the standards for the new breed were drawn up, in essence the same as those of the Russian Blue but with longer hair. The Nebelung is not yet accepted by many cat associations.

TEMPERAMENT

Nebelungs are kind, gentle, rather reserved cats, initially wary and aloof around strangers, but intensely loyal and loving once they get to know you. Although not usually overdemanding lapcats, they do need affection and attention. In households where human family members are out at work most of the day, it is best to provide a feline companion to keep a Nebelung contented. They hate being alone.

VARIETIES

There are no varieties of Nebelung.

EARS *Large and pointed.*

EYES *Green, though kittens often start off with yellow eyes that begin to go green at about six to eight months of age.*

FACIAL CHARACTERISTICS

LONGHAIRED RUSSIAN The Nebelung combines the exquisite, shimmering blue-grey of the Russian Blue with a longer, more lush coat.

HEAD *A modified, rather pointed wedge shape*

COAT *Medium-length, soft, silky, fine, double-layered hair.*

TAIL *A lush plume of hair.*

BODY *Long, lithe, rather slender, and athletic.*

LEGS *Muscular but elegant, with longer-hair "pantaloons" on the hindlegs.*

FEET *Dainty and round.*

Cymric

Cymric is Welsh for "Welsh". However, this breed has no known connection with the land of leeks and laver bread! It is, in fact, of fairly recent Canadian origin.

HISTORY

The first Cymrics appeared in Canada in the 1960s as spontaneous longhaired mutations in litters of standard pedigree Manx cats *(see pp.106–7)*. These mutations were bred together and continued to produce consistently longhaired Manx offspring. Essentially, Cymrics can be regarded, as some cat associations do, as simply a variety of tailless Manx with a medium-long, soft, heavy coat. A few associations, however, including the Australian Cat Federation, accept the Cymric as a distinct breed.

TEMPERAMENT

Cymrics are cheerful, sharp-witted cats that enjoy both outdoor and indoor life and make especially capable mousers. They will live amenably with other animals, including dogs.

VARIETIES

All patterns and colours are acceptable.

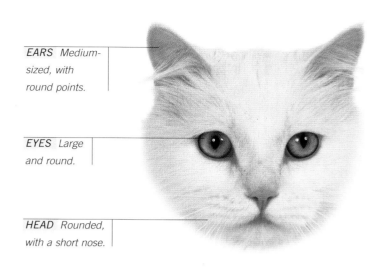

EARS Medium-sized, with round points.

EYES Large and round.

HEAD Rounded, with a short nose.

FACIAL CHARACTERISTICS

EXCLUSIVE ATTACHMENT The Cymric often builds a strong bond with one particular member of the household.

BODY Medium-sized and muscular.

TAIL Rump should feel completely tailless.

COAT Medium to long, with a dense undercoat and smooth outer layers of hair. It tends not to mat.

LEGS Short and thick, with the hindlegs longer than the forelegs.

FEET Large and round.

Non-Pedigree Longhairs

Although longhaired cats are traditionally associated with the show ring, non-pedigree longhairs grace many a home and hearth. Like the more common non-pedigree shorthair *(see pp.152–3)*, they should not be thought of as somehow "second-best" to the refined show specimen – they may not have the same illustrious parentage, but they still have the same, innate, feline appeal.

NON-PEDIGREE BICOLOURED LONGHAIR

HISTORY

Longhaired cats probably arose as the result of a spontaneous mutation within an isolated, perhaps cold, region that enabled the feature to be perpetuated through interbreeding. The modern longhair is mostly descended from Turkish and Persian cats brought to Britain during the late 19th century. Non-pedigree longhairs can be the result either of crossbreeding longhairs or of matings between longhaired cats and shorthaired cats.

TEMPERAMENT

Like all cats, the non-pedigree longhair has a personality uniquely its own, formed by heredity, upbringing, and social environment, but is nonetheless likely to be more docile than its shorthaired relation.

VARIETIES

As you would expect, a limitless number of "varieties" is possible for the non-pedigree longhair!

BODY Strong and stocky.

TAIL Medium-long and fluffy.

NON-PEDIGREE TABBY LONGHAIR As with the non-pedigree shorthair, the crossbred longhair is more likely to have tabby markings than any other because they comprise the basic feline coat pattern. The length of the fur tends to make the markings less evident, but a Tabby is nevertheless always unmistakable.

EARS Medium in size and round-tipped.

HEAD Medium in size, round, with a medium-length nose ending in a red pad. Also present is a distinctive "M" on the forehead.

COAT Long, thick, and silky.

EYES Large and round.

FACIAL CHARACTERISTICS

NON-PEDIGREE TABBY-AND-WHITE LONGHAIR This tabby-and-white is as attractive as any pedigree version.

LEGS Medium in length and thick.

FEET Large and round.

NON-PEDIGREE SMOKE LONGHAIR Although it is an indefinable colour, this is still a most resplendent cat!

Shorthaired Cats

Shorthaired cats are much more common than longhaired ones, mainly because the genes for short hair are dominant over those for long hair. Also, in the wild, long hair can tangle on things when stalking and ambushing, give enemies something to grab hold of, and become matted and likely to cause skin diseases. These are important disadvantages that natural evolution came to terms with.

A shorthaired coat, on the other hand, does not get in the way and is simple to look after and care for – wounds can be easily tended and parasites do not find it such a good environment in which to make a home. Twice-weekly grooming is sufficient and many shorthaired cats can very adequately look after their coats themselves, even without the help of an attentive owner.

Shorthaired cats fall into three principal categories: the British Shorthair, the American Shorthair, and Foreign or Oriental Shorthairs.

The British Shorthair is a sturdy cat with a strong, muscular body set on short legs, and sporting a short, plush, dense coat. It has a broad, rounded head, with a short, straight nose, and large, round eyes. European Shorthair breeds are physically identical to the British.

American Shorthairs developed from ancestors of the British and European Shorthairs, which were taken to the US by the early settlers. It is a different strain of cat, larger and leaner than the British type and with slightly longer legs, a more oblong head with a square muzzle, a medium-length nose, and large, round eyes.

In the case of Foreign or Oriental Shorthairs, the term "Oriental" does not necessarily indicate an exotic origin (although some of these cats do indeed come from the Far East); instead the name refers to a variety of breeds that share the same conformation, one that is quite different to the rounded, sturdy British and American Shorthairs. Foreign or Oriental Shorthairs have a wedge-shaped head with slanting eyes and large, pointed ears, a lithe, slim body with long legs, and a very fine, short coat. This category embraces the most well-known example, the Siamese, as well as the Korat and the Havana. In some countries, including the US, these cats are known simply as Oriental Shorthairs, or as Oriental in type, whereas in other countries, notably Britain, Australia, and New Zealand, particular colours and coat patterns are designated as being either Foreign or Oriental.

THE QUINTESSENTIAL CAT (Top right) Short hair is preferred by wild species of cat except for the manul, or Pallas's cat, which lives at high altitudes in Russia and the Himalayas. For the pet-owner, short hair means no trouble with tangles and far less grooming.

BENGAL (Bottom right) Closely related to the Asian leopard cat, the Bengal is, not surprisingly, a skilled hunter. Although owning one is like having a miniature wild cat in the house, Bengals adapt well to family life.

RUSSIAN BLUE (Left) The coat of the Russian Blue is unique among cat breeds – plush to the touch with a short, thick, double layer that is ideal for bitter Russian winters. Its old name was the Archangel Cat after the Russian port of that name.

British Black Shorthair

THE EYES HAVE IT Shorthaired black cats are a common sight everywhere, but they usually have green eyes, rather than the sparkling orange or copper eyes of the pedigree version, which provide such glorious contrast against the dense, black coat.

More than any other feline, shorthaired black cats have through the ages been the object of fear, superstition, and veneration – alternately persecuted as creatures of ill-omen and deified as bringers of good luck. In fact, such large numbers were executed during the Middle Ages in the belief that they were agents of the devil, and in an attempt by the Christian Church to purge Europe of the vestiges of paganism, that the black cat can indeed be thought of as a lucky animal to have managed to survive at all!

HISTORY

The British Black Shorthair was one of the first breeds to be shown at Crystal Palace in London during the late 19th century and was selectively bred using the best examples of British street cats. These cats are now usually produced from like-to-like matings, although they sometimes appear in Tortoiseshell litters *(see p.98)*. They themselves are used in Tortoiseshell and Tortoiseshell-and-White breeding programmes.

TEMPERAMENT

Good-natured and very intelligent, the British Black Shorthair makes an ideal cat-about-the-house.

VARIETIES

There are no varieties of the British Black Shorthair.

FEET Paws are large and round with black pads.

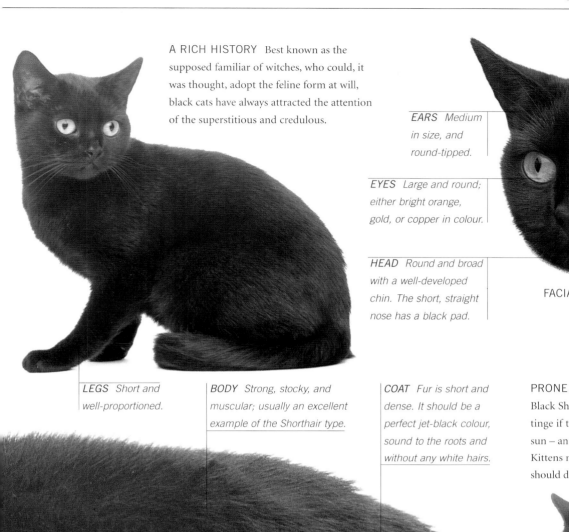

A RICH HISTORY Best known as the supposed familiar of witches, who could, it was thought, adopt the feline form at will, black cats have always attracted the attention of the superstitious and credulous.

EARS Medium in size, and round-tipped.

EYES Large and round; either bright orange, gold, or copper in colour.

HEAD Round and broad with a well-developed chin. The short, straight nose has a black pad.

FACIAL CHARACTERISTICS

LEGS Short and well-proportioned.

BODY Strong, stocky, and muscular; usually an excellent example of the Shorthair type.

COAT Fur is short and dense. It should be a perfect jet-black colour, sound to the roots and without any white hairs.

PRONE TO DISCOLORATION The British Black Shorthair's coat may take on a brownish tinge if the cat spends long periods of time in the sun – an unwelcome feature in a show specimen. Kittens may legitimately have some rustiness; this should disappear in six months or so.

TAIL Short and thick.

British White Shorthair

White shorthaired cats have always been much prized for the purity of their coats, and in many countries they are seen as a symbol of perfection. As in the White Longhair *(see p.38)*, the blue-eyed variety is genetically predisposed to deafness.

EARS *Medium-sized, round-tipped, and set well apart.*

EYES *Large, round, and orange-coloured; each eye should be equal in depth of colour.*

FACIAL CHARACTERISTICS

HISTORY
The modern breed originates from the selective breeding of street cats during the late 19th century.

TEMPERAMENT
As one would expect from its origins, the British White Shorthair is intelligent and streetwise, as well as a friendly companion.

VARIETIES
There is a trio of varieties: Blue-eyed, Orange-eyed and Odd-eyed. Non-pedigree, shorthaired white cats usually have green eyes. Additionally, the Albino Shorthair is white with pale-blue eyes, the pupils of which gleam red in reflected light.

COAT *Fur is short and dense. Colour should be pure, snowy white, and without any tinge of grey or yellow.*

HEAD *Round and broad, with a well-developed chin, a straight nose, and a pink nose pad.*

BRITISH ORANGE-EYED WHITE SHORTHAIR A perfect white shorthair with no hint of any other colour is a relatively rare, and therefore sought-after, animal. The orange-eyed variety, which does not suffer from the problems of deafness associated with the blue-eyed types, is regarded even more highly.

BRITISH ODD-EYED WHITE SHORTHAIR The variety of British White Shorthair that has one orange eye and one blue eye is a side-effect of breeding programmes designed to produce orange-eyed cats with perfect hearing. Deafness may be apparent on the blue-eyed side.

BODY *Strong, muscular, and stocky.*

TAIL *Short and thick.*

LEGS *Short, but well-proportioned.*

FEET *Paws are large and round, with pink pads.*

British Cream Shorthair

This luscious cat should look as if it has been freshly dunked in a pail of clotted cream. In practice, however, it is not easy to produce the desired pale, even coloration, and good examples are rare. Breeding from Tortoiseshells *(see p.98)* tends to produce a coat that is too red, or "hot"; and because the dominant tabby gene is difficult to suppress, many kittens retain tabby markings into adulthood. Even if these eventually fade, extreme hot or cold weather may cause them to reappear.

EARS Medium in size and round-tipped.

EYES Large and round; colour should be copper, orange, gold, or hazel.

FACIAL CHARACTERISTICS

HISTORY

Cream Shorthairs originated towards the end of the 19th century, when they started appearing in Tortoiseshell litters. For a good while, it was not known how to produce the breed except by accident. For this reason, official recognition did not come until the 1920s, by which time a breeding programme had been established. Widespread interest in the breed developed even later, becoming evident only during the 1950s.

TEMPERAMENT

The British Cream is extremely good natured, intelligent, and affectionate towards its owner.

VARIETIES

There are no varieties of British Cream.

GETTING THE BEST RESULT
Blue-Cream females mated to Blue or Cream males generally produce the best examples of this breed.

HEAD Round and broad, with a short nose with a pink pad.

COAT Short and dense, yet fine. Colour should be an even-toned cream, with as few markings as possible and no white hairs. Paler shades are preferred.

BODY Strong, stocky, and muscular.

A FUTURE SHOW CAT? The pale coat of this kitten suggests that it may eventually be good enough to show.

TAIL Short and thick.

LEGS Short, but well-proportioned.

FEET Large and round with pink paw pads.

British Blue Shorthair

An ideal body conformation, extra-plush fur, and a heavenly blue-grey colour that is set off by orange or copper eyes have given this cat a consistent number-one ranking in the Shorthair popularity stakes.

HISTORY

The British Blue Shorthair evolved during the late 19th century from breeding programmes using the very best street cats. It made an early appearance at shows, but the scarcity of studs during World War II and outcrosses to other breeds after the end of the war, caused the type to deteriorate. The introduction of Blue Longhairs *(see pp.40–41)* into breeding lines resulted in some improvement, although the fur tended to be too long. It was not until the 1950s that very selective breeding was, finally, able to restore the original Blue Shorthair type.

TEMPERAMENT

A sharp-witted and particularly affectionate cat, the British Blue Shorthair makes an excellent companion and confidant that, some owners report, has a hankering for the quiet life.

VARIETIES

There are no varieties of British Blue Shorthair, although the Chartreux *(see p.137)* is considered one by some associations.

EARS *Medium in size and round-tipped.*

EYES *Large and round; colour should be copper or orange.*

HEAD *Round and broad with a well-developed chin. The short, straight nose has a blue pad.*

FACIAL CHARACTERISTICS

BODY *Strong, stocky, and muscular.*

FEET *Large and round with blue paw pads.*

LEGS *Short and well-proportioned.*

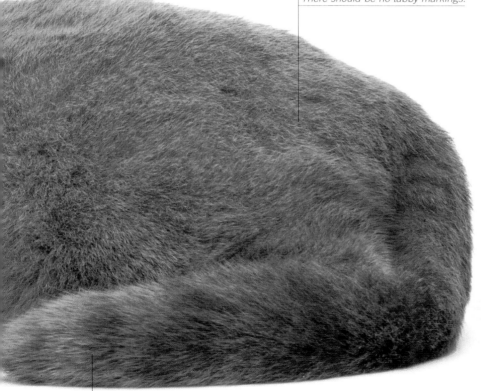

PERENNIAL FAVOURITE The British Blue Shorthair has a well-balanced, but still sometimes mischievous, disposition.

MAINTAINING THE TYPE To preserve the breed type, occasional outcrossings to Blue Longhairs and Black Shorthairs are recommended in some countries.

COAT Fur is short and dense. At one stage, a dark slate-blue colour was accepted, but now the standard requires a medium to light blue. There should be no tabby markings.

PERFECT SHORTHAIR Selective breeding of the Blue Shorthair has produced a body conformation that is a perfect example of the British Shorthair type.

TAIL Short and thick.

BLUE KITTEN British Blue Shorthair kittens are particularly irresistible and pretty. They may have faint tabby markings that should disappear within a few months.

British Blue-Cream Shorthair

This cat is a cross between Blue and Cream Shorthairs *(see pp.92–3 and p.91)*, although Tortoiseshells *(see pp.98–9)* are also used for breeding. The Australian and British standard calls for a subtly toned cat with an intermingling of the two colours, whereas the American Blue-Cream has clearly defined patches. The way that colour genes are linked to sex in some cats means that no male Blue-Creams have been recorded as having survived into adulthood.

HISTORY

The British Blue-Cream was not recognized in Great Britain until the late 1950s.

TEMPERAMENT

This cat is as affectionate and lively as its shorthaired relatives.

VARIETIES

There are no varieties of the Blue-Cream Shorthair.

GOOD TEMPERAMENT
An alert, curious nature has endeared the Blue-Cream to countless fond owners.

BODY A strong, stocky, and muscular type.

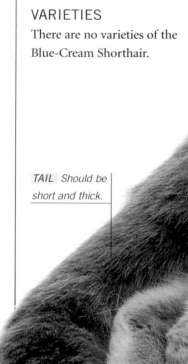

TAIL Should be short and thick.

LEGS Short and well proportioned.

FEET Paws are large and round with pads that are pink or blue or a mixture of the two colours.

COAT *Fur is short and dense. Colour should be a soft intermingling of blue and cream with no tabby markings.*

HEAD *Round and broad with a well-developed chin. The short, straight nose has a blue pad.*

EARS *Medium in size and round-tipped.*

EYES *Large and round; either copper, orange, or rich gold in colour.*

FACIAL CHARACTERISTICS

DIFFERENCE IN HAIR TYPE The cream hairs tend to be finer than the blue in the British Blue-Cream, and the coat may therefore require regular grooming when the cat is moulting.

MIXED LITTERS Litters produced by crossing Blues and Creams may contain solid-coloured kittens as well as Blue-Creams.

EXCELLENT SPECIMEN The best examples of the British Blue-Cream have very pale colouring.

British Tabby Shorthair

The epitome of cat patterning and design, the Tabby is the closest that the domestic cat comes to its pre-domestic forebears. The tabby gene is a dominant type, and the newborn kittens of other breeds often have faint, transient, tabby markings that bear witness to their original ancestry and the need for their untamed cousins to have effective camouflage in the wild. Despite the "pushiness" of the tabby gene, however, the exacting demands of the breed standard have ensured that the pedigree Tabby is no common or garden, run-of-the-mill cat!

BRITISH BROWN CLASSIC TABBY SHORTHAIR
The correct colour combination of a rich or coppery brown with dense black markings is difficult to produce, making Brown Tabbies relatively uncommon.

HISTORY

Tabby cats appear on the murals of Pharaonic Egypt, and they have been depicted by artisans and artists ever since. Indeed, the name comes from Attabiya, a quarter of old Baghdad in which a striped cloth was made, known in Britain as tabbi silk. The modern pedigree version of this venerable cat originated from crossing the best of British street cats during the 19th century.

TEMPERAMENT

The British Tabby Shorthair is a good-natured, affectionate, and intelligent cat that makes the best sort of friend.

VARIETIES

The British Tabby Shorthair is bred in two coat patterns and in several colours. The Mackerel is the more striped cat and lacks the spirals of the Classic. Brown, Silver, and Red are recognized colours in Australia, Britain, and the US, with the latter recognizing Blue and Cream as well.

BODY A strong, stocky, muscular type.

BRITISH RED CLASSIC TABBY SHORTHAIR A Classic Tabby should have a butterfly shape on the shoulders, from which three stripes run along the spine; an oyster-shaped spiral on each flank; and narrow necklace-like stripes across the chest. The abdomen is spotted and the forehead should have frown marks that form a letter "M". Both the tail and legs should be evenly ringed.

LEGS Short but well proportioned and ringed with "bracelets".

EARS Medium in size and round-tipped

EYES Large and round; copper, gold, or orange in colour.

HEAD Round and broad, with a well-developed chin and Tabby "pencillings" on cheeks. The short, straight nose should have a brick-red nose pad.

FACIAL CHARACTERISTICS

COAT Short and plush. The deep red markings should correspond to the classic tabby pattern, and be set against a rich red ground colour. Markings on each side of the cat should be identical.

NOT YOUR AVERAGE RED TOM
A pedigree Red Classic Tabby Shorthair may bear a resemblance to the neighbourhood ginger tomcat, but its rich red coat and distinctive dark red markings put it streets ahead.

TAIL Short and thick.

FEET Large and round with deep-red paw pads.

BRITISH SILVER CLASSIC TABBY SHORTHAIR Probably the most popular variety of Tabby, the Silver is also said to be the most friendly. It should have sharply defined, dense, jet-black markings that stand out against the silvery-grey ground colour. The nose pad is either brick-red or black, and the eye colour should be green or hazel in Britain, and gold, orange, or hazel in the US.

British Tortoiseshell Shorthair

Although the coat of the British Tortoiseshell, with its distinctive patches of black, cream, and red, makes it one of the most familiar of all the domestic cats, it is surprisingly difficult to breed. To produce the desired patterning, queens are best mated to a solid-coloured black, red, or cream stud, but even then the resultant litter may contain only one kitten true to type. Because of the way the genes that determine colour are inherited, almost all Tortoiseshells are female.

EARS Medium-sized and round-tipped.

EYES Large and round; colour should be either deep orange or burnished copper.

FACIAL CHARACTERISTICS

HISTORY
Like most British Shorthairs, the Tortoiseshell was developed from the best street cats. It was one of the first to make an appearance on the show benches in Great Britain.

TEMPERAMENT
The British Tortoiseshell is a sharp-witted, affectionate, and charming cat that has long been highly popular as a pet.

VARIETIES
There are two varieties. The Tortoiseshell-and-White is the same as the Tortoiseshell but for the addition of white patches. In the Blue Tortoiseshell-and-White, known as a Dilute Calico in the US, the black is replaced by blue and the red is replaced by cream.

TAIL Short and thick.

LOYAL FRIEND Affectionately known as the "Tortie", this breed has made a faithful fireside companion since the late 19th century.

HEAD Round and broad with a straight nose. Nose pad should be pink or black or a mixture of the two.

COAT Bold, clearly defined patches of black, cream, red, and white.

BRITISH TORTOISESHELL-AND-WHITE SHORTHAIR
Formerly known as a Chintz or Spanish Cat, this variety is exactly the same as the Tortie, but with the addition of white patches. Bicolours usually make the best sires.

COAT Short, dense fur, evenly patched with black, red, and cream; a cream or red blaze on the head is particularly sought after.

BODY Strong, stocky, and muscular.

LEGS Short, but well-proportioned.

BRITISH BLUE TORTOISESHELL-AND-WHITE SHORTHAIR
The black and red in the coat of the Tortoiseshell-and-White are replaced by blue and cream in this recently developed variety. The nose and paw pads are pink or blue or a mixture of the two colours.

FEET Large and round. Pads need to be pink or black or a mixture of the two.

British Spotted Shorthair

If you own a British Spotted Shorthair, look out for cat thieves! Its gorgeous coat is an eye-catcher that never fails to turn heads. Reminiscent of some of its smaller wild cousins, "Spottie", as it is affectionately known, is basically a Mackerel Tabby *(see pp.96–7)* with the markings broken up into spots.

HISTORY

A cat very similar to the British Spotted was known in Ancient Egypt, where it was revered in mythology as the killer of the serpent of evil. Like most British Shorthairs, the modern breed was selectively bred from street cats and made an early appearance at the cat shows held during the 1880s. It fell out of favour at the beginning of the 20th century, but regained popularity by the mid-1960s.

TEMPERAMENT

Spottie is good-natured, affable, and affectionate.

VARIETIES

Any tabby-type colour combination is permissible for the British Spotted, as long as the spots match the coat colour. The most common varieties are the Brown, Silver, and Red. The Australian and British standard is more specific about the distribution of markings than that of the US.

COAT Short and dense. Colour should be pale grey with black markings; dorsal stripe should be broken into spots.

BRITISH SILVER SPOTTED SHORTHAIR
The markings on the British Spotted need to be as numerous and distinct as possible. The spots can be round, oval, or rosette-shaped.

HEAD Round and broad, with a well-developed chin and the characteristic "M" of tabbies. Nose is straight and short, with a red or black pad.

EARS Medium in size and round-tipped.

EYES Large and round; colour should be green or hazel, outlined in black.

FACIAL CHARACTERISTICS

BODY A strong, stocky, muscular type.

TAIL Short and thick, with broken rings. Tail tip must be the same colour as the markings.

LEGS Short, but well-proportioned.

FEET Paws are large and round with black or red pads.

BRITISH RED SPOTTED SHORTHAIR
For this variety, the standard calls for a light-red coat, spotted in rich red, coupled with deep orange or copper eyes.

British Bicolour Shorthair

Bicoloured cats, white cats patched with another colour, are plentiful in every neighbourhood, but the upper-crust, pedigree version is much more rarely seen because of the difficulty of meeting the breed standard. The white should cover no more than half the coat, and the second colour no less than half and no more than two thirds. Ideally, the patching should be symmetrical, but in practice this is rarely possible to achieve.

HISTORY

Perhaps surprisingly, in view of the large numbers of non-pedigree bicoloured cats that have existed for as long as the domestic cat itself, the British Bicolour has only been recognized for showing since the early 1980s.

TEMPERAMENT

This is an eminently even-tempered, friendly, and intelligent cat.

VARIETIES

There are four varieties: Black-and-White (known as the "Magpie"), Blue-and-White, Orange-and-White, and Cream-and-White.

BRITISH BLUE-AND-WHITE BICOLOUR SHORTHAIR Before pedigree lines were introduced, the most well-known bicoloured cat was one owned by the Earl of Southampton, a friend of Shakespeare. A contemporary painting shows them doing "time" together in the Tower of London.

TAIL Short and thick.

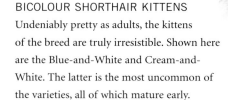

BICOLOUR SHORTHAIR KITTENS Undeniably pretty as adults, the kittens of the breed are truly irresistible. Shown here are the Blue-and-White and Cream-and-White. The latter is the most uncommon of the varieties, all of which mature early.

LEGS Short, but well-proportioned.

HEAD Round and broad. Face should be patched. The short, straight nose has either a pink pad or one that matches the colour of the patches.

BRITISH ORANGE-AND-WHITE BICOLOUR SHORTHAIR
Although very appealing in its own right, this cat's tabby markings rule out a career on the show bench.

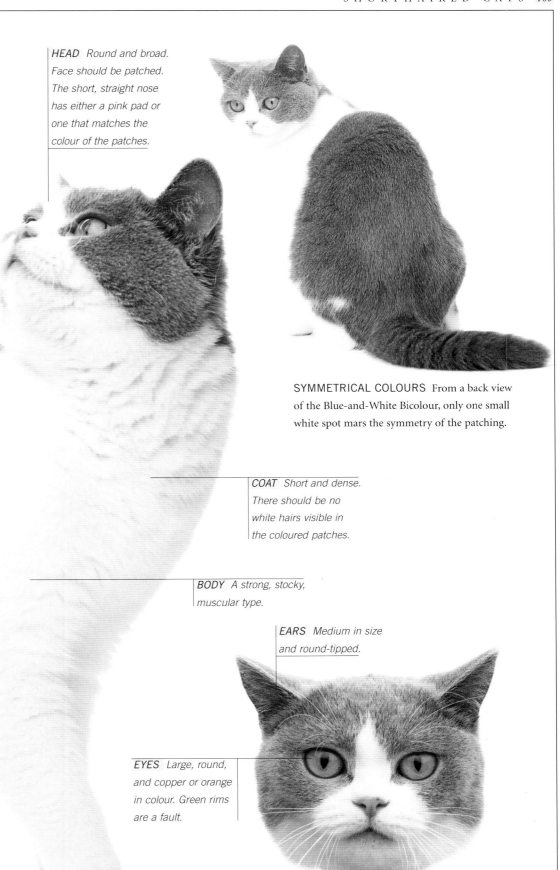

SYMMETRICAL COLOURS From a back view of the Blue-and-White Bicolour, only one small white spot mars the symmetry of the patching.

COAT Short and dense. There should be no white hairs visible in the coloured patches.

BODY A strong, stocky, muscular type.

EARS Medium in size and round-tipped.

FEET Large and round with pads that are either pink or match the colour of the patches.

EYES Large, round, and copper or orange in colour. Green rims are a fault.

FACIAL CHARACTERISTICS

British Smoke Shorthair

The magical, "now you see it, now you don't" quality of the British Smoke comes from its unusual fur. This is composed of a one-coloured topcoat over a white undercoat. When the cat is in repose, it looks solid-coloured, but when it moves the white can be seen flickering through to beautiful effect.

EARS *Medium in size and round-tipped.*

EYES *Large and round; should be copper, orange, or deep gold in colour.*

FACIAL CHARACTERISTICS

HISTORY

The British Smoke can count Silver Tabbies *(see p.97)* and solid-coloured British Shorthairs in its ancestry, which extends back to the late 19th century. These days, Smokes are usually either mated to other Smokes or, to improve the breed type, to Blue Shorthairs *(see pp.92–3).*

TEMPERAMENT

This is a pleasant-natured, affectionate, and intelligent cat.

VARIETIES

Only two varieties of British Smoke Shorthair are recognized in all three countries of Australia, Britain, and the US: the Black Smoke and the Blue Smoke.

BRITISH BLACK SMOKE SHORTHAIR The appearance of the Smoke's coat is determined by two genes: one inhibits pigmentation of the undercoat and the other enhances the tipping of the cat's topcoat.

HEAD *Round and broad with a short, straight, black-tipped nose.*

BODY *Strong and muscular.*

COAT *Fur should be short and dense. Undercoat is white or pale silver, covered by a topcoat that is tipped with black. Deep tipping is almost indistinguishable from a solid colour.*

LEGS *Short, well-proportioned legs end in large, round paws with black pads.*

BRITISH TORTOISESHELL SMOKE SHORTHAIR A variety that is not yet recognized in the US, the Tortie Smoke's coat markings produce a wonderful, hazy effect. It has pink paw pads.

TAIL *Short and thick.*

British Tipped Shorthair

Like the longhaired Chinchilla *(see pp.44–5)* and Cameo *(see pp.46–7)*, this breed has a tipped topcoat and a white undercoat, a beguiling combination that produces a distinct sparkle when the cat moves. The tipping should be evenly distributed and largely confined to the upper part of the body.

HISTORY

A complex breeding programme that incorporated cats with silver genes, Blues, and Smokes produced the cat that we know today. Known originally as a Chinchilla Shorthair, it was recognized under its present name in 1978.

TEMPERAMENT

Good-humoured and intelligent, the British Tipped makes an affectionate companion.

VARIETIES

The tips of this much-admired breed can be any British colour, with the addition of Chocolate and Lilac.

BLACK-TIPPED BRITISH SHORTHAIR Green eyes, out-lined in black, make this variety stand out from the crowd: all other varieties have orange or copper-coloured eyes.

EARS Medium in size and round-tipped.

EYES Large and round; should be bright green.

FACIAL CHARACTERISTICS

HEAD Round and broad with a straight, pink-tipped nose and a well-developed chin.

COAT Fur is short and dense. Colour should be white with black tipping on the back, flanks, head, ears, and top of the tail. The white of the undercoat should be as pure as possible.

BODY A strong, muscular, stocky type.

LEGS Short, well-proportioned legs may be marked with faint "ghost" rings.

FEET Paws are large and round, with pads that are either pink or match the colour of the tipping.

TAIL Short and thick.

Manx

A cat without a tail may seem like a contradiction in terms, but the Manx has long been established as a breed. Resembling a British Shorthair in some respects, a true, or "Rumpy", Manx should have only a small hollow where a tail would have been, although cats with residual tails are also born – these are known as "Risers", "Stumpies" (or "Stubbies"), and "Longies", depending on the tail length. The lack of a tail is not simply a quaint anomaly; the mutant gene responsible has been implicated in skeletal defects such as spina bifida, and like-to-like matings of completely tailless Manx usually results in the kittens dying before birth or shortly after.

RED TABBY STUMPY MANX
This variety has a residual tail.

TAIL Non-existent; it should be possible to detect a hollow at the end of the backbone.

HISTORY

Legend relates how this unfortunate cat lost its tail when Noah closed the door to the Ark a little too hastily: its more modern history is no less intriguing. One school of thought holds that tailless cats swam ashore to the Isle of Man, off the west coast of England, in 1588 from galleons of the shattered Spanish Armada; another that the cats arrived on merchant ships travelling from the Far East. Either way, the isolation of the island allowed the tailless trait to be perpetuated.

TEMPERAMENT

The Manx is good natured and friendly – very much a family cat.

VARIETIES

Most recognized colours, coat patterns, and colour combinations are permitted for the Manx.

FEET Paws are large and round; colour of the pads should correspond to that of the coat.

EARS Medium in size with slightly rounded tips.

EYES Large, round, and set at a slight angle toward the nose. Colour should conform to that of the coat.

FACIAL CHARACTERISTICS

BLUE STUMPY MANX Although "Stumpies" may be thought to resemble Japanese Bobtails, the two breeds are genetically very different: the taillessness of the former is caused by a dominant gene, whereas in the latter it is a recessive genetic condition.

BODY A strong, muscular, stocky type. Rump should be rounded and higher than the shoulders.

TORTOISESHELL-AND-WHITE RUMPY MANX Although Manx cats are still very much associated with the Isle of Man, where they are depicted on tourist souvenirs, coins, and stamps, examples of the breed, including the ever-popular Tortie-and-White, are now more widely distributed around the world.

HEAD Round and broad, with a well-developed chin and short to medium-length nose that is straight in Australia and Britain and more curved in the US. Colour of the nose pad should conform to that of the coat.

COAT A double type, comprising a short, very thick undercoat, which has been described as having a "cottony" feel, and a slightly longer topcoat. Appearance is glossy, and clearly defined patches of red, cream, black, and white can be seen.

LEGS Forelegs are short and set well apart; hindlegs are longer with heavy, muscular thighs that give the cat a characteristic "bunny-rabbit" gait, although this is considered a fault in the US.

RED TABBY STUMPY MANX A very rounded side view when sitting is a characteristic of the breed, caused by forelegs that are considerably shorter than the hindlegs.

American Shorthair

As the standard describes it, the American Shorthair is eminently adapted to the ethos of a country forged by frontiersmen and women: "lithe enough to stalk its prey but powerful enough to make the kill easily", with legs "long enough to cope with any terrain and heavy and muscular enough for high leaps". It is a very athletic cat, with a larger and more powerfully built body than its British relation, harder fur, and a more oblong face.

EARS *Medium in size and round-tipped.*

EYES *Large and wide; colour should match that of the coat.*

HEAD *Large, with full cheeks and a well-developed chin. The pad of its medium-length nose matches the coat colour.*

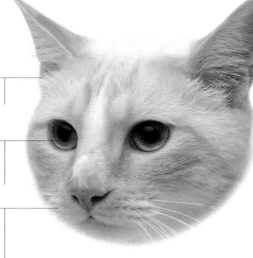

FACIAL CHARACTERISTICS

HISTORY

The American Shorthair undoubtedly sprang from the tough, hardworking cats that accompanied the Pilgrim Fathers and later settlers to the New World. The first feline colonists thrived in the American environment, adapting to the climate, landscape, and lifestyle, and developing their own unique characteristics. A brown tabby American Shorthair at the Second Annual Cat Show at Madison Square Garden in 1896 was priced at $2,500.

TEMPERAMENT

Courageous, intelligent, energetic, and hardy, the American Shorthair does its country proud!

VARIETIES

The American Shorthair is bred in any number of colours and coat patterns, of which the more popular are shown in the chart opposite.

VAN PATTERN TABBY AMERICAN SHORTHAIR
This example shows off the best features of its type: a robust, muscular build; an open, appealing face; and a general hardy disposition – a cat equally at home on the range or in the parlour.

BODY *Large to medium in size; powerful, strongly built and well balanced, with a broad, level back and well-developed shoulders, chest, and hindquarters.*

COAT *Fur is thick, dense, and hard; a soft or silky coat would be a fault. Colour is white with red tabby markings on the face, legs, and tail.*

FEET *Paws are heavy and rounded with pads that match the colour of the coat.*

LEGS *Medium in length, although slightly longer than in the British Shorthair, and heavily muscled.*

SILVER TABBY AMERICAN SHORTHAIR
This is a Classic variety of the Tabby.

SHADED SILVER AMERICAN SHORTHAIR
The Shaded Silver is exactly like its British counterpart in colour, but larger in build.

VARIETIES	COAT	MARKINGS	EYES
White	Pure white	None	Deep blue, brilliant gold, or odd-eyed
Black	Coal black	None	Brilliant gold
Blue	Pale blue-grey	None	Brilliant gold
Red	Deep, rich red	None	Brilliant gold
Cream	Buff-cream	None	Brilliant gold
Bicolour	White	Black, red, blue, or cream patches	Brilliant gold
Shaded Silver	White undercoat	Mantle of black tipping, shading towards white	Green or blue-green
Chinchilla Silver	Pure white undercoat	Black tipping on back, flanks, head, and tail	Emerald-green or blue-green
Shell Cameo	White undercoat	Red tipping on back, flanks, head, and tail	Brilliant gold
Shaded Cameo	White undercoat	Like Shell, longer tips	Brilliant gold
Cameo Smoke (Red Smoke)	White undercoat	Very deep red tipping	Brilliant gold
Black Smoke	White undercoat	Tipped with black	Brilliant gold
Blue Smoke	White undercoat	Very deep blue tipping	Brilliant gold
Blue-Cream	Blue	Clear patches of cream	Gold
Tortoiseshell	Black	Red and cream patches	Gold
Tortoiseshell Smoke	White undercoat	Black, red, and cream tips in tortie pattern	Brilliant gold
Van Pattern	White	Auburn with patching similar to Turkish Van	Brilliant gold
Calico	White	Black and red patches	Brilliant gold
Dilute Calico	White	Blue and Cream	Brilliant gold
Brown Tabby	Coppery brown	Black Classic or Mackerel pattern	Brilliant gold
Red Tabby	Rich red	Deep, rich red Classic or Mackerel pattern	Brilliant gold
Silver Tabby	Pale, clear silver	Black Classic or Mackerel pattern	Green or hazel
Blue Tabby	Pale, bluish-ivory	Very deep blue Classic or Mackerel pattern	Brilliant gold
Cream Tabby	Very pale cream	Buff or cream Classic or Mackerel pattern	Brilliant gold
Cameo Tabby	Off-white	Red Classic or Mackerel pattern tips	Brilliant gold
Patched Tabby (Tortie-Tabby, or Torbie)	Silver, brown, or blue	Black or dark grey Classic/Mackerel; red/cream patches	Brilliant gold or (Silver only) green or hazel

TAIL *Medium in length, tapering to a rounded tip.*

American Wirehair

Perhaps the "punk" of the feline world, the American Wirehair is a most distinct, and still quite uncommon, cat. The fur is unusual in that each of the guard hairs – the long, thick hairs of a cat's coat that are raised when the fur "stands on end" – is crimped along its length and hooked at the end. The fur is therefore frizzy and wiry; to the touch it is not unlike the wool on a lamb's back.

HISTORY
There are records of similar cats being seen on London bombsites after the end of World War II, but the cat as we know it today is descended from a Shorthair *(see pp.108–9)* living in the state of New York that, in 1966, gave birth to a remarkable mutant red-and-white male that had a wavy coat. The kitten was subsequently used to develop the breed, which is still relatively uncommon outside North America. New breeding lines have, however, been established in Germany, Canada, and elsewhere. Wirehairs may be shorthaired or longhaired.

TEMPERAMENT
The American Wirehair takes a keen interest in its surroundings and is considered to have an even-tempered and affectionate nature.

VARIETIES
All the colours and coat patterns of the American Shorthair are recognized for the Wirehair.

COAT Fur is of medium length and should be tightly crimped, thick, springy, resilient, and coarse. Fur on the chest and stomach is less coarse. Colour should be brown with black markings and patches of red and/or cream.

LEGS Medium in length, in proportion to the body, and well muscled.

FEET Paws are oval and compact. Colour of the pads should harmonize with that of the coat.

TORTOISESHELL-AND-WHITE AMERICAN WIREHAIR This variant is white with black and red patches.

RED TABBY AMERICAN WIREHAIR The Wirehair's springy coat creates the illusion that the tabby markings are somehow ridged or raised off the body.

EARS Medium in size, round-tipped, and set well apart.

EYES Large and round, set well apart, with a slight upward tilt at the outer edge. Colour should be brilliant gold.

HEAD Round in shape with a well-developed muzzle and chin and prominent cheekbones. Nose is of medium-length; colour of the pad should harmonize with that of the coat.

FACIAL CHARACTERISTICS

BODY Medium to large in size, and well muscled. Neck is thick and muscular.

WHITE AMERICAN WIREHAIR The unusual coat of the American Wirehair should feel springy and rather hard to the touch. Whites like this one have deep blue or golden eyes, or one of each colour.

TAIL Medium in length, tapering to a rounded tip.

BLACK-AND-WHITE BICOLOUR AMERICAN WIREHAIR This example possesses the desired brilliant gold eyes. The breed can be found in a wide range of colour and pattern combinations.

Exotic Shorthair

A composite cat! The Exotic can be said to have it all: the cobby build and irresistible snub nose and round face of a Longhair, coupled with a shorter, plush, coat that is a boon for those people who have neither the time nor the inclination for regular grooming sessions.

HISTORY

The Exotic arrived on the American scene in the late 1960s, the result of interbreeding Longhairs, American Shorthairs *(see pp.108–9)*, and Burmese *(see pp.122–3)*. As a hybrid breed, it is a healthy and robust cat.

TEMPERAMENT

As might be expected, the Exotic combines characteristics inherited from its forebears. It is as gentle and affectionate as a Longhair, but has the playful, alert intelligence of an American Shorthair.

VARIETIES

All the coat colours and patterns found in Longhairs and in American Shorthairs are permitted for the Exotic – giving over 50 varieties from which to choose. The colour of the eyes, nose, and paw pads depends on the variety, but should always conform to the coat colour.

COLOURPOINT EXOTIC SHORTHAIR Siamese-type markings, with the points a darker colour than the rest of the body, make this variety instantly recognizable.

TAIL Short and bushy, with a rounded tip; normally carried uncurled at a level below that of the back.

BLUE TABBY EXOTIC SHORTHAIR
One reason for the Exotic's consistent appeal is the affecting, sweet expression created by the round face and snub nose inherited from its Longhair background.

LEGS Short, thick, and sturdy.

GREAT INDOOR CAT Like all varieties of the Exotic, the Blue Tabby has a docile nature and habits that are less destructive than many Shorthairs, making it a classic indoor cat.

EARS Small and round-tipped; they are set wide apart and tilt forward slightly.

EYES Large and round, set wide apart; gold in colour.

FACIAL CHARACTERISTICS

BODY Medium to large in size; a solid, chunky, cobby type, with a deep chest and a short, thick neck.

HEAD Round and broad, with full cheeks, a well-developed chin, and a snub nose that should have a distinct "break".

COAT Fur is medium in length, slightly longer than other Shorthairs, but not long enough to flow. It should be soft, plush, and sufficiently dense to stand out from the body. There are no ear or toe tufts and no feathery hairs on the tail.

FEET Paws are large and round with rose-coloured pads.

BLUE EXOTIC SHORTHAIR The distinctive hallmarks of the Exotic – the beautiful, plush fur and cobby build – are shown off to perfection by this example of the breed. Although the popularity of the Exotic is mostly still confined to the US, these cats are rapidly gaining fans worldwide. They are said to be especially adaptable to the show ring.

Siamese

Imperious, importuning, impertinent, arrogant, aloof, loud, vulgar, subtle, beguiling – a Siamese is all of these and more. With its svelte, "Foreign" build, its gorgeous pointed coat pattern, and sapphire-blue eyes, this is a cat that demands attention on every level.

HISTORY

In Bangkok, the National Library possesses a collection of manuscripts, the *Cat Book Poems*, dating from possibly the 14th century, in which a Siamese-type called the Vichien Mas is depicted, and it is thought that similar cats lived in what is now Thailand for hundreds of years. Siamese were first imported into Britain in the 1880s, and the breed made its appearance in the US not long afterwards.

TEMPERAMENT

The Siamese is the most extrovert of all domestic cats, with a loud "voice" that is impossible to ignore. It is highly intelligent and usually becomes devoted to its owner.

VARIETIES

There are four classic varieties: the Seal-point, Blue-point, Chocolate-point, and Lilac-point. Newer varieties, developed by mating Siamese with other breeds, are called Colourpoint Shorthairs.

SEAL TABBY-POINT KITTEN Siamese kittens are born all-white, without points.

BODY Medium in size, long, lithe, and svelte, with an athletic appearance.

LEGS Long and slim, in proportion to the body. Hindlegs are slightly longer than the forelegs.

LILAC-POINT SIAMESE The first Siamese to be imported into England are believed to have been a gift to the British Consul from the court of Siam. Today, the breed looks slightly different from those 19th-century examples having a less round face and a paler coat. The Lilac was the last of the four classic varieties to be recognized.

SEAL-POINT SIAMESE The first variety to be recognized, the Seal-point is genetically a black cat in which the pigment has been watered down and restricted to the extremities of the body.

FEET Paws are dainty, small, and oval, with lavender-pink pads.

CHOCOLATE TABBY-POINT SIAMESE This variety has an ivory-coloured body and points broken up by milk-chocolate bars separated by a lighter background colour.

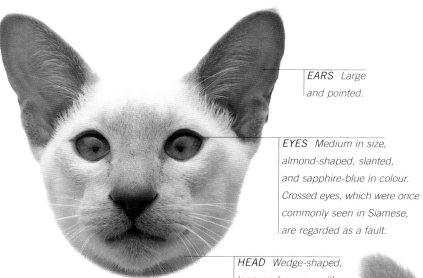

EARS Large and pointed.

EYES Medium in size, almond-shaped, slanted, and sapphire-blue in colour. Crossed eyes, which were once commonly seen in Siamese, are regarded as a fault.

HEAD Wedge-shaped, long, and narrow, with a long nose that has a lavender-pink pad.

FACIAL CHARACTERISTICS
Lilac-point Siamese

COAT Fur should be short, fine-textured, glossy, and close-lying. Colour should be magnolia with frosty-grey shading on the points – the mask, ears, legs, and tail.

TAIL Long, thin, tapering, and free of kinks.

VARIETIES	COAT	MARKINGS
Seal-point	Warm cream	Seal-brown
Blue-point	Bluish-white	Slate-blue
Chocolate-point	Ivory	Milk-chocolate brown
Lilac-point	Magnolia	Pinkish-grey
Red-point	Clear white shading to apricot	Reddish-gold
Cream-point	White shading to pale cream	Warm cream
Tabby-point	White	Tabby
Seal Tortie-point	Pale seal-brown	Seal-brown patched in cream
Blue Tortie-point	Pale blue	Blue patched in cream
Chocolate Tortie-point	Pale chocolate-brown	Chocolate-brown patched in cream
Lilac Tortie-point	Pale pinkish-grey	Pinkish-grey patched in cream

Russian Blue

The distinguishing feature of the Russian Blue is its double coat, which has a plushness that is unrivalled by any other cat. Probably the most famous, and certainly the most cosseted, example of the breed is Vashka, who was owned by Tsar Nicholas I of Russia, where these cats are considered a welcome omen of good luck.

HISTORY

The variety of names that the Russian Blue has had bears witness to the confusion surrounding its origins. The evidence for its being a natural Russian breed is supported by the large numbers that have long been found in Sweden. However, its later history is much less certain. It was known at first as the Archangel Cat because examples were brought back to Britain from the Russian port of Archangelsk by Elizabethan sailors. Later, it was known as both the Spanish Cat and the Maltese Cat, the latter name persisting in the US until the beginning of the 20th century. The breed declined during World War II, and attempts to revitalize it by using British Blue *(see pp.92–3)* and Siamese *(see pp.114–15)* outcrosses led instead to its virtual disappearance: the cat became a blue Siamese in type and almost lost its distinctive double coat. The late 1960s saw a return to the original type after concerted efforts by breeders on both sides of the Atlantic.

TEMPERAMENT

The Russian Blue is obliging, rather shy, and quiet. In fact, Blues are so quiet that it may be difficult to tell when a queen is calling.

VARIETIES

Experimental all-white and all-black Russians have been produced, but they have not attracted much interest outside New Zealand.

A DIFFICULT SURVIVAL Only a strict breeding programme has enabled this breed to survive in its original form.

HEAD Short and wedge-shaped, with a strong chin and prominent whisker pads. The medium-long nose has a blue pad in Australia and Great Britain, and a slate-grey one in the US. The thick fur makes the face appear broad across the eyes.

LEGS Long and fine-boned. In Great Britain and Australia the forelegs are shorter than the hindlegs.

FEET Small and oval in Australia and Great Britain, with blue pads. In the US, paws are more rounded, with pads either pink or mauve in colour.

EARS Large and slightly pointed. The skin is thin and only lightly covered with very fine fur, making the ears almost transparent.

EYES Vivid green in colour and set wide apart; almond-shaped in Australia and Great Britain, and more rounded in the US.

FACIAL CHARACTERISTICS

BODY Long, slender, and elegant.

A DECEPTIVELY LONG NECK The long, slender, neck of the Russian Blue is seen most clearly when it is stretched; usually the cat's thick fur makes it appear shorter.

COAT Short, plush coat with a seal-like texture. It is a double type, standing out from the cat's body because of its density. Colour should be an even blue, with a distinct sheen produced by silver-tipped guard hairs.

SLENDER BUT STRONG Fine-boned, but still muscular, the Russian Blue is an athletic-looking cat.

TAIL Long, tapering from a moderately thick base.

Abyssinian

Who could fail to be enchanted by this wild-looking creature? Certainly not the Ancient Egyptians, who, if popular theory is to be believed, worshipped the Abyssinian's antecedents as incarnations of the goddess Bast.

HISTORY

As befits its arcane aura, the Abyssinian's origins have become largely hidden with time. The breed is arguably natural, possibly old, and probably descended in modern times from a cat called Zula, who was imported into Britain from Ethiopia in 1868. Because Zula, of whom we have a photograph, did not look anything like today's Abyssinians, there are those who believe that the cat is either a product of chance matings between ordinary tabbies, or is the result of early breeders trying to produce an "Egyptian-like" cat. Other Abyssinian fanciers point out that the Romans are known to have imported cats from Egypt into Britain and may, therefore, have introduced the gene for the Egyptian look into the native feline population.

TEMPERAMENT

The Abyssinian's alert expression is reflected in its delightful personality. It is sweet-tempered, intelligent, and described by some as obedient.

VARIETIES

There is a number of varieties (see chart, below), although some are still shown in assessment classes.

EARS Large, set wide apart, and pointed, with tufts.

EYES Large and almond-shaped, rimmed in black or dark brown, and encircled by a paler area. They are amber, hazel, or green.

FACIAL CHARACTERISTICS

EGYPTIAN ANCESTRY? In profile, this Usual Abyssinian's proud, Sphynx-like bearing inevitably prompts comparison with the cats portrayed on the murals of Ancient Egypt, giving credence to the belief that this was the cat so revered by the Pharaohs.

USUAL ABYSSINIAN The original variety, the Usual was at one time known as a Rabbit or Hare Cat – a reference to the similarly ticked coat, which, as in all varieties of Abyssinian, is characterized by a distinctive agouti (a form of tabby) fur that has two to three darker-coloured bands along each hair.

TAIL Thick at the base, fairly long, and tapering, the tail is tipped with black.

VARIETY	BASE COLOUR	TICKING COLOUR
Usual	Ruddy brown	Black or dark brown
Sorrel	Copper-red	Chocolate
Blue	Warm blue-grey	Steel blue
Fawn	Medium fawn	Deep fawn
Lilac	Light pinkish grey	Darker pinkish grey
Silver	Silver	Black
Silver Sorrel	Silvery peach	Chocolate
Silver Blue	Silvery blue-grey	Deep steel blue

SILVER SORREL ABYSSINIAN
Chocolate ticking over a silver-peach base colour gives this recently developed variety a soft, graceful, charm.

BLUE ABYSSINIAN Unusually, the ticking of this naturally occurring variety is blue over a blue-grey base colour, rather than the black that might be expected.

USUAL ABYSSINIAN KITTEN Abyssinian litters are usually small and mostly male. The kittens mature early (although it may be 18 months or so before the coat develops fully) and are particularly lively and friendly.

COAT Glossy and soft, but also dense and resilient to the touch. Fur is short, but still long enough to accommodate two to three bands of black or dark-brown ticking over a ruddy brown base colour.

HEAD Round and gently wedge-shaped. The medium-size nose has a brick-red pad.

LEGS Long, slender, and fine-boned, giving the impression of being on tip-toe when standing.

BODY Medium in length, lithe and graceful, but with a muscular appearance.

FEET Small and oval-shaped, with black paw pads.

Korat

One of the oldest natural breeds, the Korat is said to have been named after the Thai province where the cat originated. Known as Si-Sawat ("royal cat") in its native land, the Korat's cloud-coloured fur makes it a symbol of rain, and it is believed to bring good fortune. With its heart-shaped head and silver-blue coat, the modern cat is not much changed from its ancestor.

HISTORY

The first Korat to be officially exhibited in Europe was entered in a British cat club show in 1896 – as a blue Siamese. A male and female pair were imported to the US in 1959, where recognition was granted in 1966. Recognition in Britain did not come until 1975, and has only recently been granted in Australia.

TEMPERAMENT

Intelligent and very sweet-natured, the Korat makes a loving companion, especially for children.

VARIETIES

Blue-point and lilac-coloured variants occur, and there may also be longhaired forms.

EARS *Large and round-tipped, set high on the head.*

EYES *Prominent, round, and luminous green. Kittens may have amber-green or yellow eyes that change hue by the time they mature.*

HEAD *Heart-shaped, with a large, flat forehead. The nose has a lion-like downward curve just above the nose-pad, which is dark blue or lavender.*

FACIAL CHARACTERISTICS

POETRY-INSPIRING "The hairs are smooth, with tips like clouds and roots like silver; the eyes shine like dewdrops on a lotus leaf." This wonderfully evocative description of the Korat is taken from the *Cat-Book Poems*, written between 1350 and 1767 and held in the Bangkok National Library.

COAT *Short, flat, silky, and fine, with a distinct sheen to its silver-blue colour. The absence of a full undercoat may make this breed susceptible to chills in colder climates. A characteristic feature of the coat is the way the fur breaks when the back is bent.*

BODY *Semi-cobby, lithe, and muscular.*

LEGS *Medium in length and slim.*

FEET *Small, oval paws with pads that should be dark blue to pinkish-lavender in colour.*

TAIL *Medium in length, and round-tipped.*

Havana

The Havana lives up to its name not only because its rich, brown coat resembles the colour of the expensive cigar tobacco, but also because it has elegance, refined manners, and a distinctive history that reeks of exclusivity.

HISTORY

During the 1950s, in Great Britain, a Seal-point Siamese *(see pp. 114–15)* crossed to a black shorthaired cat of Siamese ancestry formed the foundation of the breed, which was recognized in 1958. The British breeding programme continued to use Siamese outcrosses, but American breeders decided to ban the use of Siamese, preferring to produce a cat that was less Oriental. They called it Havana Brown, and it is recognized in Australia.

TEMPERAMENT

The Havana is an active, affectionate, and highly intelligent cat.

VARIETIES

One colour variety, the Frost, a delicate shade of lilac, is exclusive to the US, where the breed is judged by a different standard to the British. The American Havana Brown, the result of crossing the British Havana with the American Shorthair *(see pp.108–9)*, is a sturdier cat, with a medium-length torso, a rounder face, oval eyes, round-tipped ears, and longer fur.

FACIAL CHARACTERISTICS

EARS *Large, with slightly pointed tips.*

EYES *Almond-shaped, slanted, and pale to mid-green in colour.*

HEAD *Long and wedge-shaped, with a short, straight nose that should have a brown or rosy-pink pad.*

COAT *Fur is very short and glossy; colour should be an even, rich, chestnut-brown.*

BODY *Long, svelte, and muscular, with a slender neck.*

TAIL *Long and elegant.*

HAVANA BROWN
The American Havana tends to be more quiet than its British cousin.

FEET *Paws are small and oval with pads that should be either brown or rosy-pink in colour.*

LEGS *Long and slim; forelegs are shorter than the hindlegs.*

FOREIGN ORIGINS The Havana's original name of Chestnut Brown Foreign Shorthair perhaps more accurately describes its origins.

Burmese

Unlike the Balinese, the Burmese can claim a connection with the country after which it is named. Known as "Rajahs", brown cats similar to today's Burmese were recorded as dwelling in Buddhist temples in Burma as far back as the 15th century.

HISTORY

The modern breed was founded by Wong Mau, a cat imported into the US from Burma in 1930 and crossed with a Siamese tom (see pp.114–15). There may have been subsequent imports of cats from Burma, but certainly by 1936 the cats were breeding true enough to be granted recognition in the US. However, the large amount of Siamese blood that had been introduced caused the original type to be overwhelmed, and the registration was temporarily dissolved during the 1940s. Despite their Siamese content, they were given British recognition in 1952. A year later, with the American breed once more conforming to type, it was again recognized in the US. The original Burmese colour was solid brown.

TEMPERAMENT

The breed is famous for its affectionate, intelligent personality: these cats love people.

VARIETIES

Not only does the number of Burmese varieties differ on each side of the Atlantic, but also the Australian, British, and American standards: the American Burmese has a rounder body, head, eyes, and feet than the other two cats.

BLUE TORTOISESHELL BURMESE Tortie Burmese are produced by mating Reds and Creams with Browns, Blues, Chocolates, and Lilacs, and they are bred primarily to preserve the breed type, rather than for the coat colour. However, to meet the standard, this variety should have clearly defined patches of blue and cream without any barring.

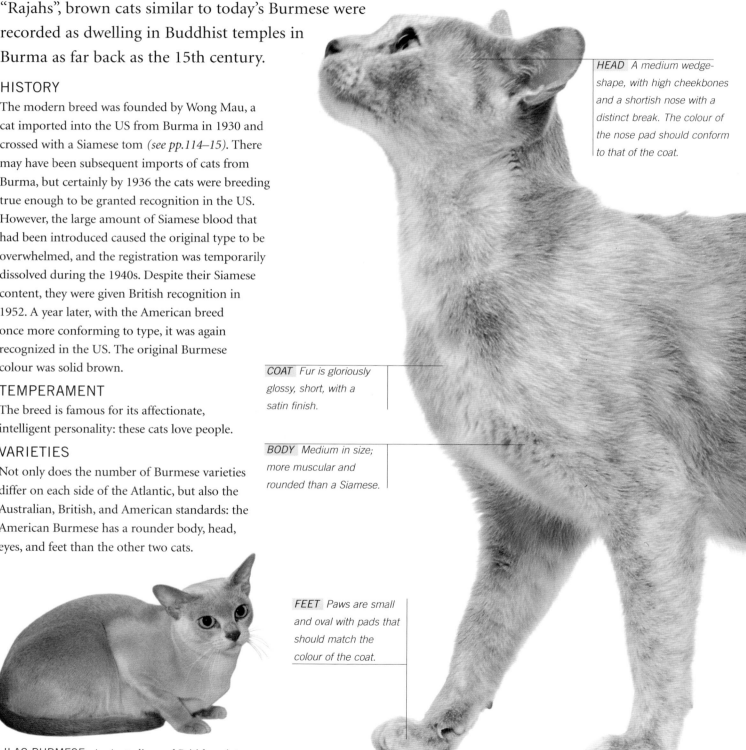

HEAD A medium wedge-shape, with high cheekbones and a shortish nose with a distinct break. The colour of the nose pad should conform to that of the coat.

COAT Fur is gloriously glossy, short, with a satin finish.

BODY Medium in size; more muscular and rounded than a Siamese.

FEET Paws are small and oval with pads that should match the colour of the coat.

LILAC BURMESE An Australian and British variety whose colour ranges from bluish-lilac to fawn.

EARS Medium in size, slightly rounded at the tips, and set well apart. They should be slightly tilted forward.

EYES Lower lids are rounder than the upper lids, giving a slanted appearance. Colour should be yellow to gold.

FACIAL CHARACTERISTICS

TAIL Medium in length, straight, and tapering only very close to the rounded tip.

LEGS Long and slim; hindlegs are slightly shorter than the forelegs.

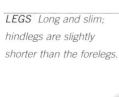

BROWN BURMESE The original and, to some, the ideal Burmese.

RED BURMESE A relative newcomer to the British scene.

AMERICAN BROWN BURMESE
A history that diverged during the mid- to late 1940s has produced two distinct types of Burmese: the Australian and British cats are more Oriental; the American Burmese is more sturdy and cobby.

VARIETIES	COAT	MARKINGS
Brown	Sable-brown	Lighter shading on underside
Blue	Silver-grey	Silver sheen
Chocolate	Milk-chocolate	None
Lilac	Pinkish-grey	None
Red	Pale tangerine	Ears are darker than back
Cream	Rich cream	None
Brown Tortie	Brown	Red patches
Chocolate Tortie	Chocolate	Red patches
Lilac Tortie	Pinkish-grey	Cream patches
Blue Tortie	Grey-blue	Cream patches

Japanese Bobtail

Idiosyncratic, unlike other shorthaired breeds, and with a decidedly Oriental expression, the Japanese Bobtail was named after both its country of origin and its "powder-puff", bunny-rabbit-type tail.

HISTORY

Although in the Far East the roots of the breed can be traced back to the 7th century, the Japanese showed little interest in this cat's show qualities until fairly recently. It was the Americans who brought the Japanese Bobtail into the limelight in the late 1960s and set the pedigree standard.

TEMPERAMENT

The friendly Japanese Bobtail is a cat full of personality.

VARIETIES

Traditional varieties in Japan are the tricoloured cats (tortoiseshell and white, and black, red, and white) that are known as *Mi-ke*, meaning "lucky". All other colours and patterns, apart from Abyssinian and Siamese types, are also recognized. The breed is recognized in both shorthaired and semi-longhaired varieties.

EARS Large, round-tipped, set well apart and at right angles to the head, giving the impression that they tilt forward.

EYES Large and oval, with a less rounded cornea than other breeds, the eyes appear slanted when seen from the side. Colour matches that of the coat.

FACIAL CHARACTERISTICS
Red-and-White Japanese Bobtail

GOOD-LUCK CAT Seated Bobtails often raise one paw, a gesture believed to bring good luck. Called *Maneki-neko*, or "beckoning cats", they appear in prints and models to welcome visitors to Japanese homes. The Gotokuji temple in Tokyo has a façade decorated with these cats, all with one paw lifted.

HEAD Should form almost a perfect triangle. Nose is long, with a pad that should match the coat colour.

BODY Medium-sized, lean, and elegant.

COAT Soft, silky, and medium in length. Colour should be red and white or black and white. Coat is not prone to shedding.

TAIL Extended, it is 10–12 cm (4–5 in) long, but in its normal, curled position, it appears to be only 5–7 cm (2–3 in).

LEGS Long and slender; hindlegs are longer than the forelegs.

FEET Paws are medium in size and oval. Pads match the coat colour.

Singapura

Singapura is the Malaysian name for Singapore, the island where, it is claimed, this cat originated. Kucinta, a Singapura, is a tourist emblem for Singapore. Like the Abyssinian *(see pp.118–19)*, this cat has a ticked coat, but with a much smoother feel.

EARS Large and slightly pointed.

EYES Large, almond-shaped, and slanted. Outlined and hazel, green, or yellow.

FACIAL CHARACTERISTICS

HISTORY

Some folk dispute the Oriental origins of the Singapura, claiming that the creator of the breed took her Burmese cats *(see pp.122–3)* to Singapore. Imported into the US in 1975, the Singapura was first shown only a year later and rapidly gained acceptance by most associations. It is still a fairly unusual breed in the US and is rare in the West.

TEMPERAMENT

Because in its native land the Singapura seeks shelter in drains, it was once known as the "Drain Cat", unfortunately suggesting a lowly feline; this name has now been dropped. Although it is reserved and somewhat shy, the Singapura loves being around people.

VARIETIES

There are no varieties of the Singapura.

DEVELOPMENT OF AN ASIAN STREET CAT

Cats similar to the Singapura are numerous not only in Singapore but also throughout Asia. However, since its introduction into the US, the breed has been developed and the standard revised, with the result that it is one of the more rare pedigree cats.

HEAD Rounded, with a well-developed chin. The short nose has a salmon-coloured pad.

BODY Small to medium in size; a muscular, moderately stocky type.

COAT Fur is very short, silky, and close-lying. Colour should be that of old ivory with bands of dark bronze and warm-cream ticking, giving a refined, delicate appearance.

TAIL Fairly short and slender, with a blunt tip.

FEET Small and oval, with pads that should be rosy brown in colour.

LEGS Medium in length and muscular.

Tonkinese

Oriental in name, but American by design, the Tonkinese is the result of crossing Siamese *(see pp.114–15)* and Burmese *(see pp.122–23)*. It is said to combine the best qualities of each.

HISTORY

Early Tonkinese, or "Golden Siamese", were developed in North America in the 1930s but were largely ignored. In the late 1960s, the breed made its debut as "Tonkinese", and these cats started attracting their fair share of attention.

TEMPERAMENT

The Tonkinese is ultra-affectionate and one of the most people-oriented of shorthair breeds.

VARIETIES

In Britain, all the recognized Burmese colours are permitted, including solids, Tortoiseshells, and Tabbies. In the US, five varieties, corresponding to the basic Siamese points, are recognized: Natural Mink, Blue Mink, Honey Mink, Champagne Mink, and Platinum Mink.

COAT Medium-short, soft, and close-lying like mink, with a natural sheen. Colour should be solid, shading to a slightly lighter tone on the underparts, with points that are clearly defined, although less distinct than a Siamese.

FEET Paws are dainty, and more oval than round. Colour of the pads should harmonize with that of the coat.

AN OUTGOING TYPE All Tonkinese, not just the Red-point, have inquisitive personalities.

RED-POINT TONKINESE A new, and uniquely British variety, the Red-point corresponds in colour to the Red Burmese, but with Siamese-type points of a darker shade.

VARIETY	COAT	MARKINGS
Natural Mink	Warm brown	Dark chocolate
Blue Mink	Bluish-grey	Slate-blue
Honey Mink	Ruddy brown	Chocolate
Champagne Mink	Warm beige	Pale brown
Platinum Mink	Soft silver	Pewter-grey

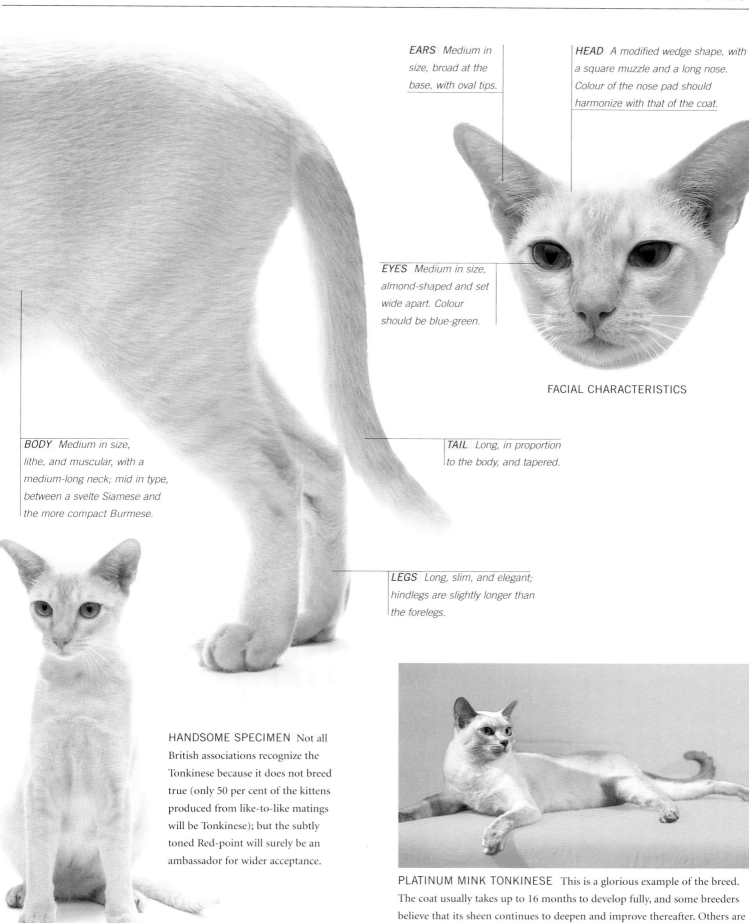

EARS Medium in size, broad at the base, with oval tips.

HEAD A modified wedge shape, with a square muzzle and a long nose. Colour of the nose pad should harmonize with that of the coat.

EYES Medium in size, almond-shaped and set wide apart. Colour should be blue-green.

FACIAL CHARACTERISTICS

BODY Medium in size, lithe, and muscular, with a medium-long neck; mid in type, between a svelte Siamese and the more compact Burmese.

TAIL Long, in proportion to the body, and tapered.

LEGS Long, slim, and elegant; hindlegs are slightly longer than the forelegs.

HANDSOME SPECIMEN Not all British associations recognize the Tonkinese because it does not breed true (only 50 per cent of the kittens produced from like-to-like matings will be Tonkinese); but the subtly toned Red-point will surely be an ambassador for wider acceptance.

PLATINUM MINK TONKINESE This is a glorious example of the breed. The coat usually takes up to 16 months to develop fully, and some breeders believe that its sheen continues to deepen and improve thereafter. Others are of the opinion that the best time to show a Tonkinese is at two years of age.

Bombay

Blacker than black, this cat possesses a truly remarkable coat that is often described as having the sheen of patent leather. It is named after the city of Bombay because of its resemblance to the Indian black leopard.

HISTORY

The breed was created in the US in the 1950s by crossing a Burmese *(see pp.122–23)* and an American Black Shorthair *(see pp.108–9).*

TEMPERAMENT

The Bombay rarely stops purring, craves human companionship, and dislikes being alone. It is quite happy to be an indoor cat.

VARIETIES

A semi-longhaired version is recognized by some European cat registries as the Bombay Longhair, or Asian Black Longhair. In Britain, the Bombay is regarded as a specific type of Asian Shorthair.

EARS Medium-sized, broad at the base with gently rounded tips. Ears should be set far apart and tilt forward slightly.

EYES Round and set far apart. They should range in colour from gold to vivid copper.

FACIAL CHARACTERISTICS

COAT Colour should be a gleaming jet-black; the fur short and close-lying.

TAIL Medium in length.

BODY A medium-sized, muscular type.

HEAD Rounded, with a full face that should taper to a short, well-developed muzzle. Nose should have a black pad.

A FAIRLY UNUSUAL BREED Still relatively rare outside the US, this cat's elegant good looks should ensure it a wider popularity in the near future.

LEGS Medium in length, in proportion to the body.

FEET Small and oval with black paw pads.

Snowshoe

A recent American breed, the Snowshoe was developed with the aim of combining Siamese-type *(see pp.114–15)* points with the white feet of a Birman *(see pp.64–5)* – the latter feature earning it the nickname of "Silver Laces". It has a modified Oriental body type, usually being larger and heavier with less extreme features, not unlike Siamese of the 1950s and 1960s.

FACIAL CHARACTERISTICS

EARS Large and pointed, set wide apart and tilting slightly forward.

EYES Large, slanting, and oval; colour should be bright blue.

HEAD A rounded, triangular shape, with high cheekbones. Medium-length nose is straight in profile and has a grey pad.

HISTORY

Three kittens of Siamese parentage that were born with white feet formed the foundation for this breed. Once a selective breeding programme was established, American Bicoloured Shorthairs *(see pp.108–9)* were used to develop Snowshoes.

TEMPERAMENT

The Snowshoe has been described as having a sparkling, "bomb-proof" personality, ideal for showing.

VARIETIES

There are two standard varieties of Snowshoe: the Seal-point has a warm-fawn body, pale-fawn stomach and chest, and seal-brown points; the Blue-point has a bluish-white body, a paler chest and stomach, and points that are a deep grey-blue.

BLUE-POINT SNOWSHOE
Still relatively rare, the Snowshoe has only two varieties, the Blue and the Seal, that are recognized by American associations. Other Siamese point colours will undoubtedly be accepted in the future.

TAIL Medium in length and gently tapering.

COAT Fur is short, glossy, and medium-coarse in texture. Mask, ears, legs, and tail should be a much darker shade of the body colour, whereas the chest and stomach are paler. Feet should be white.

BODY A medium to large, lithe, well-muscled type.

LEGS Medium in length.

FEET Paws are medium in size and oval.

SEAL-POINT SNOWSHOE The inverted facial "V" is a desirable feature.

Foreign Shorthairs

Chic cats that have the build of a Siamese and that are bred in myriad colours and patterns, Foreign and Oriental Shorthairs are among the most distinguished-looking in the feline repertoire.

HISTORY
In both the US and Britain, Siamese *(see pp.114–15)* were bred to other shorthairs to produce an elegant Foreign-type cat without point markings. Recognition was granted towards the late 1970s.

TEMPERAMENT
These cats have the same energetic and inquisitive nature as the Siamese.

VARIETIES
Varieties include Black, White, Blue, Lilac, Red, Cream, Silver, Cameo, Chestnut, Cinnamon, Caramel, Black Smoke, Chestnut Smoke, Cameo Smoke, Tabby, and Tortoiseshell. Eye colour is green in most cases, but can be blue or orange in the American White, and must be blue in British Whites. Amber eyes are allowed in the Black, and colours from copper to green are legitimate in the Cream and Red. In Australia and Britain, solid-coloured types are known as Foreign Shorthairs, whereas Tabby, Ticked, and Spotted cats are called Oriental Shorthairs. There is a move, however, towards a redefinition of terms and a regrouping of varieties.

EARS Large and pointed.

EYES Medium in size, almond-shaped, and slanted.

HEAD A Siamese wedge-shape with a long nose and lavender-coloured nose pad.

FACIAL CHARACTERISTICS
Foreign Lilac Shorthair

FOREIGN BLUE SHORTHAIR This is a cat that deserves a high profile.

BODY Medium in size; a long, svelte, lithe, type. Neck is long and slender.

COAT Fur is short, fine-textured, and close-lying. Colour should be pinkish-grey, with a frosty-grey tone.

TAIL Long, thin at the base, and tapering to a fine point.

FOREIGN BLACK SHORTHAIR This variant perfectly demonstrates feline elegance.

ORIENTAL TICKED TABBY SHORTHAIR Each hair in this variant has bands of dark shading.

FOREIGN LILAC SHORTHAIR The Havana breeding programme *(see p.121)* in Britain during the 1950s gave rise to the development of this variety. If two Havanas produced from crossing Russian Blues and Seal-point Siamese are mated together, the litter will contain Foreign Lilacs.

EARS Large and pointed.

EYES Medium in size, almond-shaped, and slanted; green in colour and rimmed with chestnut.

HEAD A Siamese wedge-shape with a long, pink-padded nose.

FACIAL CHARACTERISTICS
Oriental Chocolate Tabby Shorthair

ORIENTAL CHOCOLATE
TABBY SHORTHAIR

LEGS Long, slim, and elegant; hindlegs are higher than the forelegs.

FEET Paws are dainty, small, and oval, with lavender-coloured pads.

ORIENTAL TABBY SHORTHAIRS Oriental Tabbies were produced originally by mating non-pedigree tabbies with Siamese. Later on, however, Tabby-point Siamese were used in the breeding programme. All colours and tabby patterns are now accepted.

ORIENTAL BLUE TABBY SHORTHAIR

Burmilla

As the name suggests, the Burmilla is the product of crossing a Burmese *(see pp.122–3)* with a Chinchilla *(see pp.44–5)*. It possesses the body conformation of a Burmese but has a softer, tipped, or shaded coat. The development of the Burmilla can be said to have filled a need in the cat world: that of a tipped, silver shorthair of Foreign type.

HISTORY

During 1981 in Great Britain an accidental mating between a Lilac Burmese queen and a Chinchilla stud, both owned by Baroness Miranda von Kirchberg, produced four kittens that were to become the Burmilla's founder members. The possibility of establishing a new, true breed was quickly realized, and with that aim the Burmilla Cat Club came into being in 1984. The Burmilla is seen at an increasing number of shows and has won innumerable friends and admirers, but it is not yet widely accepted by cat associations.

TEMPERAMENT

This cat is renowned for its excellent, even-tempered disposition.

VARIETIES

The Burmilla is bred with a silver or golden ground colour tipped in black or any of the Burmese or other standard colours.

BODY Medium in length, and lithe but muscular.

LEGS Medium length and slim. Forelegs are slightly shorter than the hindlegs.

FEET Paws are a neat, oval shape with black pads.

EARS *Medium to large, set moderately apart. They are broad at the base, have rounded tips, and tilt forward slightly.*

EYES *Large, set well apart, and outlined in black. All shades of green are accepted.*

HEAD *Gently rounded, with a medium width between the ears. Nose is short with a terracotta nose pad outlined in black. Traces of tabby markings and a distinct "M" decorate the forehead.*

FACIAL CHARACTERISTICS

BLACK-TIPPED BURMILLA The Burmilla is rapidly becoming one of the most popular of the new shorthaired breeds.

BROWN-TIPPED BURMILLA The pads of the Brown-tipped Burmilla and the pencilling around the eyes and lips are brown, corresponding to the colour of the tipping.

COAT *Fur is short, but longer than the Burmese, and dense and soft in texture; it has a rough feel at the tips.*

BLACK-TIPPED BURMILLA Gentle shading that contrasts against a silver undercoat and delicate tabby markings visible on the points lend this variety a quiet air of distinction.

TAIL *Medium to long, it should taper to a round tip. It is ringed in the same colour as the tipping.*

Cornish Rex

Looking as if it has just returned from the hairdressing salon with a rather old-fashioned perm, the Rex cats are named after the Rex rabbit, which also has a curly coat.

HISTORY

Although crinkly coated kittens are recorded to have appeared in both Europe and the US after World War II, the breed was not taken seriously until 1950, when a litter of farm kittens in Cornwall, England, included a lovely cream male with wavy fur that was mated back to its mother and found to breed true. In 1966 another, similar, kitten appeared in Devon, which, when crossed with the Cornish type, produced cats with straight fur – proving that the Cornish and Devon coats were caused by different genes and that the two cats should be developed separately. Rex cats were recognized in Britain in 1967 and are now accepted for showing all over the world.

TEMPERAMENT

The Cornish is affectionate, highly intelligent and very playful.

VARIETIES

All coat colours and patterns, apart from bicoloured, are recognized. Those with Siamese-type points are known as Si-Rex.

EARS *Large and slightly rounded, set high on the head.*

EYES *Medium in size and oval-shaped. Colour should harmonize with the coat.*

HEAD *Wedge-shaped with curly whiskers. The long nose should have a pad that harmonizes with the colour of the coat.*

FACIAL CHARACTERISTICS

COAT *Silky, short, and close-lying, with no guard hairs. Colour should be a mixture of chocolate, red, and cream patches. Fur should be particularly curly on the back and tail.*

BLUE CORNISH REX The Blue's coat has a distinct sheen.

BODY *Long and slender with a naturally arched back.*

TAIL *Long and slender, tapering towards the end, and extremely flexible.*

LEGS *Very long, straight, and slender.*

CHOCOLATE TORTOISESHELL CORNISH REX
A Foreign-type cat, the Cornish is characterized by curly, very short, fine fur that is less coarse than the Devon's. It has few, if any, guard hairs, so that its coat usually consists solely of down and awn hairs.

FEET *Neat and slightly oval. Colour of the pads should harmonize with that of the coat.*

Devon Rex

Curly coated and originating in England's South West, the Devon Rex is an enchanting, pixie-like cat with extremely large ears as its most prominent characteristic.

HISTORY

The first Devon Rexes appeared as spontaneous genetic mutations some ten years after the Cornish ones. Although similar in many respects, cross-breeding trials have shown that the two breeds are genetically distinct.

TEMPERAMENT

Loving and playful, the Devon Rex makes an excellent family pet. Tranquil and home-loving by nature, they are fast runners and agile jumpers and will adapt easily to an indoor existence, although they love to play outside.

VARIETIES

All colours and patterns are accepted.

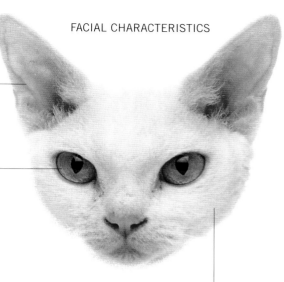

FACIAL CHARACTERISTICS

EARS Strikingly large, set low on the head, with rounded tips. They may be tufted.

EYES Large, oval-shaped, and wide set. Colour should harmonize with that of the coat.

HEAD A modified wedge in shape, with very prominent cheek bones and a short muzzle. The curly whiskers tend to be brittle.

COAT Very short, fine, wavy, and soft, although slightly coarser than the Cornish. Colour should be pure white, without any markings. Grooming is minimal.

TAIL Long, fine, and tapering, well covered with fur.

BODY Medium in size, slender, hard and muscular, with a broad chest.

WHITE DEVON REX Also Foreign in build, the Devon has a unique pixie face that differentiates it from the Cornish. Its fur is also different in feel, containing all three types of hair that make up the coats of other cats. The Devon's habit of apparently wagging its tail when particularly happy has earned it the nickname "poodle cat".

LEGS Long and slim.

FEET Small and oval in shape. Colour of the pads should harmonize with that of the coat.

Selkirk Rex

The most recently developed breed of Rex cats does not hail from the southwest of England, like the Cornish and Devon Rexes, nor from the Selkirk region of Scotland. Its origins lie in the United States and it was named after the Selkirk Mountains, which, although often erroneously described as being in the US, are in British Columbia, Canada.

FACIAL CHARACTERISTICS

EARS Medium-sized, set well apart, with broad bases, and tapering to a point.

EYES Copper, gold, yellow, or green, complementing the coat colour. Blue in white individuals.

HISTORY

In 1987, by spontaneous mutation, a shorthaired but curly coated dilute-calico female kitten arrived in an otherwise normal litter of domestic cats. When mature, this kitten was mated to a champion pedigree Black Longhair (see pp.36–7). The resultant litter of six kittens comprised three straight-coated and three curly coated individuals. The latter trio were the foundation of the breed.

TEMPERAMENT

Intelligent, playful, and affectionate. An ideal family cat.

VARIETIES

Selkirks come in all colours and patterns, including the pointed ones. They can be short- or longhaired.

TORTOISESHELL SELKIRK REX The Selkirk is a medium to large, solidly built cat that is heavier than one might at first imagine.

COAT Thick and plush with soft, loose curls. It can be short or long. Longhairs have longer, plume-like tail curls and a longer ruff.

HEAD Similar in shape to a British Shorthair, but rather more rounded.

BODY Stocky and muscular. This is a medium- to large-sized cat with heavy boning, particularly the male.

LEGS Medium boning.

FEET Large and round.

TAIL Medium in thickness, tapering, and with a rounded tip.

TABBY-AND-WHITE SELKIRK REX
The curious coat of this ideal family pet has an attractive soft feel.

Chartreux

It is thought that the Chartreux breed was first developed in the Middle Ages by monks in the French monastery of La Grande Chartreuse (famous for its green liqueur). This affectionate, sweet-natured cat makes an ideal companion. Most Chartreux do not miaow but rather emit a delightful chirrup. They also have a tendency to adopt a "praying" attitude, sometimes begging for titbits in this way.

EARS *Medium in size, set high on the head, and pricked.*

EYES *Orange to deep copper with a slight upward slant at the outer edge. The expression is sweet and intelligent.*

FACIAL CHARACTERISTICS

HISTORY

In Great Britain, selective breeding has brought the Chartreux so close in type to the British Blue Shorthair (*see pp.92–3*) that no distinction is made between the two. In North America, however, it is given its own class where a sturdier cat than the British Blue is called for, with a less rounded face and a higher proportion of grey in the coat.

FRENCH BEAUTY The Chartreux has a pleasant rounded face with a fairly narrow muzzle, full cheeks, and a strong bottom jaw.

HEAD *Rounded and wedge-shaped, with a straight nose of medium width, and a small, narrow muzzle.*

TEMPERAMENT

Chartreux make devoted family cats that fit in well with other pets, including dogs. Many Chartreux quickly adapt to a harness and lead and can be taken outdoors for walks.

COAT *Short to medium length, with a plush, woolly texture. Colour is a grey shade that can range from light ash to slate grey. Coat hairs have silver tips that give a charming, faintly luminous sheen.*

VARIETIES

There are no varieties of Chartreux.

BODY *Large, muscular, and well rounded, with a deep chest and broad shoulders.*

TAIL *Thick at the base, but tapering to a round tip.*

LEGS *Quite short, strong, and muscular.*

FEET *Round and small compared to the body.*

Egyptian Mau

Mau or Miw was the Ancient Egyptian name for the divine household cat, and of all domestic felines the Egyptian Mau is probably the most majestic.

HISTORY

Cats similar to the Egyptian Mau go far back into history, particularly in the Middle East, and it is believed that the Mau is a natural breed originating in the area of Cairo. The Mau first appeared in Europe at a cat show held in Rome in the mid-1950s, and from there was exported to the US in 1953, with initial recognition coming 15 years later. It is now recognized in Britain.

TEMPERAMENT

The Egyptian Mau is loving and playful and is said to be good at learning tricks. It is one of the few breeds that enjoys walking on a lead. One of the bravest of cats, it tends to stand its ground rather than flee when trouble brews, but when it does decide to run, it is the fastest mover of all domesticated cats.

VARIETIES

There are five varieties: the Silver has a silver body with black markings; the Bronze has a light-brown body with dark-brown markings; the Pewter has a rose-grey body with black or brown markings; the Smoke has a pale silver body with black markings; and the Black has the same colouring as the Smoke, but without the white undercoat.

EARS *Medium to large in size, set well apart, and moderately pointed, with tufts.*

EYES *Almond-shaped; pale-green in colour.*

HEAD *A slightly rounded wedge in shape, with a short nose. There should also be a scarab mark on the forehead.*

FACIAL CHARACTERISTICS

PEWTER EGYPTIAN MAU A popular belief is that the Mau may be descended from the cat symbolized by the Ancient Egyptian gods Ra and Bast. This theory is given credence by the pattern on the Mau's brow that resembles the sacred scarab beetle, which is often found on the foreheads of cats depicted on Egyptian murals.

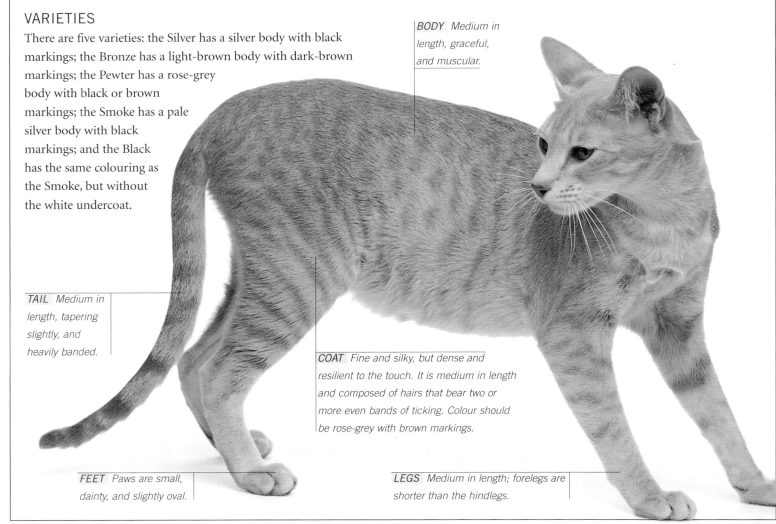

BODY *Medium in length, graceful, and muscular.*

TAIL *Medium in length, tapering slightly, and heavily banded.*

COAT *Fine and silky, but dense and resilient to the touch. It is medium in length and composed of hairs that bear two or more even bands of ticking. Colour should be rose-grey with brown markings.*

FEET *Paws are small, dainty, and slightly oval.*

LEGS *Medium in length; forelegs are shorter than the hindlegs.*

Sphynx

A birthday-suit cat! The virtually hairless Sphynx, a cat without its traditional covering of fur, is not to everyone's taste, but it is an undoubted attention-grabber.

HISTORY

Hairless cats are said to have been bred by the Aztecs, and there are references to the "Mexican Hairless" in books from the turn of the 19th century. However, the modern cat was developed only after 1966 from a mutant kitten born in Ontario, Canada. It is rare outside North America, where it is a recognized breed.

TEMPERAMENT

The Sphynx is an affectionate cat that enjoys being cuddled.

VARIETIES

The Sphynx can have any recognized coat colour or pattern. The eye colour should harmonize with the colour of the coat.

EARS Very large and round-tipped.

EYES Deep-set, lemon-shaped, and slanted; eye colour should complement the coat.

HEAD Neither round nor wedge-shaped, but slightly longer than it is wide and with strong cheek bones; the short nose has a pad that conforms in colour to the coat. The Sphynx has no whiskers.

FACIAL CHARACTERISTICS

HARLEQUIN SPHYNX To the touch, Sphynx skin feels like that of a warm peach. These cats should be bathed in warm water from time to time; they are easy to dry with a soft towel.

BLACK-AND-WHITE SPHYNX Lacking the insulation of hair, the Sphynx can easily get cold and is obviously designed to be an indoor cat.

BODY Medium in size, fine-boned but muscular, with a barrel chest.

TAIL Long, hard, and tapering.

LEGS Long and slim, with a bow-legged stance caused by the barrel-shaped chest.

COAT Hairless, apart from a fine down on the face, ears, feet, and tail. Skin is wrinkled on parts of the head, body, and legs, but should be taut elsewhere.

FEET Paws are neat and oval-shaped with long toes. Colour of the pads should conform to that of the coat.

Bengal

This beautiful and rather expensive cat originated in the US by crossing a domestic tabby Shorthair *(see pp.108–9)* with a Leopard Cat. The latter is the commonest wildcat of southern Asia and is found, usually leading a solitary life, in a variety of habitats from jungles and pine forests to mountainous regions. The Bengal is one of the most beguiling felines around and must rank high on the list of fairly recent breeding successes.

HISTORY
The development of the Bengal in the 1970s was the result of an investigation into the apparent natural immunity of Leopard Cats to feline leukaemia. The hybrid was found to combine the striking coat colour and markings of the wildcat with the gentle temperament of a domestic shorthair.

TEMPERAMENT
Bengals make lively, loving, and intelligent companions, adapting very well to life in the family. However, those within three generations of the original cross-mating (by now very few) may be a bit on the wild side.

VARIETIES
Bengals come in a variety of colours, including Brown/Black Spotted, Brown/Black Marbled, Snow/Spotted, and Snow/Marbled; both of the latter have an ivory, creamy white, or fawn background.

HIDDEN PATTERN Although Bengal kittens are born spotted, their initially rough fur disguises the patterning for three to four months.

COAT Medium-short, thick, and plush, with a luminous sheen. The soft, dense fur of the cat's underparts is paler than the colour of the rest of the body. Markings may be randomly scattered spots, leopard-like rosettes, or horizontal bands. Legs are barred and the tail is ringed with a dark tip.

EARS Medium-sized with wide bases.

EYES Almond-shaped and quite large. The commonest colour is green, but they may be gold, hazel, blue-green, or, sometimes in Snow-coloured cats, blue.

FACIAL CHARACTERISTICS
Brown Spotted Bengal

BROWN SPOTTED BENGAL Black and Brown Bengals appear to have gold dusted over their coats, while Snow-coloured varieties display a pearly sheen.

TAIL Long and muscular.

BODY Long, sleek, and muscular.

HEAD Wedge-shaped, with puffed whisker pads. Nose is short.

LEGS Strong and relatively short. Hindlegs are somewhat shorter than the forelegs, giving a "stalking" appearance.

FEET Quite large and rounded.

BROWN MARBLED BENGAL Although it will live happily indoors, the Bengal likes some freedom and the opportunity to roam every now and then. Ideally, it should have access to a garden or outside run.

Ocicat

Despite the name and appearance of this exquisite little cat, it is not a smaller relative of the wild spotted South American cats the Ocelot and Margay. It is, in fact, the result of selective breeding of domestic cats by a cat fancier in the US in 1964.

HISTORY

Mrs Virginia Daly was hoping to develop Abyssinian-pointed Siamese by crossing Siamese (see pp.114–15) with Abyssinians (see pp.118–19). To her surprise, a handsome spotted golden male, very much resembling a young ocelot, was born in a litter from a second-generation Siamese–Abyssinian cross. In subsequent years, the American Shorthair (see pp.108–9) was introduced to increase the size of the breed and to add silver to the colour range. Crossing with Abyssinians, which beneficially extends the gene pool, is still allowed. The Ocicat is widely recognized by cat associations.

TEMPERAMENT

Belying its looks, this is a thoroughly domesticated, loving, and even-tempered cat. It adores attention and hates being left alone. Like its Siamese ancestors, the Ocicat is very vocal and will protest loudly if it feels affronted. Active and extrovert, it likes outdoor access and does not make a very good indoor cat. Some Ocicats find it difficult to live with other cats.

VARIETIES

Permissible colours are Silver, Chocolate/Silver, Fawn Silver, Blue Silver, Lilac Silver, Sorrel Silver, Chocolate, Sorrel, Lilac, Blue, Fawn, and Tawny.

EARS Moderately large, with rounded tips and vertical hair tufts.

EYES Large, almond-shaped, and rimmed by dark fur.

HEAD Slightly curved from muzzle to cheek. A modified wedge shape with a broad muzzle and a short nose.

FACIAL CHARACTERISTICS

CHOCOLATE OCICAT This medium to large cat has a long muscular body. It moves with grace and fluency, keeping low to the ground like a wild ocelot – which it somewhat resembles – when stalking its prey.

TAIL Fairly long and slim with a slight taper.

COAT Fur is short, glossy, fine, close-lying, and ticked with several colour bands. Spots lie in rows along the spine but are more randomly scattered on the body; they should be clearly defined against the lighter background.

BODY Long, well muscled, and lithe.

DOG TRAITS The Ocicat is an athletic cat that enjoys exercise. Often they can be trained to walk on a lead, respond to voice commands, and even retrieve thrown objects rather like a dog.

LEGS Medium length and muscular.

FEET Paws are compact and oval with five toes on the front foot and four on the back.

USUAL OCICAT Ocicats are generally very healthy animals and, although an exotic breed, they do not demand any special attention. The coat does not need much grooming.

Scottish Fold

This rather curious-looking cat remains a controversial example of artificial selection in breeding. The folded-over ears that characterize the Scottish Fold may predispose the animal to deafness and infestation with ear mites or other form of outer-ear disease. Although rare and not officially recognized in Great Britain, the breed became popular in North America and was recognized there in 1978.

HISTORY

If records are correct, the gene for folded ears has been present in European domestic feline populations for almost 200 years, having arrived, some say, from China. The modern Scottish Fold arose from a kitten born as a natural mutation on the Perthshire farm of William Ross in 1961. It was exported to the US in the early 1970s. The kittens are born with normal pointed ears that then start to fold down between two and three weeks of age.

TEMPERAMENT

An exceptionally sweet-natured and gentle cat that loves family life and is particularly good with children, the Scottish Fold does tend to attach itself to a human "favourite" within the household. Nevertheless, although it can adapt to mainly indoor life, the cat enjoys time outdoors and, understandably in the light of its ancestry, makes a superb working farm cat that is highly skilled in hunting.

VARIETIES

Any of the American Shorthair colours *(see pp.108–9)* and almost all patterns are accepted with the exception of Chocolate, Lavender, and dark Siamese points.

BLACK SMOKE-AND-WHITE SCOTTISH FOLD
Although the Scottish Fold has an appealing owl- or pixie-like appearance, it is debatable whether encouraging the breeding of characteristics that may predispose to disease is ethical.

BODY Powerful, rounded, and cobby; well padded and medium in size.

TAIL Medium in length and flexible.

EARS This cat's defining features are small and neat, rounded at the tips, and set wide apart. The front of the ear should fold over completely to cover the opening of the outer ear canal.

HEAD A wide, round head set on a short, sturdy neck.

EYES Large, round, and set well apart.

FACIAL CHARACTERISTICS
Black-and-White Scottish Fold

COAT Fur should be short, dense, resilient, and thick enough to stand away naturally from the animal's body.

LEGS Sturdy, muscular, and short.

FEET Neat, round paws.

TORTOISESHELL SCOTTISH FOLD Regularly check the ears of a Scottish Fold. Keep them free from wax by carefully swabbing them with cotton-wool buds dipped in warm olive oil.

Munchkin

The Munchkin is the feline equivalent of the Dachshund dog, a breed developed in the 1980s that has stirred up much controversy. Described as a "freak dwarf" by some, this breed originated in a spontaneous natural mutation that was then artificially selected for breeding into a distinct type. It is not the first cat breed to be engineered for human aesthetic appeal. Certainly, it has gained growing numbers of adoring fans, and, although still an experimental breed, Munchkins seem to be as healthy as other cats and free from defects, including the spinal problems that can afflict Dachshunds.

HISTORY

In 1983, a pregnant black queen with short legs was found living under a pick-up truck in Louisiana, in the United States. Blackberry, as she came to be named, gave birth to a litter of kittens, half of which also had short legs. In later litters Blackberry continued to produce around 50 per cent of kittens with the same inherited trait. She and one of her sons, Toulouse, were the basis on which the Munchkin breed was formed. They are recognized by TICA, but not by the American CFA or the British GCCF.

TEMPERAMENT

Sociable, friendly, and active, Munchkins seem to retain playful kittenish qualities throughout adult life. Despite their short legs they can run fast and jump higher than you might imagine.

VARIETIES

Standard Munchkins have short legs and carry the gene that causes this. Non-standard Munchkins are produced by Munchkin parents but do not carry the gene. They come in a variety of coat patterns, colours, and coat lengths.

BLACK-AND-WHITE MUNCHKIN Many Munchkin enthusiasts consider these little cats to be Peter Pans that retain their kittenish ways and personalities throughout life, ever ready to play and investigate the world around them.

BODY Medium length and compact.

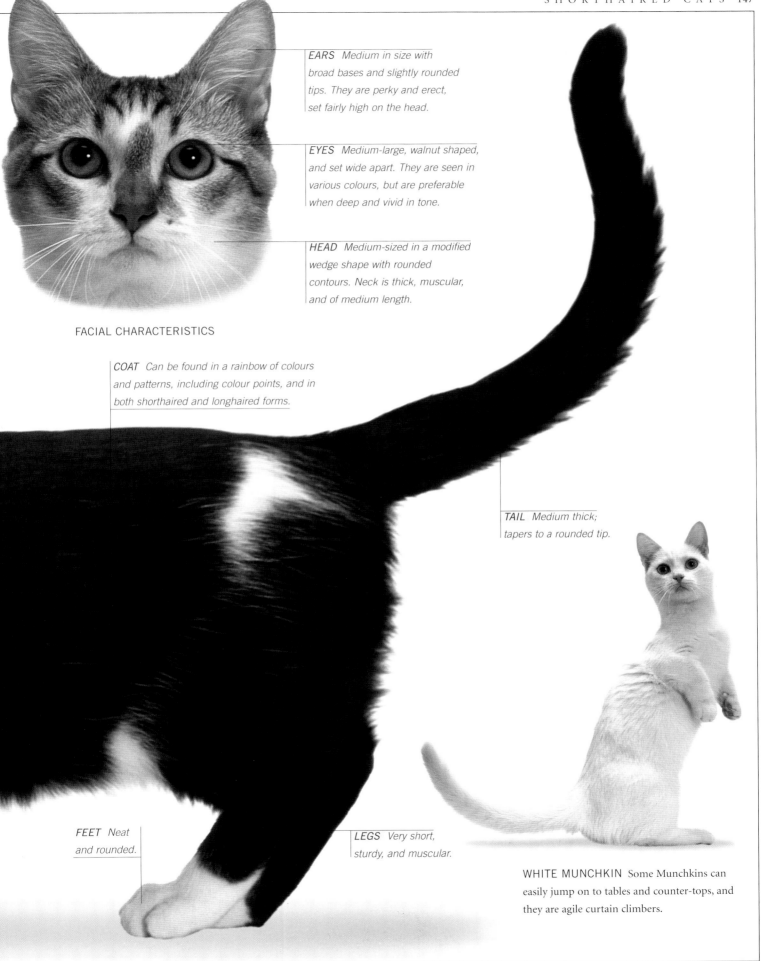

EARS *Medium in size with broad bases and slightly rounded tips. They are perky and erect, set fairly high on the head.*

EYES *Medium-large, walnut shaped, and set wide apart. They are seen in various colours, but are preferable when deep and vivid in tone.*

HEAD *Medium-sized in a modified wedge shape with rounded contours. Neck is thick, muscular, and of medium length.*

FACIAL CHARACTERISTICS

COAT *Can be found in a rainbow of colours and patterns, including colour points, and in both shorthaired and longhaired forms.*

TAIL *Medium thick; tapers to a rounded tip.*

FEET *Neat and rounded.*

LEGS *Very short, sturdy, and muscular.*

WHITE MUNCHKIN Some Munchkins can easily jump on to tables and counter-tops, and they are agile curtain climbers.

American Bobtail

At first sight, you might well imagine that what you are seeing is a truly wild cat, the Bobcat of North America. Not so. This spectacular domestic cat looks wild but, in fact, has one of the most agreeable natures of any companion breed. It is a truly American, naturally selected cat that, as its name suggests, sports a short tail – on average, just 2.5–10 cm (1–4 in) long.

HISTORY

Although bobtailed cats were to be found in America for hundreds of years, true development of the breed only began in the late 1960s. The American Bobtail is one of the latest breeds to be recognized by the CFA of the United States.

TEMPERAMENT

The American Bobtail has an absolutely superb temperament and is intelligent, loving, loyal, and devoted to its owners. It likes to play and is excellent with children and elderly people. It is easily trained to walk on a lead and, if started when a kitten, makes a very good car traveller.

VARIETIES

The American Bobtail can be found in both shorthair and longhair forms.

HEAD A broad, modified wedge shape, with a wide nose and plenty of nose leather.

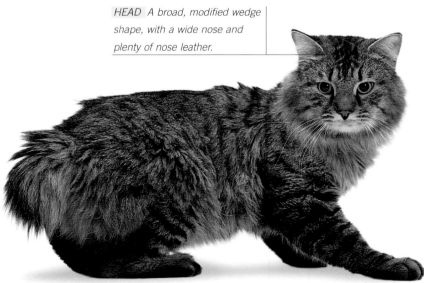

JEWEL THIEF American Bobtails are attracted to bright, shiny objects and are apt to purloin them whenever possible. It is, therefore, best to keep jewellery boxes and drawers closed when these cats are about!

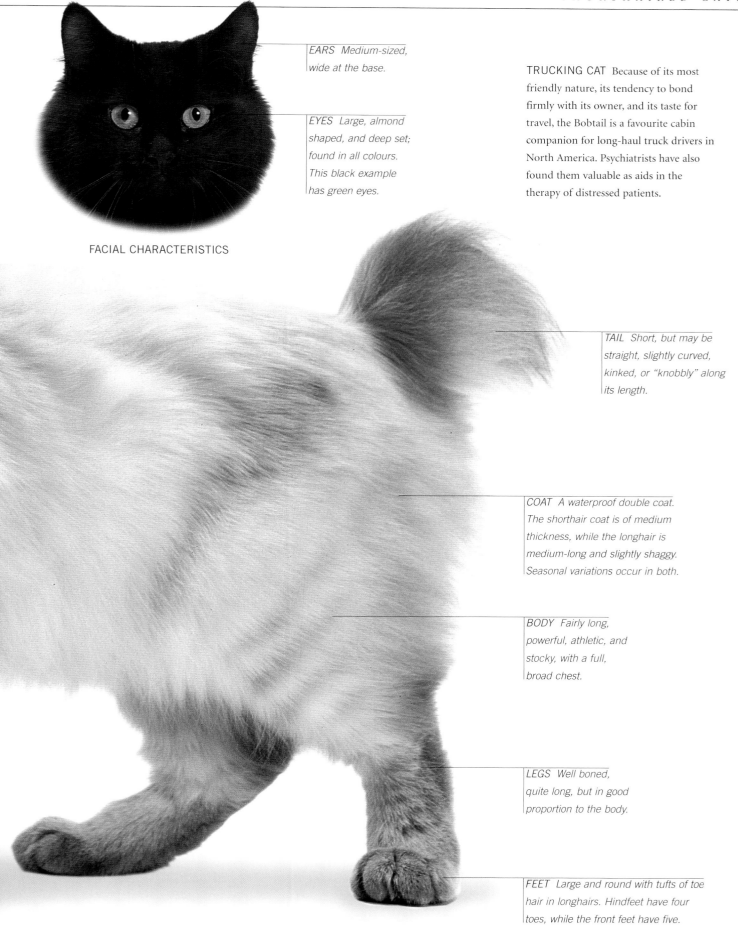

EARS Medium-sized,
wide at the base.

EYES Large, almond
shaped, and deep set;
found in all colours.
This black example
has green eyes.

FACIAL CHARACTERISTICS

TRUCKING CAT Because of its most
friendly nature, its tendency to bond
firmly with its owner, and its taste for
travel, the Bobtail is a favourite cabin
companion for long-haul truck drivers in
North America. Psychiatrists have also
found them valuable as aids in the
therapy of distressed patients.

TAIL Short, but may be
straight, slightly curved,
kinked, or "knobbly" along
its length.

COAT A waterproof double coat.
The shorthair coat is of medium
thickness, while the longhair is
medium-long and slightly shaggy.
Seasonal variations occur in both.

BODY Fairly long,
powerful, athletic, and
stocky, with a full,
broad chest.

LEGS Well boned,
quite long, but in good
proportion to the body.

FEET Large and round with tufts of toe
hair in longhairs. Hindfeet have four
toes, while the front feet have five.

LaPerm

One of the most appealing of the Rex-type cats, the LaPerm is a relatively new arrival on the cat-fancy scene. As its name suggests, the LaPerm sports a coat that looks as if it has been Marcel-waved. Even its eyebrows and whiskers are curly. A playful, people-loving animal, it behaves in many ways more like a lapdog than a cat.

GENETICALLY GOOD With hardy farm-cat forebears and no in-breeding, the LaPerm is genetically a very sound breed, free of the defects and tendency to certain diseases found in some other, more established breeds.

HISTORY

The LaPerm was developed in Oregon, USA, in the 1980s. An abandoned farm kitten was taken in by Linda Koehl. To the lady's surprise, the kitten grew a delightful crimped coat within a few weeks. The subsequent line of cats turned out to be superb small pets with apparently no genetic defects and exhibiting the hearty constitutions of their farmyard forebears.

TEMPERAMENT

Incredibly loving and inquisitive, LaPerm cats relish being cuddled. They are generally happy to follow their human companions about, and they come obediently when called.

VARIETIES

Both short- and longhaired varieties occur, and a wide range of colours is accepted. LaPerms do not breed true; in every litter there will be some non-curly kittens that nevertheless display all the other breed characteristics. The breed is recognized by TICA and the CFA, but not yet by the British GCCF.

FEET Medium-sized and round.

LEGS Long in proportion to the body.

TAIL Long and tapering, with wavy hair.

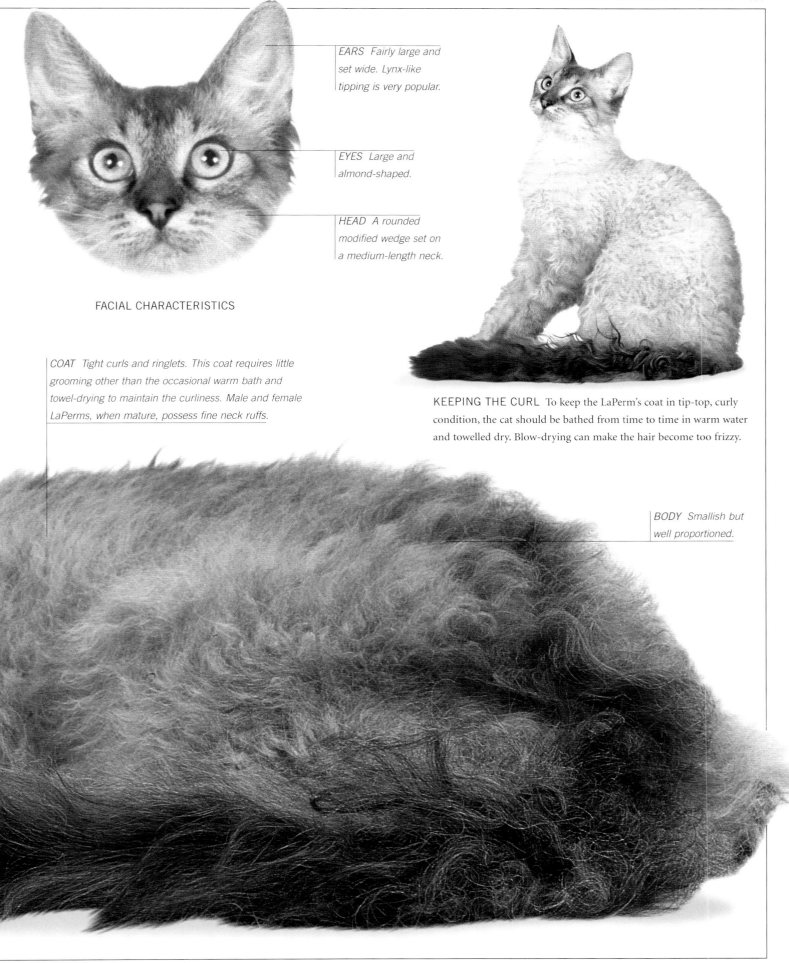

EARS Fairly large and set wide. Lynx-like tipping is very popular.

EYES Large and almond-shaped.

HEAD A rounded modified wedge set on a medium-length neck.

FACIAL CHARACTERISTICS

COAT Tight curls and ringlets. This coat requires little grooming other than the occasional warm bath and towel-drying to maintain the curliness. Male and female LaPerms, when mature, possess fine neck ruffs.

KEEPING THE CURL To keep the LaPerm's coat in tip-top, curly condition, the cat should be bathed from time to time in warm water and towelled dry. Blow-drying can make the hair become too frizzy.

BODY Smallish but well proportioned.

Non-Pedigree Shorthairs

All cats, pedigree or crossbred, are aristocrats, with blood-lines that run back to the sacred cats of the Pharaohs – the humble moggie no less than the most dignified of Grand Champions. All have their own individuality but share the same charm, elegance, and feline mystique.

HISTORY
Shorthaired cats have graced human society for thousands of years. They were differentiated from pedigree types only in the late 19th century, when the best examples of British street cats were selectively bred for showing.

TEMPERAMENT
Moggies are the original fireside companions, chosen not for their venerable parentage, but because they are appealing and lovable in their own right. In a receptive household, all make firm and lasting friendships.

VARIETIES
"Varieties" are dependent only on the ingenuity and resourcefulness of mother nature.

AMERICAN NON-PEDIGREE
SILVER SHORTHAIR The American
moggie has its own unique attraction.

BODY Strong
and muscular.

BRITISH NON-PEDIGREE
GINGER-AND-WHITE SHORTHAIR
Although the patching is uneven and
there are obvious tabby markings, the
contented dignity of this Ginger-and-
White quells any notion of its being
a poor relation to its pedigree
counterpart.

LEGS Short and
well proportioned.

FEET Paws are
large and round,
with pink pads.

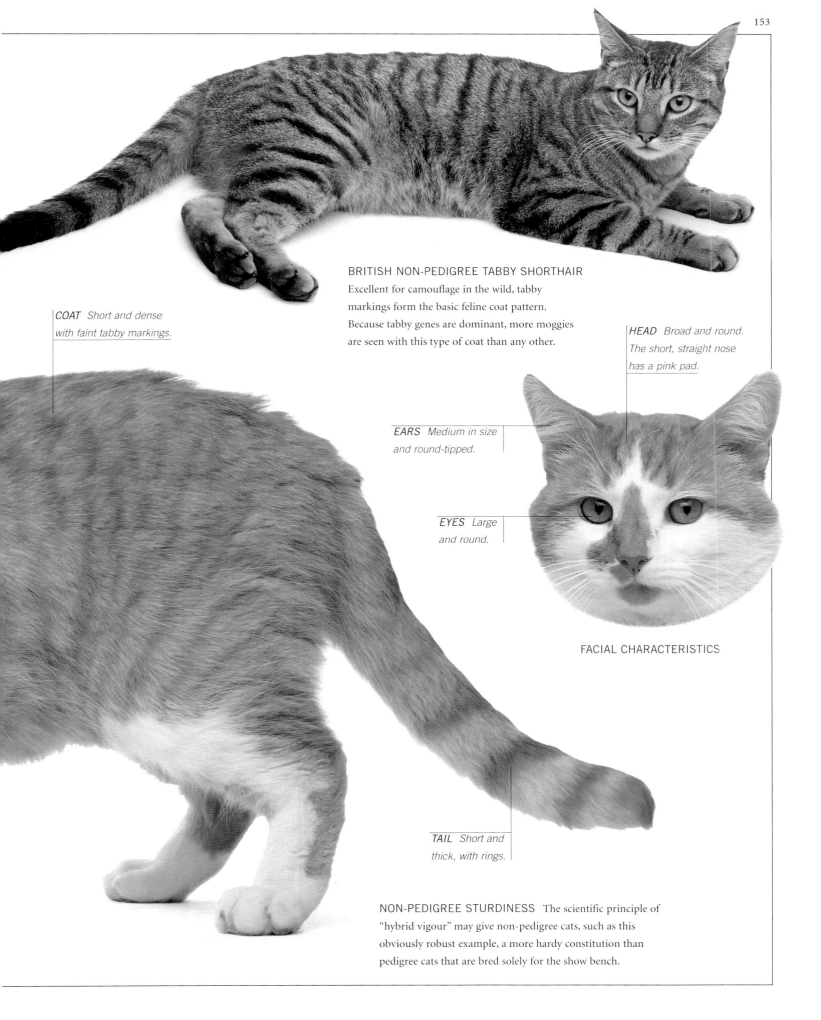

BRITISH NON-PEDIGREE TABBY SHORTHAIR
Excellent for camouflage in the wild, tabby
markings form the basic feline coat pattern.
Because tabby genes are dominant, more moggies
are seen with this type of coat than any other.

COAT Short and dense
with faint tabby markings.

HEAD Broad and round.
The short, straight nose
has a pink pad.

EARS Medium in size
and round-tipped.

EYES Large
and round.

FACIAL CHARACTERISTICS

TAIL Short and
thick, with rings.

NON-PEDIGREE STURDINESS The scientific principle of
"hybrid vigour" may give non-pedigree cats, such as this
obviously robust example, a more hardy constitution than
pedigree cats that are bred solely for the show bench.

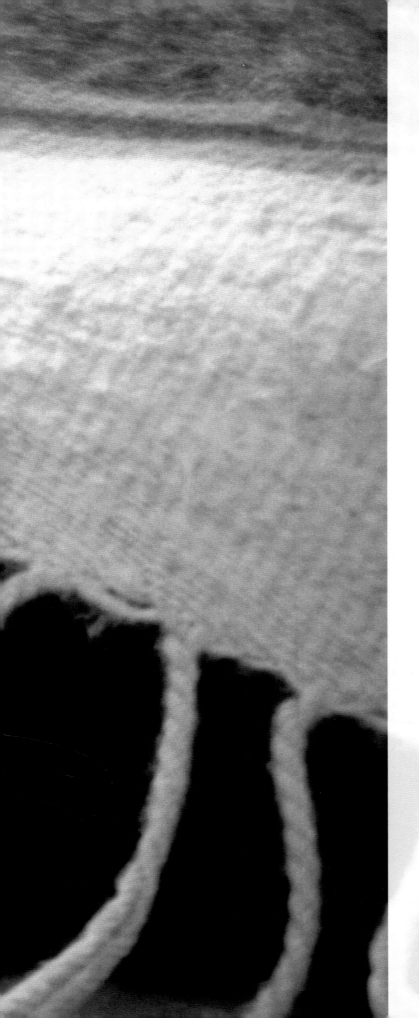

Keeping a Cat

It may happen that a cat chooses to come and live with you. That is how it has been for me on a number of occasions. It begins with trial visits in the style of a *Good Food Guide* inspector; your establishment, the cat's possible future home, is given the once-over – more than once, usually! And, in the manner of a food inspector, close attention is paid to the quality and ready availability of meals, but also, and very importantly, to the warmth of the reception given and the comfort of the place. If you are "picked" in this way by a cat and are not one of that bizarre minority of folk who inexplicably count themselves to be ailurophobes, without a scrap of feeling for felines in their souls, you have got your cat – or rather your cat has got you.

People decide for a variety of reasons that they want to acquire a cat. It is almost never for rodent control, but may be for companionship or, most often, simply because cats are great to have around. What other domestic animal combines sophistication with friendship, while being able to warm your lap, deter mice, grace any room, and give early warning of impending earthquakes? All provided at a highly economical running cost.

HIDE AND SEEK Cats love to curl up in cosy, sheltered spots – under a rug, for example. They may do this simply to keep warm or in readiness to ambush any toy mouse that might pass by!

Your New Cat

There's more to deciding to share your home with a cat than simply looking up your local breeders in the telephone book. Are you fit to be a cat companion?

Questions to ask include: what other animals live in the house and how might they interact with a new arrival? Will the cat be permanently confined indoors because you live in a high-rise apartment? If the cat is to be allowed outdoors, can arrangements be made to have a cat-flap fitted to a door or window? Have you the time and patience to give certain kinds of cat the grooming they regularly require? What arrangements can you make for the pet's welfare during your holidays? Can you afford the basic equipment needed, daily supplies of high-quality cat food, and the cost of both preventive medicine and any unexpected course of medical treatment?

WHAT KIND OF CAT?

Careful thought and preparation must precede the acquisition of a cat. You must first decide what kind of cat would be mutually suitable. If you are planning to show and/or breed cats, obviously only a pedigree animal will fit the bill. But if you simply want a cat friend, a cat-about-the-house, there are the humane-society clinics and reception centres stuffed with abandoned, unwanted cats – most of them on Death Row, with dates of execution set if they are not given a good home by that time. Should you be new to cats, do not get the idea that there is such a thing as a "best" cat. All cats are individuals. All are aristocrats.

Now, more decisions to be made. Do you prefer a kitten or an adult cat? Kittens, like kids, have their problem periods as they grow up. Are you able and prepared to cope? Should you choose a tom or a queen? Entire toms *can* make marvellous companions, but they remain essentially a mixture of Arnold Schwarzenegger and Don Juan – regularly off to war or obsessed with their latest amorous encounter. And some toms do leave their strong characteristic odours around, marking your house as their territory or attracting rival males to leave droplets of smelly urine on the doorstep. Of course, queens tend to bring forth kittens with monotonous regularity, and crossbred kittens are not easy to find homes for. Again, are you prepared for all this?

PLAYFUL KITTENS Happiness to three kittens is a wastepaper basket.

CHOOSING A KITTEN

1 *Check the kitten thoroughly to ensure that it is in good condition. Part the hair to look for signs of parasites, particularly the fine "coal dust" that indicates the presence of fleas.*

2 *You should also inspect the kitten's ears carefully. Ensure that there are no discharges and that the ears do not contain dirt that may indicate infection or parasites.*

3 *The eyes should be bright, clear, and free from discharges.*

One humane, effective, and relatively simple solution to some of the problems posed above is neutering.

Choices must also be carefully made, and not purely on grounds of aesthetics, if you want a pedigree cat. Longhairs need regular grooming and will take far more of your time than shorthaired breeds do. Russian Blues or Longhairs generally make better indoor cats than most shorthaired breeds. By contrast, Abyssinians and Somalis adore their freedom and are not suited to life in an apartment. Some breeds, like the Siamese, demand lots of attention and fuss. A few, such as the Sphynx, need special care and handling. And all pedigree cats, particularly the more glamorous breeds, can attract the attention of cat thieves.

BUYING A CAT

When choosing your cat, pedigree or crossbred, it is best to avoid pet shops. Deal instead with a recommended breeder, a humane society, or a friend or neighbour. How do you pick the right cat or kitten? Some folk believe that the cat of your life might be found in the stars. If you know the date of a particular animal's birth, there are astrologers willing to draw up its personal horoscope. By matching it up with your own, they say, you can increase the chances of a perfect relationship. For example, Virgo cats (born between 24 August and 23 September) are predicted to be excellent, conscientious, dedicated, and down-to-earth cats especially suited to Capricorn and Taurus owners.

For most of us, however, more mundane considerations must influence our selection. In essence the difficulties about choosing one's cat are similar to those involved in buying a second-hand car. How do you spot the faults? Is it really in good running order? It is unlikely to be an expensive mistake if you acquire a crossbred cat with, metaphorically speaking, its gearbox full of sawdust or its mileage clock wound back, but if you are buying pedigree stock

4 *It is important to look at the mouth for evidence of plaque build-up, sore, inflamed gums, and abnormal teeth. Hold the kitten's head from behind as shown here and gently prise open its mouth.*

5 *The area beneath the tail should be clean, dry, and free from evidence of diarrhoea or urine scalding.*

6 *The cat should be alert and interested, show no evidence of pain when handled, and react amicably when picked up. Remember to be gentle when picking up a young kitten, since its ribcage is delicate and can be easily hurt.*

you *must* get expert advice before parting with large sums of money for potential show champions.

For all cats, pedigree or not, the following list of points should be checked by the prospective owner. Just as if you were buying a gleaming new car, do not meekly accept the salesman's word, but look at the cat's condition and state of health carefully and critically. Any responsible vendor will not object to your thoroughly examining a prospective new pet. If all is well, buy the cat – if possible on approval – and then have the animal overhauled by the veterinarian as soon as possible. *Never* buy a cat from a back-street pet shop or from a "cat farm", since young cats are very susceptible to disease and infection, and these can spread easily. It is *never* sensible to buy a kitten younger than ten weeks old.

Choosing a pedigree animal demands more than just fitness checks. The quality, points, and prize-winning potential of any individual can only be gauged by an expert eye. You should therefore take along somebody who is knowledgeable about the

A CAT SHOULD:

- Appear alert and interested in its surroundings;
- Move around readily with its head held straight;
- Be able to spring to the ground easily from table height;
- Have clear, bright eyes without any white film (the "haw") showing;
- Have clean ears, mouth, and nose, without discharges;
- Have clean, white teeth without accumulations of tartar, and salmon-pink gums and tongue;
- Have a smooth, clean skin, with sleek fur composed of a full bushy undercoat and a glossy topcoat.

A CAT SHOULD NOT:

- Suffer from diarrhoea;
- Sneeze, cough, or wheeze;
- Appear to be in pain when touched or handled;
- Show any trace of blood;
- Have any holes, breaks, or blemishes in its coat.

breed you want to buy and who knows what you are hoping for in the cat.

Pedigrees are expensive but, if you cannot quite afford the full price, you may be able to obtain a bargain by buying a "pet-quality" cat, or by making a breeding agreement. Pet-quality cats are ones that do not reach the standards required for showing, but that nevertheless make perfectly good pets. Under a breeding agreement, you buy a show-quality cat, and return it to the breeder at pre-arranged times for breeding. You must agree who will own any subsequent kittens, and put whatever is agreed in writing.

All pedigree animals should be registered under an individual name, with details of their colour and parentage, when they are about five weeks old. Unless this is done, they will not be permitted to enter a cat show in a pedigree class.

When selecting a cat, always look for one that is playful, alert, and willing to be handled. With kittens, go for the bolder, quick-to-come-forward individual, rather than the most retiring one, since it may be a weaker or more sickly specimen.

Check that a kitten has been vaccinated against feline enteritis and feline influenza at least one week before purchase, and that adults were vaccinated as youngsters and given regular boosters thereafter. Vaccination certificates signed by a vet should be provided as proof. If you have other cats and are anxious to keep them free from feline leukaemia, ask a vet to carry out a simple blood test on the new animal and to provide a certificate stating that the test result was negative.

MAKING NEW FRIENDS After a few moments of uncertainty, a firm friendship is in the making between kitten and puppy. Such introductions will almost always be successful but require careful "refereeing" by the owner.

HOUSE-PLANT HAZARDS

The average house is full of potential hazards for cats, and you should think carefully about the risks before the pet's arrival. House plants should be of non-poisonous varieties. Do not allow access to the following species, especially if your cat is prone to nibble plants:

- Aloe vera
- Azaleas
- Caladium
- Calla
- Christmas rose
- Chrysanthemum
- Creeping Charlie
- Creeping fig
- Crown of thorns
- Common or cherry laurel
- Daffodil
- Dieffenbachia
- Dumb-cane
- Easter lily
- Elephant ears
- Emerald duke
- English holly
- False Jerusalem cherry

- True ivies
- Lily of the valley
- Majesty
- Mistletoe
- Nephthytis
- Oleander
- Philodendron (Tree lovers)
- Poinsettia
- Pothos
- Red princess
- Rhododendron
- Saddle leaf
- Spider mum
- Sprengeri fern
- Swiss cheese plant
- Tulip (bulbs)
- Umbrella plant
- Weeping fig

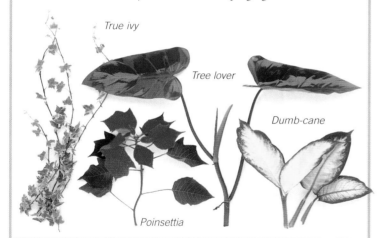

True ivy

Tree lover

Dumb-cane

Poinsettia

HOUSEHOLD HAZARDS

Some of these substances can poison a cat not only by being licked and ingested, but also by being absorbed through feline skin.

- Aspirin
- Antifreeze
- Bleach
- Cleaning fluids
- Deodorants and deodorizers
- Detergents
- Disinfectants
- Drain cleaner
- Fungicides
- Herbicides

- Household polishes
- Insecticides
- Liniments
- Potpourri liquids
- Shoe polish
- Simmering aromatic oils
- Snail/slug bait
- Suntan lotion
- Tar
- Wood preservatives

OTHER HAZARDS

Think of your cat as a child and proof your house against any possible accidents by using common sense.

- Keep cats away from hot ovens, boiling liquids, and fires. Use a safety guard around an open fire;
- Keep washing machine, refrigerator, freezer, and oven doors shut;
- Ensure that rubbish bins are inaccessible to cats;
- Do not let your cat chew electric cables and disconnect power when not in use;
- Put valued objects, such as fragile ornaments, out of the cat's reach;
- Do not leave sharp kitchen utensils out;
- Do not leave toxic household products in accessible places. Beware of antifreeze-contaminated puddles of water in the garage;
- Do not leave polythene bags out – if a cat climbs inside it may suffocate;
- Do not leave small objects where your cat may chew and swallow them;
- Do not put a hot electrical iron where a cat could knock it over;
- Do not allow cats on to a high balcony or windowsill.

THE NEW ARRIVAL

Only when you have prepared yourself by obtaining all the basic equipment should you bring a new cat to your home. Transport your cat in a proper carrying container. These come in various designs and materials – stout cardboard ones can be purchased cheaply from pet stores, humane societies, and vets.

If you are obtaining an adult cat from a friend, try to bring with it some familiar piece of cat furniture, such as its bed or litter tray. Once at your house, allow the cat to explore thoroughly on its own, introducing it to one room at a time without interference from children or other pets. Keep other animals away until the new arrival has had a chance to roam around the place. Then, allow the "resident" animals into a room where you are holding the latest addition to the family. Supervise the initial encounters carefully and give both sides equal amounts of affection and attention. There is bound to be some antipathy between the animals since cats are so territorial; this may last hours or weeks, but it will gradually fade to become a reasonable accommodation on both sides and a generally good friendship.

Kittens are generally accepted more readily than adult cats by other pets.

THE FIRST WEEK

Spoil and fuss over the new cat during its first week with you, and be ready to play with it. Find out from the previous owner what its feeding routine and particular dietary fancies are and try to oblige them. Keep the cat indoors for about one week, and make sure you accompany the animal when you allow it to make its first outdoor exploration. *Never* allow a newly arrived cat, even if it is an adult, to stay out on its own at night.

Basic Equipment

Cats are not expensive to house, but they must be provided with certain items of basic equipment, such as somewhere to sleep, a litter tray, feeding and drinking bowls, a collar, a carrying box, and basic grooming equipment.

USEFUL EXTRAS

If your cat is able to go outside, a cat-flap is a useful addition. It should be fitted no higher than 6 cm (2–3 in) from the base of the door or windowsill. All flaps should be lockable. Some cat-flaps have magnetic strips along the sides that help avoid draughts by creating a tight seal.

You could also consider supplying a scratching post or pad, a playpen – useful for kittens until they acclimatize to their new home – and some toys.

Bristle and wire brush

Wide-toothed comb

Fine-toothed comb

GROOMING EQUIPMENT As well as a brush and combs, such as those shown here, you will need nail clippers *(see p.175)*.

TOYS You can buy toys from pet shops, or simply supply your cat with things like empty cotton reels that will give it endless enjoyment. Avoid soft rubber toys; they can cause choking and other problems.

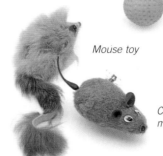

Balls

Mouse toy

Clockwork mouse

Litter tray

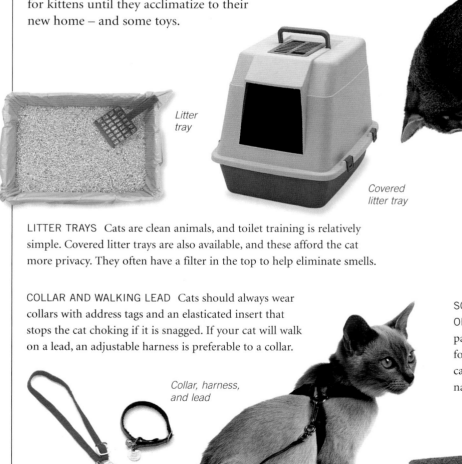

Covered litter tray

LITTER TRAYS Cats are clean animals, and toilet training is relatively simple. Covered litter trays are also available, and these afford the cat more privacy. They often have a filter in the top to help eliminate smells.

COLLAR AND WALKING LEAD Cats should always wear collars with address tags and an elasticated insert that stops the cat choking if it is snagged. If your cat will walk on a lead, an adjustable harness is preferable to a collar.

Collar, harness, and lead

SCRATCHING POST OR PAD These are particularly useful for indoor cats, who can sharpen their nails on them.

FEEDING AND WATER BOWLS Each cat should have its own dishes. They must always be kept clean and separate from the household crockery.

Plastic bowl

Plastic food-and-drink bowl

Earthenware bowl

CAT BED Beds can be purchased in a wide variety of designs, from traditional wicker baskets to beanbag types, from cat igloos made out of plastic to the good old cardboard box lined with newspaper.

CAT CARRIERS

Cat carriers are available in a range of designs, some suitable for long-distance transport by road, sea, or air, others really only to be used for short trips to the vet or cattery.

CARDBOARD CARRIER This collapsible carrier made of cardboard is cheap and easy to store, but it may not be secure enough to contain a robust and irate tom, particularly if the cardboard has perished in places. It is difficult to clean and disinfect.

WIRE CARRIER This airy, plastic-covered wire carrier is easy to clean. Ensure the door does not bend open at places when under pressure from a cat.

WICKER CARRIER This type of carrier is not easy to keep clean. Make sure that the door is securely closed before use.

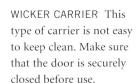

PLASTIC CARRIER This is the strongest and best – but most expensive – type of cat carrier. It is well ventilated, not too gloomy, and has optional food and water fittings. It is very secure, easy to clean, and is suitable for short- and long-distance trips.

Food and Nutrition

The cat is a creature built to eat meat. This is not to say that cats do not like or need some vegetable matter in their diet. Among wild species, the flat-headed cat of Malaysia and Indonesia has a particular love of fruit and sweet potatoes.

Although proteins play important roles in a cat's diet, particularly at certain times of life, a purely protein diet for a cat would be unnecessarily expensive and wasteful. There are also health aspects. Proteins produce many waste products after digestion, and these have to be eliminated by the kidneys, organs that may be under great pressure in older animals. A luxurious menu consisting of nothing but raw *filet de boeuf* contains far too little calcium and too few vitamins for healthy feline living.

Variety, then, is the watchword for your familiar's diet, and it will enable a cat to balance its diet instinctively. Accustom a kitten to a broad selection of foods. Even if you inherit an old animal that is set in its ways and seems determined to fast until death unless fed on nothing but crayfish or caviar, there is a fair chance that a bit of culinary effort will succeed in enticing him out of his monotonous diet.

When acting as chef to a newly arrived puss, introduce your carefully considered diet gradually. Change him from the old menu to the new bit by bit over a period of a couple of weeks or so.

Besides variety, the other important factor in feeding your cat is freshness. Do not give him stale food or food you bought because it was cheap but that may have been on the store shelf so long that it has lost its nutritional value.

PROTEINS

As mentioned above, protein is one of the essential parts of a cat's diet and should form at least 25 per cent of the diet of an adult cat, or 35 to 40 per cent of a kitten's. The daily protein requirement of an adult cat is 3 g of protein per 450 g (1 lb) of body weight. For a kitten, this should be increased to 8.5 g per 450 g (1 lb) of body weight.

Protein foods include the pre-packed special cat foods you can buy, as well as fresh foods such as meat, poultry, fish, eggs, milk, and cheese.

Proteins are built of chemicals called amino acids, one of which – taurine – is very important for good health in cats. Taurine deficiency may occur if cats are fed on strict vegetarian diets or on commercial dog food. Blindness or heart disease can develop in taurine-deficient felines.

FATS

In addition to proteins, your cat needs fats as an important source of calories, particularly as the animal gets older. Fats should form 15 to 40 per cent of the ration, and they have the advantage that they do not load the kidneys with waste products.

It is essential to avoid feeding fats that are old or rancid – although a hungry cat may accept such foods, they can make it ill. Fats are usually found in the protein foods mentioned above, but can be

VARIETY OF FOOD Accustom your cat to a varied diet from a very young age, if possible.

specially augmented by adding one teaspoonful of fat to the food of older animals that no longer absorb nutrients very well and have lost their layers of insulating fat. The best sources of high-quality fat are soft animal fat (chicken fat or bacon grease), butter, and lard.

FILLER FOODS

Cats also often get their energy in the form of filler foods such as carbohydrates, bulk, and fibre. These are not essential but can be included to make up to half of the ration if desired. Filler foods include fruit and vegetables and starchy foods such as bread, pasta, and cereals.

FOOD-AND-WATER BOWL A double feeding bowl for water and food is very useful. Cats should always have water available.

MINERALS AND VITAMINS

Minerals of all kinds are essential for a cat's growth and the maintenance of its vital functions. If you feed your cat a well-balanced, varied diet, mineral deficiencies are most unlikely to occur. The same is true with regard to the vitamins, and special vitamin supplements are not normally necessary for the healthy cat unless recommended by the vet. The cat does not have the same need as a human of vitamins B12, C, and K in its diet.

WATER

As long as fresh, clean water is always available, do not worry about how much of the stuff your feline friend is drinking, unless you have settled for the lazy man's diet of nothing but food pellets. It is well known that animals can survive perfectly well on a diet of fish and beef without ever drinking water. A meat diet has a high water content, and the cat's kidney is capable of concentrating the urine and thereby saving water; about two and a half times more than the human kidney. Of course, outdoor cats may be tippling at a favourite puddle.

If your cat really does seem to do without H_2O, there is no cause for concern – it is quite a common phenomenon. As well as the water in the food itself, all creatures get a large proportion of their daily water requirements by chemical action – the fats and carbohydrates in their food are "burned" within their bodies, producing water molecules.

Yeast tablets

Mineral/vitamin powder

Cat "sweets" containing vitamins

Fortified milk-food powder

DIETARY SUPPLEMENTS Extra vitamins and minerals may be given to your cat.

Cleverly, cats also lose very little water through panting or sweating, and only an insignificant quantity evaporates during breathing. Even big wild cats like lions have been known to go without a drink for up to ten days. Nevertheless,

MYTHS AND FALLACIES

Eating grass

Having laboured like a French chef over your moggy, do not be alarmed if he or she still insists on chewing grass and weeds at the first opportunity. Grass is good for cats. It contains certain vitamins and also acts as an efficient emetic, helping the animal regurgitate unwanted matter such as fur balls. If you and your cat share a high-rise apartment without ready access to a garden, grow him some grass from seed in a window box. Chewing grass is not a sign that the cat feels ill.

Mousing

Cats hunt mice, birds, insects, and so on for sport, not as a food source. True, they may on occasion eat part or all of their prey, but basically they are in it for the fun of the game. So you need not

Contrary to popular myth, eating grass is a normal occurrence.

think that by underfeeding or, indeed, not feeding your cat, he will be encouraged to clear your premises of small rodents. The opposite is true. Well-fed cats are the best mousers. They have the stamina, energy, and quick reactions required for the sport. Mickey, a well-fed tabby of Burscough, Lancashire, UK, killed over 22,000 mice in 23 years before dying in 1968 – an average of nearly three mice each day of his life.

Flies

"Cats that catch flies and eat them go thin" is a very common saying. Although there is the possibility that a cat eating a blue-bottle might also take in disease bacteria, the problem is a minute one. Occasionally worm eggs might be carried by flies from one cat to another, but other than this slight risk, fly-eating cats rarely come to much harm.

a supply of fresh, clean water must be made available at all times for your cat.

We should perhaps pause at this point to doff our hats in memory of Jack, a black tom that lived in Brooklyn, New York. In 1937, at the age of three, Jack gave up water-drinking in favour of milk laced with Pernod. As he grew older, he demanded stiffer and stiffer saucers of "milk", until it was more a question of lacing the Pernod lightly with milk than the other way round. Jack finally gave up the ghost in the bar where he lived when he was eight years old. Unsurprisingly, at the post-mortem Jack's liver was found to be in a distinctly sad state.

THE FASCINATION OF WATER Water is both an essential and fascinating element to all cats, so do not be surprised to find yours playing in it.

SEASONING AND SUPPLEMENTS

Most cats are discerning and prefer intelligent seasoning of their food. I have had cats who adored curried chicken and spaghetti with clam sauce – very civilized and utterly beneficial. If you are cooking some of your pet's meals, season with iodized salt to taste (your taste). Enough iodine, which is a trace element, can be assured in this way. It is particularly important in pregnant queens where iodine is needed to prevent resorption of the foetuses within the womb. Stock bouillon cubes make a gravy containing all essential salts.

If you are using proprietary dry or soft-moist food, remember that these products tend to be low in fat content. Add eight teaspoonfuls of fat, butter, or lard per 500 g (1 lb).

ORGANIC AND ANTI-OXIDANT FOODS

The arguments for human benefits in eating chemical fertilizer-free and pesticide-free organic food most probably also hold

EATING WELL As for human beings, a good-quality, balanced diet in appropriate quantity, prepared and served hygienically, is important for a cat's health and longevity.

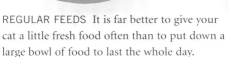

REGULAR FEEDS It is far better to give your cat a little fresh food often than to put down a large bowl of food to last the whole day.

good for cats. To cater for this, pet-food manufacturers are now producing cat foods made from naturally grown, unadulterated ingredients, some of which are claimed to have the added advantage of being hypoallergenic, containing, for example, no wheat gluten, which may cause allergic reactions in certain individual cats.

Recently, new anti-oxidant cat foods, rich in such things as vitamins C and E, have been developed. It is thought that the anti-oxidants mop up damaging

chemicals called free radicals, which attack genetic material in the cat's body cells and are associated with the diseases of aging. Hopefully such nutritional advances will lead to longer life for our feline friends.

HOW MUCH TO FEED

Scientists have calculated that the daily requirements of a cat on a diet containing 25 per cent protein is 15 g (½ oz) of food per 400 g (1 lb) of body weight, but this is a theoretical guide only. In practice, like their human companions, cats vary widely in appetite. The ancient Greeks believed that cats put on weight as the moon waxed and lost weight as it waned. Overweight cats – and I have met plenty – are at increased risk of health problems, just like their overweight owners. The obese animal is more likely to end up with osteoarthritis, heart disease, or diabetes. So, if your cat is losing his figure, do not feed treats and titbits in between meals. Instead, feed him or her twice daily, not on demand, provide light foods – your vet will advise you on this – and watch that milk! Milk is fattening and, unlike water, not essential for cats.

See the bottom of the next column for a rough guide to daily food quantities for kittens and cats of different ages.

Fresh food and water are a must for cats, whose noses are as sensitive as

that of a *Guide Michelin* inspector. Cats will stalk away from the first hint of staleness. Giving fresh food frequently is the best way to avoid waste and the risk of tummy upsets.

Under abnormal circumstances, cats can go without food for weeks and lose

PLANNING YOUR CAT'S MEALS

AGE	MEALS PER DAY	AMOUNT G (OZ)
Weaning to 3 months	4–6	80–190 (3–7)
4–5 months	4–6	275 (10)
6–7 months	3–4	370 (13)
7–8 months	3	370 (13)
9 months and over	2–3	400 (14)
Pregnant queens	3–5	420–460 (15–16)
Senior citizens	3–6	300–370 (10½–13)

40 per cent of their body weight without dying, although if they lose 10 to 15 per cent of the total water in their bodies that is usually fatal.

THE MAJOR FOODS

So many different foods are available that the suitable combinations are infinite. I will therefore deal only with the main kinds.

CAT CONNOISSEURS Your cat will truly welcome a diet that has been well thought out rather than just thrown into a bowl.

Canned food

These products consist of meat and/or fish, salts, jellying agents, vitamins, colouring chemicals, preservatives, sugar, water, and sometimes cereals.

Advantage: It is very nutritious.

Disadvantages: Canned food is relatively expensive and encourages faster build-up of plaque and tartar on the teeth than other types of food. You are buying a fair quantity of water, particularly where the "jelly" is much in evidence. Also, the canning and storage time may result in a drastic reduction of the vitamin level, particularly heat-unstable vitamins such as vitamin B.

Soft-moist products

These look good, taste not quite so good and contain meat,

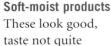

soya bean, fats, vitamins, preservatives, colouring chemicals and often thickening agents and sugar.

Advantages: Like canned foods, they are usually very nutritious and can make up a large proportion of the diet; you are buying less hidden water than is often the case with canned food, and they can be stored reasonably well.

Disadvantages: They are expensive, do not store as well as canned or dry foods, and are generally too low in fat.

Dry food

These mini-biscuits contain cereals, fish, meat, yeast, vitamins, fats, and colouring agents.

Advantages: Many kinds are fairly well balanced, they are cheaper and contain less water than canned or soft-moist food,

store well and are pleasant to handle. They combat tartar.

Disadvantages: They are frequently much too low in fat content for cats. If fed as the only food, they have been suspected of causing bladder problems and difficulty in passing urine. Their low water content, with the salt analysis of some brands, may produce "sludge" in the cat's urine, which can block up the animal's waterworks. Where much dry food is fed, adequate fresh water must be available at all times and, best of all, the pellets may be moistened with gravy, milk or water. Use dry foods sparingly if at all for cats with a history of urinary troubles. Probably the best rule is to give some dry food to all cats but as part of a varied menu. Some dry cat foods are now being formulated in a way that helps to diminish fur-ball build-up in the stomach or to clean the teeth and combat tartar production.

TYPES OF FOOD Canned food is popular and nourishing. It is also practical, stores well, and is sterile. Soft-moist products are nutritious but low in fat, and most cats like mini-biscuits.

Meat

This may be beef, lamb, or pig. Except for pork, which *must* be cooked, it is good to give minced raw meat to your cat occasionally. Get it from the butchers, not from the knacker's yard, where it is likely to be cheap but teeming with bacteria. Cooked meats should be baked or grilled rather than boiled, to retain nutrients and tasty juices. If meat is boiled, however, the water should be seasoned and used as a gravy on some drier item of food. Offal (lungs, tripe, and udder, for example) should always be cooked. All cooked meat should be cut into small cubes.

Poultry

Scraps of cooked birds left over from the family table provide good pickings for puss. Few humans pick a chicken clean of such parts as the kidneys or parson's nose, which are greatly prized by cats. Most bird bones are very splintery and should on no account be fed to your pet.

The same holds true for rabbit as it does for poultry.

Eggs

Eggs are a good source of protein, but are better fed cooked and chopped rather than raw. Egg white should never be fed raw, since it contains a chemical which neutralizes an essential B vitamin. A total of two eggs per week is the maximum for a cat. Separated egg yolks can be given more often if you wish.

Milk

Not all cats like milk. If yours does not drink milk, why worry? Water is always necessary for cats, but milk is not. Some cats cannot digest the milk sugar (lactose) in cow's milk and get diarrhoea after drinking it.

Cheese

This is an excellent source of protein, either when given raw, in which case it should be grated or cubed, or cooked with some other item.

SEPARATE FOOD BOWLS If you live in a multi-cat household, the best way to prevent cats fighting over food is to ensure that each one has its own dish.

Fish

Fresh fish, chopped and boned if from a species larger than a herring, is admirable up to once or twice a week. In Britain, fish is often fed raw, but in America it is generally cooked. Cooked fish is better steamed or baked rather than boiled, again to retain maximum nutrients. Canned fish such as sardines can be given whether in oil or tomato sauce. The oil has a beneficial effect on the bowels and helps to dispel stomach fur balls that can accumulate, particularly in longhaired cats. Diets composed of nothing but fish are unbalanced and tend eventually to produce problems as the cat grows older. However, it is not true to say, as some books do and as folklore has it, that too much fish releases poisons or causes the disease named "fish eczema" *(see pp.182–3)*.

Vegetables

Boiled potato can be added to meat or fish, forming up to about one third of a meal. Start a cat early on foods like cooked greens, boiled young spinach, scraped raw carrot, and peas.

Starchy foods

Crumbled, toasted bread can be used like potato and mixed with gravy or fish stock, as can pasta such as macaroni, spaghetti, or noodles. Cereals can also be fed to cats. Corn flakes, wheat flakes, porridge, or baby cereal can all be used with milk, particularly for the first meal of the day and for kittens.

Fruit

If your cat fancies the occasional segment of tangerine or slice of apple (and it is surprising how many do – particularly Siamese), good for it! It is thought, incidentally, that 75 per cent of all cats are partial to the odd sweet grape.

VARIETY FEEDING A broad diet is preferable to feeding just one type of proprietary "balanced" cat food day after day.

A Cat in the House

In order to create a mutually respectful rapport with your cat, establish a few ground rules as soon as it walks into your home. Allow it its own space, but ensure that it respects your space and your belongings too!

LITTER TRAINING Kittens quickly learn how to use their litter trays. Have them in place by the time the kittens reach three or four weeks of age.

A LIFELONG FRIENDSHIP It is important that children learn the proper handling of family pets as early as possible.

HANDLING YOUR CAT

While it is a good thing to handle your pet, remember always to support the full body. Do not just let it dangle from its "armpits" – the cat will resent this and may possibly struggle or even bite. Pick up an adult cat by putting one hand under the chest, just behind the front paws, and the other under the bottom, tucking the tail in. Once up, let it sit in the crook of your arm with its forepaws on your shoulder or held in your other hand.

Kittens should be handled with great care, since their ribcages are very soft and can easily bruise internally if roughly treated.

Although queens pick up and carry kittens by the scruff of their necks, you should avoid doing this except for brief periods when grabbing cats that may be uncooperative or agitated. Scruffing a cat by taking firm hold of the loose skin at the back of the neck does not hurt the animal, but it is a rather undignified procedure. Where a cat has had an injury to its body, particularly a fracture, scruffing is allowable.

HOUSE TRAINING

Cats are neat and nimble, and housing them indoors does not present the problems associated with dogs. They can, where necessary, be kept permanently indoors and will happily adopt as their territory even the smallest flat. Some breeds are particularly suited to this cloistered life. Sanitation arrangements and scratching instincts need to be given special attention in order to keep a cat healthy and happy.

Spend some time, especially with younger cats, teaching them how to behave. The earlier you begin, the better. When kittens first start to eat solid food at three to four weeks of age, introduce them to toilet training. Place the litter tray in a convenient, easily reached, but quiet spot, and as soon as the animal looks like urinating or defecating (easily spotted as they crouch, tail raised and with a certain faraway look in their eyes), pop them on it. Never rub a kitten's nose in any "mess" that it makes. Felines are clean and train quickly. Very old cats may become forgetful or lose control on occasion. Bear with them.

A litter tray should be made of metal or plastic and be large enough for the cat to stand in. It should be lined with newspaper and then covered with a 4-cm (1½-in) deep layer of peat moss or proprietary cat litter. Ashes can be used, though they are rather dusty. Sawdust is messy when dry and quickly becomes soggy and smelly when wet. Remove the soiled litter daily, and clean and disinfect the tray weekly, using any household disinfectant except those containing phenol, carbolic acid, or any coal-tar chemicals – these can be poisonous to cats. Rinse a disinfected tray thoroughly.

CAT-FLAPS

Some types of cat-flap can be activated by small magnets attached to a cat's collar. To train a cat to use a flap, begin by fastening the flap open and allowing the cat to familiarize itself with the hole. Then, use bits of food to entice your pet through the flap, helping to push it open.

PRIVATE DOOR Cat-flaps are easily fitted to doors and the intelligent cat soon learns the knack of using one.

OBEDIENCE

All cats should be taught to recognize their own name. Use it regularly, particularly at feeding times. Make a point of having regular set times for feeding, grooming, and playing. Cats can be trained to do little tricks, like begging for food, but this can be achieved only by kindness and reward in the form of titbits of favourite food, and always depends on the animal being in the right mood. You cannot force cats to do anything against their wills. Nevertheless, it is possible to dissuade them from undesirable habits, like biting or jumping on people. From the earliest age, firmly but gently pick up the cat, place it on the floor, and say "No". Some antisocial behaviour will be reduced if the cat can be allowed outdoors or given a scratching pad.

SCRATCHING

Scratching is, in more ways than one, a very touchy subject, particularly if your cat has no eye for interior decoration and takes it out on your highly polished cabinet or the sofa that was your mother-in-law's wedding present. The answer is to provide a substitute scratching object of the right texture to give the cat the most satisfactory "feel". A log complete with bark, a vertical post on a stand wrapped in coarse sacking, or one of the compressed blocks of corrugated paper sold in pet shops will do. Cats have to be trained to use these devices. At the first sign of Puss contemplating the furniture, grab him and take him to the official scratching point. With a little patience he will get the message.

USEFUL EQUIPMENT A typical cat scratching post – it looks tempting and will probably save some wear and tear on your furniture.

The surgical removal of a cat's claws under anaesthetic by a vet is possible, but such mutilations are illegal in Great Britain and Australia and frowned upon in New Zealand.

SLEEPING ARRANGEMENTS

A special bed in a box or basket can be provided, but it is not absolutely essential. Most cats pick their sleeping places around the house quite independently. However, young kittens should be given a box (a simple cardboard one will do) where they can sleep snug, draught-free, and out of harm's way. A lining of newspaper covered by a piece of blanket that is changed regularly should be placed inside. To avoid contamination, never feed a kitten in its sleeping box.

Why do I not believe in having my cats sleeping with me? Cats, like any animals that live close to the ground, sniff each others' backsides, investigate drains, and can be too intimate with germ-carrying rodents. They are more likely to transmit infections to humans if draped across the pillow eight hours out of every 24. There may be a risk of suffocation of a very small baby if a cat is allowed into the room in which the infant is sleeping.

LEAVING YOUR CAT

A cat can be left alone in a house or flat for as long as 24 hours, provided that adequate food, water, and litter are left. If you are likely to be away from your home for longer than a day, arrange for a neighbour to call in regularly (once every 24 hours at least) to replenish food and water and empty the tray. Neighbours are preferable to catteries – there is less risk of your pet picking up disease, and the animal is not wrenched away from familiar surroundings.

EXERCISE

Luckily for some of us, cats do not need active exercising by their owners, although it seems likely that exercise is beneficial to their health.

Kittens exercise themselves in play and will get endless pleasure and activity out of a ping-pong ball to chase around or a cardboard box to jump in and out of. For the permanently housebound adult cat, a climbing frame and scratching post should be provided. As I pointed out earlier, if you live in a high-rise apartment or near heavy traffic, your cat is best kept indoors at all times. Restless breeds that need to spend more time outside (Rexes, Somalis, and Abyssinians, for example) should be avoided for such dwellings. Although even adult indoor cats usually keep themselves fit by stretching and playing by themselves, it is a good idea, and a lot of fun, to play with your cat.

Taking cats for walks on leads is not as easy as taking dogs. Some cats object, and they must never be forced to walk farther than they choose. Training a cat to a lead should begin early with a newly weaned kitten. Walks should at first be in the house, later in the garden, and then, if things go well there, finally on the pavement. A long, thin, leather or, better, cord lead should be used for cats. Breeds that are more amenable to lead-training than others are Siamese, Burmese, Russian Blue, Foreign White, Foreign Black, Foreign Blue, and Foreign Smoke.

WALKING ON A LEAD Only some cats are content to be taken for walks on a lead. Attach it to the cat's collar or to a harness.

The Travelling Cat

With the right preparations in advance, it is possible to reduce the amount of stress that travelling has on your cat. Moving house – a very necessary reason for travelling – does not normally trouble a family cat. It retains its well-loved human companions and usually many items of furniture that it knows well.

CAT CARRIERS There are two designs of cat carriers for routine journeys. Although cosier, the wicker basket is not as easy to clean and disinfect as the plastic-covered wire model.

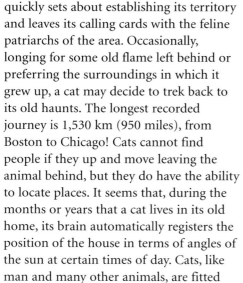

that emits a chemical based on the naturally produced cat facial pheromone. Undetectable by humans, this is a mood-modifying hormone that exerts its effect by being breathed in by the cat and passing then through the bloodstream to the brain. It is utterly safe, not a drug, and certainly worked well on my bunch of Birmans. In the UK it is available as Feliway.

CARRIERS

Every cat owner should have a cat carrier. For short journeys – to visit the vet, for example – one of the disposable cardboard carriers that you can buy from vets, humane societies, or pet shops is suitable. For longer journeys a more substantial container is needed. This must be escape-proof, well ventilated, and easy to clean. Although the wicker-basket form is very popular, it is not always secure enough, and it is difficult to clean and disinfect thoroughly. A vinyl, polyethylene, or fibreglass carrier is preferable. In cold weather, the carrier should be lined with a blanket or a special fur fabric insulator. A thin blanket is sufficient for warm weather.

After arriving at its new home, the cat quickly sets about establishing its territory and leaves its calling cards with the feline patriarchs of the area. Occasionally, longing for some old flame left behind or preferring the surroundings in which it grew up, a cat may decide to trek back to its old haunts. The longest recorded journey is 1,530 km (950 miles), from Boston to Chicago! Cats cannot find people if they up and move leaving the animal behind, but they do have the ability to locate places. It seems that, during the months or years that a cat lives in its old home, its brain automatically registers the position of the house in terms of angles of the sun at certain times of day. Cats, like man and many other animals, are fitted with internal biological clocks. If the cat is

uprooted to a new home where the sun's angle at a particular hour is slightly different, and it wants to put it "right", it works by trial and error, moving in one direction and then the other in order to improve the angle. All of this computation is done subconsciously. Even when the sun is obscured by cloud, the cat can probably locate it by means of rays of polarized light. There may also be, as in birds, a biological compass built into the feline skull, which helps it to navigate. All of which means that cats have an uncanny sense of direction.

When the cat reaches the vicinity of its old house, it completes its journey by noting familiar sights, sounds, and smells. A recent development that can help a cat adjust well to new surroundings, alleviate anxiety, combat the stress of new arrivals, and, incidentally, reduce scratching and urine-marking of furniture, comes in the form of a spray or "plug-in" room diffuser

ACCLIMATIZATION It is a good idea to let your cat try out its carrier in advance of taking it on a journey.

CATTERIES This is an average cattery. The indoor accommodation is snug and dry and is provided with an individual run. The general design with plenty of fresh air is better than totally enclosed layouts, but the spread of diseases could still occur easily. I prefer a double gate with secure locking devices to prevent accidental escapes when people enter and leave the cats' quarters. Two cats from the same home can usually share accommodation. Always visit and inspect any cattery before booking your pet in for a stay.

In hot conditions, a damp towel should be placed over the carrier (without obstructing the ventilation holes) to keep the temperature inside from rising.

When first introducing your cat to its carrier, do so in a closed room. Cats do not generally like carriers and the journeys associated with them, and some protest vigorously at being boxed up. Make sure that the cat uses its litter tray before being placed in the carrier.

Unless your cat is one of the very few that are accustomed to car travel and will lie peacefully on the back seat, take no chances and confine it to a carrier when going anywhere. If the journey lasts more than half an hour, stop regularly to allow your cat to use its litter tray and have food and drink. Do all this inside the car with doors and windows closed to avoid an escape.

In hot weather, you should not leave a cat (or any other animal) for long periods in a closed car. Hyperthermia (overheating), which may end fatally, can occur remarkably rapidly, particularly in an excited and apprehensive animal, which most are when enclosed. You should always make sure a window is partially open if a cat is left in a car on a summer's day for even the shortest period of time.

Tranquillizers or sedatives can be given to cats that are upset by travelling, as can other drugs for those affected by motion sickness, but try to avoid using them. Seek the advice of your vet if you have a cat that absolutely hates transportation.

PET TRAVEL SCHEME
Taking a cat to another country needs careful planning. In 2000, the Pet Travel Scheme (PETS) was inaugurated in Great Britain allowing pet cats (and dogs) to enter and

re-enter the United Kingdom without being subjected to a miserable six months in quarantine (see box, p.173). Although this scheme is sometimes referred to as a "pet passport", the animal is not given a one-off travel document similar to that of its owner that lasts ten years. The procedure

LONGER JOURNEYS These two excellent designs of cat carrier are approved for air, sea, and land transport. They are airy, strong, and secure models that can be firmly locked and are constructed of materials that are easy to clean and disinfect.

is rather more complicated, covers one journey at a time, and only works with animals (including returns) from certain eligible countries (*see table, opposite*).

The other most important factors are the regulations governing importation of animals that are in force in the country of destination. Check with your travel agent, shipping agent (if involved), airline freight company, and, most important of all, the consulate of the country you are going to, regarding any quarantine, health-certificate rules, and transportation conditions.

Cats coming from Australia have to have an additional certification stating that they have not been in contact with Hendra virus for 60 days before departure for the UK. Hendra virus, first discovered in 1994 in Australia, causes a serious disease of horses and human beings and may be carried by cats.

The Pet Travel Scheme was developed to allow entry of pets from Europe and other approved countries to the UK. Jersey and Guernsey have their own Pet Travel Schemes. The Republic of Ireland is *not* part of the PETS scheme, so cats have to go into quarantine when entering or re-entering the UK. There are no quarantine requirements for the import of cats into European countries or the United States, but rabies vaccination is often required and the animals must be certifies to be in "good health". For more information concerning PETS contact your vet, the local DEFRA office (Department for Environment, Food, and Rural Affairs) or the PETS helpline in the UK on 0870 241 1710.

If a pedigree cat, destined for breeding or showing, is being transported from one country to another you should approach one of the cat associations such as the GCCF or CFA for information on additional necessary documentation that should accompany the cat from the country of origin. This will include such things as pedigree certificates and, for males, Certificate of Entirety or Certificate of Neutering.

AIR TRAVEL

The most common form of animal transport for international journeys is air travel, and its speed makes it ideal for long distances. You must use a cat container that is approved by the International Air Transport Association (IATA). There are rules to ensure that cat carriers are spacious enough, strong with secure doors, well ventilated, provided with food and water bowls accessible from the outside, and correctly labelled with official "Live Animal" stickers, a 24-hour contact telephone number, and the consignee's name and address. For travel interstate within Australia and to and from New Zealand, airlines provide containers. Basically, containers must be leak-proof, escape-proof, and uncrushable.

Before taking your cat to the airport:
• Give the animal a light meal and a drink two hours before despatch;
• If your vet has recommended a tranquillizer tablet, give it as directed or just before you hand the cat over.

RAIL AND SEA TRAVEL

In general, the recommendations for containers for air travel should apply here also. The State Rail Authorities throughout Australia insist that the cat, in its carrier, travels in the luggage wagon, although the owner must provide the carrier. Sea travel for cats takes longer than flying and there is no veterinary care. Unless the owner is also on board, daily attendance must be provided by one of the crew. Sea-sickness is, however, rare in cats.

EATING AND DRINKING Before taking your cat on any journey, regardless of length, make sure that it eats, drinks and, preferably, uses its litter tray.

THE PET TRAVEL SCHEME (PETS)

The Pet Travel Scheme allows pet owners to take their animals out of the country with them, without having to quarantine them on their return. The scheme operates as follows:

OUTWARD:
1. **Microchipping:** The cat must be implanted with an authorized microchip according to manufacturer's instructions and national guidelines.
2. **Vaccination:** The cat must be vaccinated against rabies. Animals must be over three months old and have already been fitted with a microchip.
3. **Blood testing:** Thirty days after the rabies vaccination, a blood sample must be taken and the owner provided with a declaration of the date of sampling by the vet. This sample is sent to a government-approved lab to check that an adequate level of protection against rabies has been reached.
4. **PETS certificate:** The owner should obtain a PETS certificate, which can only be issued by a government-appointed vet and is valid for travel from six months after the blood sample giving a positive result was taken. This certificate expires on the date the rabies vaccine booster is due. As long as the booster is given by the due date, a new PETS certificate can be issued without the need for another blood sample. There are three licensed rabies vaccines in the UK. Booster vaccines are given annually.
5. **The route:** Only approved routes and transport companies are eligible for the scheme. Owners should speak to the approved carrier to discuss how their pet will travel. Most cats travelling by air must go as freight cargo; if travelling by sea, they must be contained in a crate or the owner's car in the hold. Pets remain with their owners in their car during a journey through the Channel Tunnel. You are not permitted to bring cats into the country in any other way, including on private planes or boats.

INWARD (return):
In order to enter the UK under PETS, you will need:
1. **PETS certificate:** This will prove that the pet has been microchipped and vaccinated.
2. **Tick and tapeworm treatment certificate:** This is an official certificate of treatment against ticks and tapeworm (*Echinococcus multilocularis*). This treatment must be administered by a vet 24–48 hours before the return trip to the UK, and owners are given an official certificate from the vet saying this has been done. (It may take a few days for a vet to obtain the necessary certificate, so arrange this well in advance of the inward journey).
3. **Declaration of residency:** Before entry or re-entry into the UK, the owner must sign an official declaration (available in advance of the journey from DEFRA) stating that the animal(s) have not been outside any of the PETS-qualifying countries in the previous six months.

MICROCHIPPING As part of the Pet Travel Scheme it is essential that your cat is microchipped. This is a quick and painless task that your vet will perform. The information on the microchip can be accessed using a special scanner.

PETS ELIGIBLE COUNTRIES

EUROPE:		
	Germany	Netherlands
	Gibraltar	Norway
Andorra	Greece	Portugal
Austria	Iceland	San Marino
Belgium	Italy	Spain
Cyprus	Liechtenstein	Sweden
Denmark	Luxembourg	Switzerland
Finland	Malta	Vatican
France	Monaco	

FURTHER AFIELD:		
	Falkland Islands	New Zealand
	Fiji	Reunion
Antigua and	French Polynesia	Singapore
Barbuda	Guadeloupe	St Helena
Ascension Island	Hawaii	St Kitts & Nevis
Australia	Jamaica	St Vincent
Bahrain	Japan	USA
Barbados	Martinique	Vanuatu
Bermuda	Mauritius	Wallis & Futuna
Canada	Montserrat	
Cayman Islands	New Caledonia	

Grooming

More fastidious than dogs in keeping up appearances, cats will groom themselves regularly and often.

Rows of hooked, horny, and backward-pointing scales (*papillae*) on the cat's tongue form an efficient comb for raking the skin and fur.

   As well as keeping the coat clean, neat, and glossy, grooming helps cats to remove dead hair and skin cells and to tone up the superficial blood circulation and underlying muscles.

Domestic cats, and particularly longhairs, do need extra grooming beyond the cleaning that they give themselves or one another, and it has to be provided by the owner. Longhaired cats moult all the year round and need daily grooming. In good weather, groom your cat outdoors. If you have to groom it indoors, choose the bathroom or porch, and stand the cat on a sheet of plastic or newspaper.

FASTIDIOUS CLEANING These three pictures show various classic stages in a cat's self-grooming routine. Sometimes the fussy self-cleaning of cats anxious to remove foreign substances from their coat can lead them to swallow toxic things. If your cat is spending an unusually long time grooming itself, you should investigate to make sure it has not got anything nasty stuck to its coat and that it is not suffering from any skin problems.

GROOMING PRELIMINARIES
Particular attention should be paid to the cat's head when grooming. Begin with the ears, eyes, and teeth.

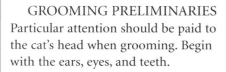

1 *Look inside each ear for any signs of dirt or the accumulation of dark-coloured wax. Clean out the ears using one or two twists of cotton wool lightly moistened with olive oil.*

2 *Check the eyes. Longhairs in particular may suffer from a blocked tear duct, which will result in dark staining below the innermost angle of the eyelids. Crusts of dried mucus may have accumulated in the corner of the eye. Clean the area gently with a warm, weak solution of salt in water. Persistent tear-staining or marked eye discharge requires veterinary attention.*

3 *Inspect the teeth for tartar encrustations. Get your cat used to having its teeth cleaned once a week with a soft toothbrush (its own!), salt, and water, or by using a special pet toothpaste. Once formed into a chalky deposit on the teeth, tartar will need to be removed by the vet using descaling instruments or an ultrasound machine.*

Grooming a Shorthair

Shorthaired cats possess less exuberant upholstery than longhaired cats, and are better at self-cleaning, so they need grooming only twice a week.

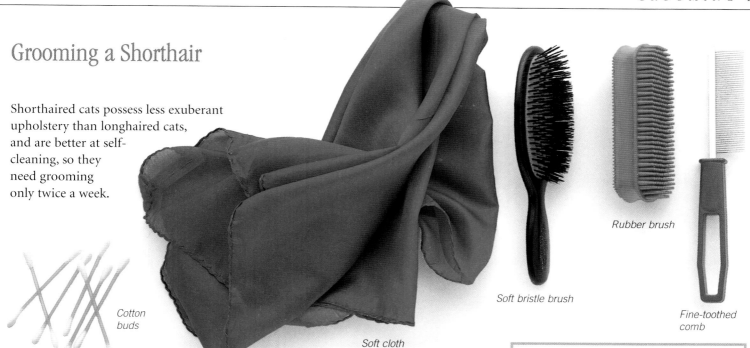

Cotton buds

Soft cloth

Soft bristle brush

Rubber brush

Fine-toothed comb

1 *With a fine-toothed metal comb, work down the cat from its head to its tail. As you comb, look for black, shiny specks, since these indicate the presence of fleas.*

2 *Use a soft rubber brush to brush along to the lie of the hair. If your cat is Rex-coated, this brush is an essential grooming item, since it will not scratch the cat's skin.*

3 *After brushing and combing, rub in some bay rum conditioner. This removes any traces of grease from the coat and brings out the brilliance of its colour.*

4 *Finally, to bring up the glossy quality of a shorthaired cat's coat, "polish" the fur with a piece of silk or velvet or a chamois leather cloth.*

CARE OF THE CLAWS

If in any doubt as to how to trim claws, let a veterinarian show you how, or let him or her clip them.

CLIPPING NAILS Use very sharp scissors, human toe-nail clippers, or "guillotine-type" claw clippers. Hold the cat firmly in your lap and press the pad of its paw with your fingers to make the claws extend.

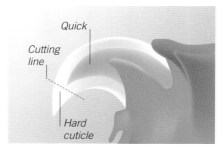

Quick

Cutting line

Hard cuticle

CAT'S CLAW Examine the claw carefully. The main part includes the pinkish-coloured quick, which contains nerves and blood vessels. Do not cut this. The white tips are dead tissue and can be cut, but not closer than 2 mm (¹⁄₁₀ in) to the quick.

Grooming a Longhair

Daily grooming really is an essential ritual for longhaired cats. Without it, balls of matted hair can form in the coat, and they gradually build up in size until the only solution is for the veterinarian to remove them. Two grooming sessions a day, of 15 to 30 minutes each, should suffice to keep a longhaired cat's coat in peak condition.

If, despite your best grooming efforts, you do come across badly matted hair on your cat's coat, hold the fur with one hand and try to tease out the mat with the other. Never cut it off with scissors – it is all too easy to "tent" the cat's pliable skin and cut it. If you cannot free the knot easily, consult a vet.

Wire and bristle brush

Wide-toothed comb

Fine-toothed comb

Toothbrush for tidying the face

Slicker brush

Cotton buds

Roller comb

1 *Once a week, as a preliminary step, powder the entire coat in sections, using either a proprietary grooming powder or a mixture of corn powder and talcum powder. This adds body and separates the coat hairs.*

2 *Using your hands, distribute the powder evenly into the coat, making sure that no section is more heavily powdered than another. Most cats love what they perceive as an unsolicited, all-over body massage!*

3 *With a pure bristle brush (which does not cause static or break hairs) use a "brushing up" action to lift the fur and to begin the process of removing debris and dead hair.*

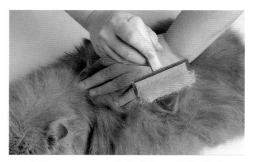

4 *When you are satisfied that all the fur has been thoroughly lifted, change actions and brush down and up, all over the body, including the tail and the cat's underside.*

5 *Change to a fine-toothed comb to tease out any snarls and tangles.*

6 *Depending on your preference, you may consider gently plucking out the hair growing at the tips of the ears to give them a more rounded appearance, but this is not essential.*

7 *As a tidy finishing touch, use a toothbrush to make the ruff stand out and to brush around the face, down the front, and down the legs. Be careful not to go too close to the eyes.*

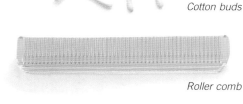

Washing

If your cat's coat gets very dirty, you should give it a wet or a dry bath.

If your cat violently objects to water, give it a dry bran bath. Use this method only on shorthaired cats that are not too dirty. First heat 500 g–1 kg (1–2 lb) of bran in an oven at 150° C (302° F) for 20 minutes. Then stand your cat on a newspaper and massage the warm bran into its coat. When you have covered all the fur with bran, comb it out.

Washing by the wet method is shown in these photographs. However, you can consider yourself very lucky if your cat behaves as calmly as this one! You might want to consider a professional groomer.

1 Use a bowl, sink, or bath. Close all windows and doors. Put a rubber mat in the bath to stop the cat slipping. Pour on water at blood heat (test the temperature with your elbow).

2 Pour on some non-irritant baby or cat shampoo while holding the cat firmly with your other hand.

3 Work up a lather in the coat by massaging gently with your fingers. Take particular care with the head, and avoid getting water or lather in the ears and eyes.

4 Rinse thoroughly with warm water – a spray attachment is useful for this.

5 Wrap the cat in a large, warm towel.

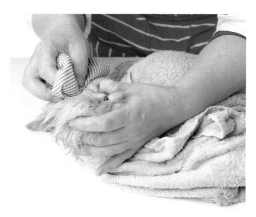

6 Now wash the cat's face with cotton wool or a soft cloth dipped in warm water.

7 Keep the cat in a warm place until completely dry. A hairdryer, if it does not upset the cat, can be used – check the heat with your hand. Then comb the dry fur out.

Health Care

Although it is not necessary for a cat owner to have an in-depth veterinary knowledge, it does pay to know a little about the potential problems a cat may face during its life.

CHOOSING A VET

Before your cat is ill, find a vet in your area to give your new feline a thorough check, provide the necessary vaccinations, and tell you about any preventive medicine or special care it may require. The vet should also provide a 24-hour service that can deal with genuine emergencies.

Obviously it is best to find a veterinary practice that works extensively with small animals. Other cat owners, breeders, and humane-society clinics in your vicinity will point you in the right direction. It is almost always possible to visit your cat doctor's surgery by prior arrangement in order to see all the facilities available.

A vet undergoes many years of training in animal medicine and surgery, including the particular problems of *Felidae*, so if trouble strikes or you have questions on

SEEING A SPECIALIST Some veterinarians specialize in cat diseases or in problems of a particular part of the body.

any aspect of cat management, be guided by him or her. Do not try to lecture the vet after having read this book. The vet is in the best position to provide you with unbiased advice.

If you are not satisfied with the veterinary care of your cat, you are free to obtain a second opinion – something that all vets are ethically bound to agree to.

COMMON AILMENTS

Cats may have nine lives but they are, like humans and other creatures, occasionally out of sorts and sometimes downright ill. The study of feline diseases and their treatment by medicine and surgery are important areas of veterinary science, and much research is currently being done – such as, for example, work on the virus FIV that has been identified as producing a feline immune-deficiency syndrome that, although not transmittable to humans, is similar in some respects to the AIDS virus. No matter how skilled your vet may be, it is a cat owner's responsibility to have some working knowledge of the common feline ailments. The owner is usually the first to spot that all is not well with an animal, and he or she must know when to seek professional attention and how to assist the patient's return to health.

This section of the book describes the symptoms of the most common diseases of cats and explains what you should do about them and what treatment is available from the vet. Simple, useful first-aid techniques are included, but the emphasis is on seeking veterinary help for all but the mildest and briefest of conditions.

The mouth
Symptoms associated with mouth problems are salivating (slavering), pawing at the mouth, exaggerated chewing motions, and tentative chewing as if dealing with a hot potato.

The mouth should be inspected from time to time to see that all is in order. If tartar – a brown, cement-like substance – accumulates to any extent, it does not produce holes in the teeth; instead it damages the gum edges, lets bacteria in to infect the teeth sockets, and thus loosens the teeth. (There is always some gum inflammation with tartar.) To prevent the build-up of tartar, brush your cat's teeth once a week with a soft toothbrush or cotton wool dipped in salt water, and take it to the vet once a year for descaling treatment.

Check that there are no foreign bodies stuck between the teeth. Pieces of bone often become wedged between the teeth and against the roof of the mouth. Fishbone pieces sometimes lodge between two adjacent molars at the back of the mouth. You can probably flick a foreign body out with a teaspoon handle or similar instrument. If there is no foreign body, look for smooth, red, ulcerated areas on the tongue. These can be caused by licking an irritant substance, but are more commonly caused by a virus of one sort or another.

Ulcers of this type are associated with profuse slavering, unwillingness to eat, and dullness. Seek veterinary help. A major aliment may be underlying the troubled mouth, and medication to control pain, inflammation, and secondary infection will be required.

Make sure that none of your cat's teeth are loose or diseased by touching each tooth gently with your finger or a pencil. If any teeth wobble, or the cat gives a sign of pain, take it to the vet. Do not give aspirin to relieve toothache because it is poisonous to cats.

ADMINISTERING EYE-DROPS To apply ophthalmic ointment, hold the nozzle parallel with the eye and squeeze the ointment on to the surface of the eyeball.

CHECK THE EYES Protruding "third eyelids" always indicate some form of illness.

Do not worry if many teeth have to be removed from an elderly cat. Food such as minced cooked liver, fish, and cereals with milk are easily taken, even by toothless cats. Having no teeth at all is better than having septic gums and rotten teeth that create misery.

The eyes

Signs that all is not well with a cat's eyes are when they are sore, runny, or watery, or when there is a blue or white film over the eye. The protrusion of a white skin (the haw, third eyelid, or nictitating membrane) over some or most of one or both eyes from the inner corner is another common eye symptom.

If the eye is obviously sore and inflamed, if the eyeball has a blue or white area on it, or if the lids are swollen, then it is probably infected, wounded, or irritated by foreign matter, like grass seeds. Such eye conditions always need professional attention; if they are left untreated, the eye may be progressively damaged, resulting eventually in loss of sight.

Bluish or whitish films that appear on the normally transparent front of the eye (cornea) are not cataracts. Cataracts are opacities of the lens behind the pupil that also produce a blue or white effect, but deeper in the eye. In dim light, when the pupil is dilated, more of the opaque lens shows and the cataract seems to enlarge. The opposite happens in bright light.

Some old cats may seem to have bluish lenses, but these are not necessarily cataracts. Many are caused by changes (similar to those that occur in middle-aged humans) in the refractive properties of the lenses, which remain clear and transparent. Such cats are not going blind.

The partial covering of the eye by the third eyelid is a common and curious phenomenon. It is not a sign that the cat is going blind, and it often happens in otherwise apparently healthy cats. It can be a result of weight loss, when the eye sinks back as the fat padding within the eye socket is reduced. It may be an early symptom of feline influenza and associated respiratory viruses. If it occurs, keep a careful watch on the cat and, should other symptoms develop, see the vet. If this condition persists without other signs, try giving more food and give 50 micrograms of vitamin B12 daily in the food or as a tablet.

The vet has a number of ways of dealing with the varieties of eye disease. He can use local anaesthetic drops to numb the eye for the removal of irritant objects, and can apply drugs not just by ointment and drops but also by injection under the conjunctiva, the pink membrane round the eye. He can also examine deep into the eye with the ophthalmoscope and can identify infecting bacteria by taking swabs of the cat's tears. Eye conditions such as squints, blocked tear ducts, and cataractous lenses can be dealt with by surgery.

The nose

The main problems associated with the cat's nose are running, watery nostrils, snuffling, and sneezing. The appearance of symptoms like those of the common cold in humans generally means an outbreak of feline influenza, which needs veterinary attention. After recovery from cat flu, many cats remain snuffly and catarrhal for months or even years.

If your cat has snuffles, bathe the delicate nose tip with a little warm water, soften and remove any caked mucus, and gently anoint a little petroleum jelly into the nose.

The ears

Ear problems can be suspected if your cat starts shaking its head, scratching its ear, or tilting its head to one side, which is sometimes associated with loss of balance and a staggering gait. (In rare cases, the latter symptoms can be due to diseases of the brain in which the ear itself is not involved.) Other symptoms include the sudden "ballooning" of an ear flap, the presence of tiny white "insects" moving slowly around inside the ear, and a bad-smelling, chocolate-coloured, or purulent discharge.

If ear trouble flares up suddenly, pour liberal quantities of mineral oil (paraffin oil) warmed to body heat into the affected

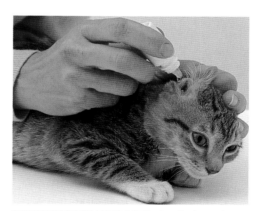

ADMINISTERING EARDROPS Apply drops into the ear, fold the outer ear over, and massage gently for a moment.

ear. Do it in the garage rather than the lounge so that the cat does not fleck excess oil all over your curtains.

Head-tilting and loss of balance may indicate middle-ear disease. This is an inflammation of the middle ear, which lies behind the eardrum. Infection usually enters this area via a channel (the Eustachian tube) that runs from the throat, so it often follows throat and respiratory infections. It needs immediate veterinary treatment, since the modern drugs used by the vet can reach the inflammation in the middle ear and in almost all cases prevent permanent damage to the balancing organs and the spread of the infection to the brain.

ITCHY EARS Repeated scratching of the ears requires investigation.

The sudden ballooning of a cat's ear flap is due to bleeding within the flap and the formation of a big blood blister, or haematoma, usually caused by the cat scratching its own ear vigorously but sometimes caused by a blow or bite from another animal. It annoys the cat because the ear feels strangely heavy, and it will shake its head to try to dislodge the "weight"; but it is not painful like an abscess unless secondarily infected, which is uncommon. The condition is identical to that seen in boxers who are repeatedly punched around the ears. Left untreated, the blood inside the haematoma clots and shrinks into a gnarled scar, causing the ear to crumple and resemble a cauliflower.

The vet can prevent a cat taking on the appearance of a prize fighter by giving a general anaesthetic, draining off the blood, usually through an incision, and then stitching the ear in a special way that may involve attaching steel buttons for a week or so. It is not a serious condition and the success rate following surgery is very high. Nevertheless, the cause of the original scratching (mites, canker, or whatever), must be treated to avoid a recurrence.

If your cat is simply an ear-flicker and the ears seem dry but contain the "insects" – actually otodectic mange mites – referred to already, give some ear-mange drops (available from the pet shop). Any discharge means that the cat has canker and may need antibiotic treatment.

The chest

Cats can suffer from bronchitis, pneumonia, pleurisy, and other chest conditions.

Common signs of chest ailments are coughing, gasping, and laboured breathing.

Coughing and sneezing – all the miserable signs of a head cold – may be symptoms of feline influenza, which is also caused by a virus. It may be mild or severe, and is sometimes fatal. In such cases, the damage may be done by secondary bacterial infections of the lung. It is not a cold, wet-weather disease particularly; many major outbreaks occur in summer and it is often found in epidemic form in catteries during the hot holiday months. Protect your cat against feline influenza by ensuring that it is vaccinated and boosted regularly. There is no connection between human and cat forms of flu.

Laboured breathing without cold symptoms may be a sign of pleurisy or of heart disease in older cats.

Keep a cat with chest trouble warm and dry. Do not let it exert itself, and give it nutritious food, either finely minced or in liquid form. The odd drop of brandy or whisky can be spooned in. Keep the nostrils unblocked as far as possible by sponging the nose and greasing it with a little petroleum jelly.

More serious cases will be treated by the vet using antibiotics, drugs to loosen

THE EFFECTS OF CAT FLU This poor little kitten shows the typical face of a feline-influenza patient.

mucus in the lungs, and, where the heart is involved, special cardiac medicines. Where fluid accumulates in the chest in pleurisy cases, the vet may tap this off under sedation. Very many cats with heart problems can live happy, long lives once a diagnosis has been made and maintenance treatment prescribed.

An interesting and rather disturbing finding in a recent study by American vets is that cats exposed to tobacco smoke in their environment – feline passive smokers – have a significantly increased risk of developing the serious cancer malignant lymphoma.

The stomach and intestines

Signs of stomach or intestinal disorders are vomiting, diarrhoea, constipation, and blood in the droppings. There are numerous causes for any of these symptoms, and sometimes more than one symptom will be observed at the same time. Here the most common causes have been dealt with and no attempt has been made to describe all the diseases that involve the abdominal organs.

Vomiting may be simple and transient, due to a mild infection of the stomach (gastritis) or the presence of a fur ball. However, if it is severe, persistent, or accompanied by other major signs, it can indicate the presence of serious conditions such as feline infectious enteritis, tumours, or obstruction of the intestine.

Diarrhoea may be mild, when it is probably caused either by feeding too much liver or by a bowel infection, or it may be serious, as in some cases of feline infectious enteritis.

Constipation may be a result of age and faulty diet, or may indicate an obstruction. Blood in the stools may be caused by the scratching of the intestinal lining by gobbled bone splinters, or be a side-effect of an acute attack of food-poisoning.

Use your common sense and, if any of these symptoms persist for more than a few hours or are accompanied by profound malaise and weakness on the part of the cat, you need skilled help.

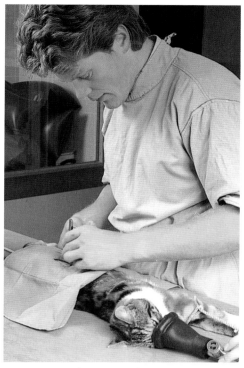

NEUTERING This queen is being spayed while under gas anaesthetic.

In mild cases, or until the vet arrives, remember that water and salt loss through vomiting or diarrhoea can have serious consequences. To combat dehydration and weakness, spoon small quantities of glucose and water, seasoned to your taste with table salt, into the cat as frequently as possible. Where vomiting is the prime symptom, do not give solid food but concentrate on giving the liquid replacement. Half a teaspoonful of Maalox or baby gripe water can be given, but do not give milk or brandy.

Where diarrhoea is the main symptom, concentrate on fluid administration. It is safe to introduce about a third of a cupful of strong, sweetened coffee cooled to body temperature via the rectum through a human enema syringe. It must be done slowly and gently. A little arrowroot powder or crushed arrowroot biscuit in water can be given by mouth, but do not administer human kaolin and morphine diarrhoea mixtures.

In the early stages of constipation you can try spooning two or three teaspoonfuls of mineral oil (liquid paraffin) into the cat. The tiny, ready-to-use, disposable enemas available at the chemist are excellent and very effective. Use a half to one tube as

directed for humans on the accompanying instructions. Where constipation is a chronic problem, add bulk to the diet in some form (see p.184).

Severe or persistent cases of constipation will need veterinary attention. The vet can examine the alimentary tract with his fingers, by X-ray, possibly by barium meals, by gastroscope, and sometimes by exploratory operation.

Viral infections

Feline infectious enteritis (FIE), one of the major virus diseases of cats, not only affects the intestines, it also attacks the liver and white cells of the blood. It can be fatal in a matter of hours and the symptoms are variable. Diarrhoea is not always present. Although the vet cannot kill the virus, he may use antibiotics against secondary bacterial infection. He will certainly be concerned to protect the cat from dehydrating through fluid loss, and this may mean giving transfusions of saline under the skin. The best cure for feline infectious enteritis, a terrible scourge, is prevention. Have your cat vaccinated and boosted regularly.

Feline infectious anaemia (FIA) is a disease caused by *Hemobartonella*, a microbe that is probably transmitted by insect (including flea) and cat bites. The symptoms can be long-lasting and often rather vague. They include weakness, loss of weight, pallor, loss of appetite, and, sometimes, jaundice. There is no vaccine available at present. Treatment of acute cases may include blood transfusion.

Feline infectious peritonitis (FIP) is a viral disease. It usually attacks cats under three years of age. Symptoms can include progressive swelling of the abdomen, loss of appetite, and fever. Again, no vaccine is presently available. Treatment is possible but the prognosis is generally very grave.

Feline leukaemia (FeLV) is similar to the disease in humans and is caused by a virus that, however, cannot infect people or other non-feline species. Symptoms are highly variable since the disease can target variously the abdomen, the kidneys, the

thymus gland, or the eyes. Treatment is very difficult but the preventive measures in the form of a vaccination programme are very effective.

Feline immunodeficiency virus (FIV) infection can also result in a bewildering range of symptoms affecting almost any part of the cat's body. Infected cats can be symptomless for many years. It is thought that spread of the disease is through bites contaminated with virus carrying saliva. There is no specific treatment that can kill the virus and no vaccine against it yet exists.

The urinary system

Problems in the urinary system are marked by difficulty passing urine, blood in the urine, loss of weight, and thirst.

When a cat strains to pass urine, the owner may think it is suffering from constipation, but it may have "gravel" in the urine. Cats on mainly dry-food diets, cats taking insufficient water, and tomcats castrated very early are more prone to "gravel", which is a deposit of salt crystals in the bladder that can eventually block up the water pipe (urethra) of male animals. When the bladder is overfull and tight as a drum, the cat is in considerable pain, will resent being handled, and may actually turn to look at its hindquarters and spit angrily. Take your cat to the vet for treatment. Do not try squeezing the cat's swollen bladder yourself because it is very easily ruptured.

Blood in the urine generally indicates bladder infection (cystitis). This complaint is more common in female cats and also requires veterinary treatment.

Loss of weight and thirst, particularly in old cats, can be due to kidney disease, although other diseases, including diabetes, can also cause these symptoms.

Preventive measures against urinary problems include making sure that your cat always eats a good proportion of moist food and has plenty of fresh water available. Do not have a tom castrated too early.

The vet can deal with urinary problems by using special urine-active antiseptics and antibiotics. He can catheterize a cat's bladder painlessly to free blockages and take urine samples for analysis. The kidneys can be X-rayed by contrast radiography and, if necessary, the bladder and urethra can be operated upon quite safely.

Genitalia

In female cats the most common symptom of a genital infection is a purulent discharge – which may be white, pink, yellow, or chocolate-coloured – from the vagina. Cats that are known to be pregnant should be taken to the vet immediately. In non-pregnant queens it can be a sign of womb infection (usually following kittening) or the onset of the hormonal disease pyometra. This is commonest in queens that have never had kittens or have had just one litter. It looks like a septic infection and can make the animal very ill through absorption of the pus-like fluid that distends the womb, although in many cases the pus is sterile. It is not an infectious disease although secondary bacterial invasions are a danger.

If you are not planning on breeding, have a female spayed when young. If discharges are seen, clean the vulval area with warm water and weak antiseptic and take the little lady along to the vet.

The vet may prescribe hormone treatment together with drugs to reduce the amount of fluid in the womb and antibiotics to tackle any opportunist bugs. His main weapon is normally surgical: the removal of the diseased womb (hysterectomy) through a side or mid-line incision under general anaesthetic. If the cat is in a weak and toxic state because of the diseased womb, the vet may delay operating for some time in order to try to strengthen her with vitamins, anti-toxic drugs, and antibiotics.

The skin

There are many kinds of skin disease in cats. Tell-tale signs include thin or bald patches in the fur, scratching, and wet or dry sores.

Itchy thinning of the hair over the trunk with points of oozing red scabs is one of the most common skin diseases. Often named "fish eczema", this complaint has nothing to do with eating fish but is glandular in origin.

Skin parasites – fleas, lice, ticks, and mites – are most numerous in hot weather. Fleas and, less commonly, lice and ticks can cause damage to the coat. The presence of just one single flea on a cat – terribly hard to track down – may set up widespread itchy skin irritation as an allergic reaction to the flea's saliva, injected when the flea sucks. In late summer, orange specks in the fur of the head and ears or between the toes reveal the presence of harvest mites. Irritating mange caused by an invisible mite can cause dry, moth-eaten-looking areas around the head and ears.

If you see or suspect the presence of any of these skin parasites, obtain one of the anti-parasitic powders, aerosols, or skin-absorbed drops from your pet shop, chemist, or vet. The latter can also clear a cat's fleas by means of an injection of a drug such as aslufenuron.

DETECTING AND DEALING WITH FLEAS

1 *If you look closely, you will see a flea in this cat's coat. Parting the fur makes the flea easier to see against the white skin.*

2 *To treat skin parasites, use a proprietary powder (or an aerosol) on the coat. Avoid the cat's eyes, nose, and mouth.*

3 *With powder, gently stroke it into the coat, working "against the grain".*

4 *Comb any excess powder out of the coat, this time going with the grain.*

DESPERATE MEASURES This cat had an advanced case of ringworm and had to be shaved for treatment. Most cases are far less dramatic.

If necessary, have the cause of your pet's tatty upholstery investigated by the vet. He can prescribe different drugs for the various types of disease, but he may need to do sample-analysis to diagnose some conditions. To detect ringworm, for example, which takes a very subtle form in cats compared to that in humans or cattle, it may be necessary to do an ultraviolet light examination of fungus culture from a hair specimen. Ringworm can now be treated by drugs given orally and mange can be treated externally by baths, creams, and aerosols, or by tablets, which work via the bloodstream. "Fish eczema" is treated by hormone tablets.

Roundworms

Capable of causing bowel upsets, particularly in kittens, roundworms can also spread to humans and occasionally damage babies severely.

Rid your cat of roundworms by using one of the modern worming drugs at regular three-month intervals throughout its life.

Tapeworms

Although tapeworms do not often cause the cat much trouble, they can occasionally spread to humans.

To prevent infestation, keep your cat free of fleas, because they act as host to tapeworm larvae. If you see tapeworm segments (they look like grains of boiled rice) in the stools or stuck to the hair around the anus, give the cat a dose of a modern tapeworm drug such as niclosamide. The very safe worming drug mebendazole eradicates roundworms and tapeworms and should be used regularly.

Bites and other wounds

Cats do fight and often get bitten, particularly unneutered toms. Bites tend to go septic and they can prove troublesome. They may produce abscesses, which on the torso take the form of soft, low swellings covering a wide area. Hidden by the fur, and not always easy to detect by probing with the fingers, the only clue to their presence may be if the cat shows signs of pain when handled. On the limbs or tail, where the bone lies close to the surface, it is common for bacteria to reach the surface of the bone when an attacker's canine teeth pierce the skin. If not treated quickly, bites to the tail can become gangrenous. Septic wounds of the feet can show themselves as dramatically enlarged "club paws".

As soon as you detect a bite wound, carefully clip the hair around it down to the skin with scissors. Make a strong solution of Epsom salts (magnesium sulphate crystals) dissolved in warm water, and apply it to the wound as frequently as possible. Antiseptic ointments are of little value since the bacteria have been "injected" by the biter's teeth. A single long-acting shot of penicillin from the vet is a prudent measure.

Where the animal is found to have an abscess, swollen limb, or septic tail, professional treatment is always essential.

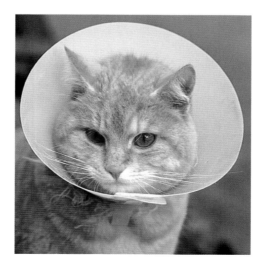

PROTECTING WOUNDS To stop a cat from interfering with surgical wounds, inflamed ears, or other conditions of the head, a home-made collar is effective.

Other types of wound in which the skin is torn should be bathed in weak antiseptic and warm water, dried, and then sprinkled with an antiseptic powder.

Veterinary treatment is needed for wounds that are of a size to need stitching. Small wounds, if contaminated with soil, for example, and particularly old or puncture wounds, benefit from antibiotic therapy.

Humans bitten or scratched by cats should regard their wounds as potentially dangerous. There is the possibility of infection with the germs of "cat-scratch fever" or with the bacterium often found in cats' mouths, *Pasteurella septica*.

Lumps and bumps

You may find a growth, thickening, or swelling somewhere on your cat's body, perhaps on a leg, eyelid, or on the tummy. In most cases, these are unlikely to be tumours, benign or otherwise. Blood blisters (haematoma), inflammation, or matted hair are much more common.

Tumours do occasionally arise in cats, and a small percentage may be malignant (cancerous). If they are caught early when they are small, it is easier for the vet to remove them. Tumours tend to develop slowly, while inflammatory conditions such as abscesses generally appear quickly.

OLD AGE

Inevitably, time catches up with cats. A study in the US has suggested that the average lifespan for indoor cats is a little over 14 years, while for outdoor cats this plummets to a mere two years. Should your pet survive beyond 17 years, it is doing very well indeed. Very few reach 20, although the record at present stands at 34 years 2 months and 4 hours, achieved by Granpa in 1998. Certainly cats tend to live longer than dogs – the oldest recorded dog reached 29 years, and the majority do not pass 16 years.

Old cats need special attention and understanding. After years of faithful companionship, it would be a churlish owner who did not give a thought to coping with feline geriatrics.

AGING BEAUTY This venerable 17-year-old cat
is still in excellent condition.

Old cats change physically and frequently
become rather thin. This may also be
accompanied by a change in appetite, with
an increased or decreased demand for food.
They may become more thirsty. Certainly
some of these changes are the result of a
failing liver and kidneys, conditions that,
in the absence of other symptoms, are
difficult for the vet to deal with.

If your cat's appetite increases, give more
food at each meal or, better still, more
meals daily. High-quality protein food
(fish, meat, and poultry) and a variety of
vegetables and fruit are essential for the
feline senior citizen. Give more water
or milk if it is wanted, since denying the
increased thirst would be dangerous.

Age may bring fussiness, and increased
amounts of high-quality protein may
produce bowel sluggishness and
constipation, as happens in some old
people. Although oily fish, such as tinned
pilchards, help the free movement of the
bowel, the basic fault generally is that, in
providing rich and tasty morsels to the
old-timer, owners do not give enough
bulky roughage, the stuff that gives healthy
exercise to the intestines. A little mineral
oil mixed with the food can be used
occasionally as a laxative (say two
teaspoonfuls once or twice weekly), but
the regular daily use of mineral oil is bad
since it cuts down absorption of vitamins
A, D, and E in the cat's diet.

If your cat will not take fibre in its food
in the form of bran or crumbled toasted
wholemeal bread, the daily use of a bulk-
acting granular laxative is the answer. An
ideal one is made from certain plant seed
husks. When mixed with meat or fish,
laxatives of this type are usually accepted
by cats. Once swallowed, the seed husks
absorb liquid and swell, becoming bulky
enough to stimulate contraction of the
lazy intestine-wall muscles.

In old age, a special watch should be
kept on the mouth. Clean the cat's teeth
once or twice weekly (see p.178). Regular
servicing by the vet throughout life should
have stopped the build-up of tartar, but a
fondness for soft snacks may encourage
rapid tartar formation with secondary
gum damage, inflammation of the tooth
sockets, and loose teeth. Catch these things
early because septic areas in the mouth
and bad teeth can only contribute to
kidney and liver degeneration. General
anaesthesia for major mouth surgery
(such as multiple extractions) can be
risky in old age, so do not neglect mouth
hygiene in earlier years.

There is a tendency for cats to lose
personal pride when past their prime.
They either forget or cannot be bothered
to groom themselves. Groom daily with
a comb and brush; with longhaired cats,
look out for knots building up in the coat.

Some old warriors lose control of their
bowels or waterworks on the odd occasion.
This may be forgetfulness, or it may
be that the nerve control of the valves
involved is weakening. If accidents become
troublesome, let your vet check the animal.
Cystitis can be a cause of involuntary
leaking and should be treated. Lazy bowels
may simply need more of the bulk content
already mentioned.

Deafness or failing eyesight usually arise
gradually, if at all, and the owner should
be able to compensate for the loss of these
senses. For example, remember that a deaf
cat cannot hear if you are moving furniture,
vacuuming the carpet, or bringing a strange
dog into the room – all potential dangers
in the immediate vicinity from which a cat

with good hearing will quickly remove
itself. If you have a blind cat, keep its food
dishes in the same place and protect it
from open fires and similar dangers; also,
try to avoid rearranging the furniture.

Although there is no elixir of life
available yet for man or his pets, there are
some drugs, which the vet may prescribe,
that can counteract some of the symptoms
of old age. One such drug is sulphadiazine,
which is claimed to combat senility, lack of
lustre, greying of hair, and general lack of
interest and vitality where such signs are
due solely to old age. There is also a range
of anabolic hormones that encourage
tissue building, oppose wastage of bodily
protein, speed the healing processes, and
generally increase appetite, alertness, and
activity. The vet must decide whether your
cat is suitable for treatment with any of
these compounds.

GETTING TO GRIPS It can be useful to restrain
a cat by wrapping it in a blanket or towel.

NURSING CARE
Whether your pet's ailment is mild or
serious, you will normally have to be
prepared to do some nursing. There
are some essential nursing techniques
to be learned.

Handling a cat for examination
The way your cat should be handled for
examination depends on the cat. You may:

- Cradle it in your arms if the animal is quiet and not in pain.
- Place the cat prone on the table and hold all four legs so it cannot use its claws.
- Hold the cat by the scruff and press down firmly on to a flat surface to restrict its ability to scratch.
- Use the perspex-cylinder method, in which the cat is placed in a stout plastic or perspex cylinder 10–12 cm (4–5 in) in diameter and 20–30 cm (8–12 in) long, depending of the size of the cat.
- For a head examination, wrap the cat in a large, strong cloth or blanket.

Administering medicine

Although the vet will try to select drug preparations as attractive as possible to cats, liquids and crushed tablets mixed with food are usually detected quickly. The cat then marches off highly offended, going without a meal rather than taking its medicine.

The key technique to master is how to hold the cat's head, by bending it back on the neck until the mouth automatically opens a fraction. Then keep the mouth open by pushing the lips on each side between the teeth with your index finger and thumb. If giving a tablet, drop it accurately on to the groove at the back of the tongue. Give a quick poke with the index finger of the other hand (or, very carefully, with the blunt end of a pencil if your feel uncertain about your finger's safety), pushing the tablet over the back of the tongue. Close the mouth immediately.

With the same grip on the head, liquids can be dropped in slowly. Do not be impatient and flood your pet's mouth with fluid. The cat will only choke, panic, and splutter furiously.

Injections

These are given by the vet and are normally the quickest, easiest means of giving drugs to cats.

Pre-tranquillizing

If your cat is as wild as a mountain lion but has to be taken to the vet's surgery for some reason, it is often possible to make things easier for all concerned by giving Valium or some other sedative under the vet's instructions before leaving home.

Taking temperatures

The accepted method of taking a temperature is by gently inserting a well-lubricated thermometer into the rectum. Generally, this is not worthwhile as most cats object to an undignified intrusion, become excited, and cause the temperature to climb. If you want to try, the normal temperature is 38–39° C (100.5–101.5° F).

FIRST AID

Cats do occasionally appear to have nine lives. Their bodies are so elastic and wiry that they often survive being run over by a car tyre without suffering fractures or serious damage. Nevertheless, hit by cars, air-gun pellets, stones, falling masonry, or drunkards' boots, trapped in doors, falling from great heights, or savaged by dogs, a cat sometimes seems to need every life it can lay claim to. These serious crises produce skeletal and soft-tissue damage, which the vet will have to treat in the operating room. It is important to know how to give useful first-aid emergency treatment until the animal can be taken to the vet.

Collapse and accident

If the cat is injured or unconscious, do not move it unless it is in danger. If you have to move an injured cat, slip a sheet under it and carry it as in a hammock or with one hand grasping the scruff of the neck. Lay the cat down in a quiet, warm place indoors and cover it with a blanket. Place a hot-water bottle, wrapped in a cloth, next to it. Do not give it anything to eat, but you may try to spoon in a few teaspoonfuls of warm sweet tea. Do not give alcoholic stimulants or aspirin.

Check the cat's pulse, which can be felt on the inside of the thigh where the leg joins the body. If the breathing is irregular or non-existent, loosen the collar, open the mouth, and remove any foreign body or saliva, blood, or vomit. In extreme cases, give artificial respiration.

Bleeding

If some part of the cat's body is bleeding badly, put a thick pad of cotton wool, lint, or a folded handkerchief on to it and press firmly.

Drowning and choking

In life-or-death cases of drowning or choking, where you cannot easily remove whatever is causing the obstruction, you must literally swing a cat. Pick it up by its two hindlegs and whirl it round and round. This will cause centrifugal force to drive blockages from the airways. Do not be namby-pamby about this; swing the cat hard – it is difficult to dislocate a cat's legs. If this does not work, try artificial respiration.

For artificial respiration, first make sure the tongue is not lying back in the mouth. Place both palms on the chest over the ribs and push down firmly to expel air from the lungs. Do not press too hard, or you may cause injury. Alternatively, use "mouth-to-mouth" respiration, by taking the whole of the cat's muzzle in your mouth and blowing in air steadily for three seconds, pausing for two, and then repeating the operation.

A WARM BED When it is necessary to provide heat for cats, a hot-water bottle covered by a blanket fits the bill.

Reproduction

Few babies are more attractive than the cubs, or kittens, of cats, big or small. The successful breeding of, say, snow leopards or ocelots, is a notable and welcome event – the more the merrier for such endangered species. With domestic cats, however, the owner has a special responsibility. While pedigree kittens are usually in demand, crossbred animals are often regrettably a burden on the market.

Queens reproduce easily and fruitfully during most of their adult lives. With a relatively short gestation (pregnancy) period and an average litter size of almost four, cats can multiply almost as prodigiously as rabbits. It is grossly irresponsible to allow your cat, male or female, to produce unwanted kittens that end up being put down.

Unneutered toms run the risk of more fighting wounds than their neutered colleagues, and for queens there are the stresses and strains, and possible complications, of repeated pregnancies. If you do not want your cat to have or to father a litter, or if you cannot be certain of finding good homes for any kittens born, have your queen neutered (spayed) or your tom castrated (doctored), or talk to your vet about the pill.

Cat reproduction follows the basic pattern of other mammals but with certain interesting modifications. Owners of unneutered queens, pedigree or crossbred, should acquaint themselves with the basic biological facts of life, feline-style.

THE MIRACLE OF BIRTH One of the great joys of owning a cat is being around a queen when she is giving birth and raising kittens. Remember, though, that kittens must be wanted and assured of a good home for life.

Sexual Behaviour

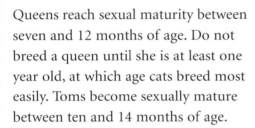

Queens reach sexual maturity between seven and 12 months of age. Do not breed a queen until she is at least one year old, at which age cats breed most easily. Toms become sexually mature between ten and 14 months of age.

THE OESTRUS CYCLE

Queens come into heat (oestrus) according to a seasonal rhythm. The heat period lasts for two to four days and occurs at roughly two-week intervals. The cycle is usually repeated two or three times in spring (mainly March and April) and in summer (mainly June and July), with sometimes a third period of activity in September.

SEXUAL POSING A queen begins to rub and roll.

Obviously, some queens do their own thing and have heat cycles somewhat outside these peaks. When a queen is in heat she will adopt a characteristic posture: front end flat on the ground, rear end stuck in the air, and hindlegs "pedalling" an invisible bicycle.

PREVENTING PREGNANCY

If you do not intend to breed from a female cat, a good time to have her neutered (spayed) is when she is four months old. This operation, done by a qualified vet under general anaesthetic, consists of removing both ovaries and part of the horns of the womb. The incision is usually made in one flank. There is very little risk of strain involved in the operation; the kitten is bouncing around again 24 hours after the operation. Sutures are generally removed seven to ten days after the operation, and there are rarely any after-effects.

Tom kittens can be castrated when four months old, though I recommend waiting until they are a couple of months older. This allows for the penis to grow in diameter and avoids troublesome clogging up with urine sludge later in life. Castration is the painless removal of the testicles by a vet. Although it can be done under local anaesthetic up to six months, after that age a full general anaesthetic is used. "Doctored" toms do not necessarily become fat, sluggish, and

lazy, although their urine loses its pungent aroma and they become sweeter characters.

Some folk think spaying and castration are cruel denials of a cat's natural desires. In practice, a castrated tom is spared the bites, abscesses, and other unfortunate consequences of cat fights. And it is humane to prevent unwanted pregnancies.

Both spaying and castration can be carried out at any age, though a vet will not usually spay a queen who is more than a couple of weeks pregnant. It is also best to avoid operating on a queen that is in heat; at these times the high level of sex hormones in her blood slows the speed of clotting when the vet operates.

In females, an alternative to surgery is the contraceptive pill or injection. A drug like megestrol acetate can be used in pill form in two ways: daily for two months during the breeding season, or weekly for up to 30 weeks during the non-breeding season. Injectable heat-suppressing drugs, such as proligestone, can be given at any point in the sexual cycle.

Diabetic cats and certain others should not be put on the pill. Prolonged use of these products can also, in some cases, result in mammary gland (breast) enlargement and, possibly, abnormalities of the uterus. It is vital that you discuss the best procedure for your cat with your vet.

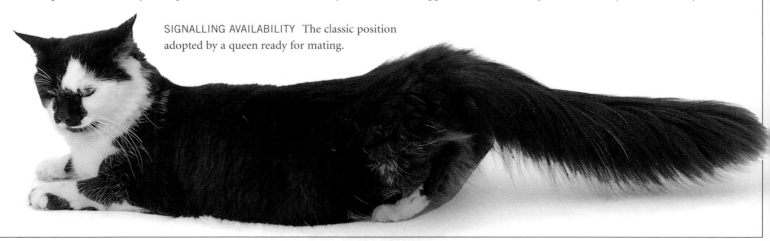

SIGNALLING AVAILABILITY The classic position adopted by a queen ready for mating.

Mating

"The cat, if you but singe her tabby skin,
The chimney keeps, and sits content within;
But once grown sleek, will from her corner run,
Sport with her tail and wanton in the sun:
She licks her fair round face, and frisks abroad
To show her fur, and to be catterwaw'd."

The Wife of Bath (Prologue), Alexander Pope

FIRST APPROACH Initial contact between tom and queen.

CHOOSING A STUD

If you plan to breed from your pedigree queen, you will, unless you also have a similarly blue-blooded tom, have to find a reputable breeder. Make enquiries at a cat club, cat show, or your vet's surgery. A first-class breeder of the kind you must seek will have spacious, secure, hygienic, and warm accommodation for the tom and queen. All the animals at the stud should be free of feline leukaemia virus. You should ask to see veterinary certificates verifying this and produce similar ones, together with vaccination certificates, for your cat. A stud fee will be payable, though if the first mating should not prove successful, a second attempt is normally granted free of charge.

Discuss with the breeder the approximate date (always impossible to predict with complete accuracy) when you should deliver your queen.

RECOGNIZING OESTRUS

So how do you know when a queen is ready to mate? Before the oestrus (heat) begins in earnest, she will be more affectionate than usual, rubbing and rolling with exaggerated enthusiasm. When heat sets in, she will start to "call" – howl in a most imperious manner – and show marked restlessness and a longing to go out of doors so she can go in search of a feline Don Juan.

Her call may be a low, plaintive love song or, in the case of a Siamese, a powerful aria worthy of the renowned soprano Maria Callas. Most noticeable of all is the mating posture described and illustrated opposite. Once the queen begins to call, telephone the breeder and arrange to take your cat round. Do not go through with the lover's tryst if either of the cats is off-colour.

THE QUEEN'S CYCLE

Oestrus

Oestrus resumes 2–4 weeks after weaning

Lactation period 6–8 weeks

Gestation period 58–72 days

Birth – litter of 1–10 kittens

20 1 2 3 4 5 6 7 8 9 10 11 12 13 14 15 16 17 18 19

SEASONAL CYCLES If your queen becomes pregnant, the cycle from oestrus through gestation, birth, and lactation, to the resumption of oestrus lasts, on average, 20 weeks. Feline heat cycles are seasonal and tend to start in January. Within any phase, two or three two-week cycles occur. Each oestrus lasts two to four days.

COITUS

After you arrive at the breeder's premises, the queen will be placed in adjoining quarters to those of the tom, and separated by wire mesh. They will be allowed to mix when the female begins to make advances to the male. The couple will be allowed to mate three or four times and then perhaps left together for a further two to three days. You will then be able to return to collect your hopefully pregnant animal.

When you bring the queen back home she may well still be in heat – do not let her go out of the house for a few days. It is not unknown for superfecundation to occur – this is a condition in which offspring from two toms, one of them perhaps the crossbred and cross-eyed tom that rules your neighbourhood, are conceived contemporaneously. In such cases the litter will consist of a mixture of pedigree and non-pedigree kittens.

Whether it is in the breeder's carefully supervised cattery or up on the roof, once a queen is with a tom, as with many mammals, the cats' rituals of courtship and mating progress through a series of clearly defined phases, as described on the following page.

Mating

1 *The provocative rolling of the queen stimulates the tom's interest.*

2 *The queen goes into the typical mating position. Her body is pressed to the ground, her back hollowed, and her hindquarters raised.*

3 *The tom mounts the queen and seizes the scruff of her neck between his teeth.*

4 *The male often "pedals" with his hindlegs immediately prior to the brief act of coitus.*

5 *The neck-bite and the stimulation of the male's bony, spiny penis at this point trigger ovulation by means of nerve signals sent to the pituitary gland in the brain.*

6 *Ejaculation occurs immediately the penis is introduced into the vagina, and may be accompanied by a howl from the queen.*

7 *The tom separates from the queen and moves off a little way. Sometimes he will sit or lie watching her. Here, he is grooming himself.*

8 *After mating, the queen too goes off by herself. She may give a luxurious display of rolling, rubbing, and stretching.*

9 *The above sequence is repeated after five to ten minutes, and may subsequently occur many more times.*

Pregnancy

The length of pregnancy in the cat is between 56 and 71 days, but the average length is 65 days.

The average litter size of the domestic cat in the UK is four kittens, while in the US it is 3.88 (only statisticians have ever seen 0.88 of a kitten!). Larger cats tend to have more kittens in a litter.

It is known that more eggs are ovulated and probably fertilized than kittens are born. The reason for this is that death and resorption of the early foetus is common in the cat. It occurs without producing any noticeable symptoms in the queen.

Kittens born earlier than 58 days tend to be delivered dead or very weak, and those born later than 71 days are generally bigger than normal and may also be dead. Such late, big kittens can cause birth problems – consult your vet if the 71st day of pregnancy arrives without the queen displaying any sign of labour. Older queens tend to have smaller litters and towards the end of their lives may only produce a single, often quite big, kitten. Such mature mums may also have difficult births.

The largest litter on record comprised a remarkable 19 kittens. They were delivered by Caesarean section in 1970 to Tarawood Antigone, a brown Burmese owned by Mrs Valerie Gane of Kingham, Oxfordshire, England. The father was half Siamese. Of the 19, one was female, 14 were male and four were stillborn.

HANDLE WITH CARE Picking up a heavily pregnant queen should be done even more carefully than usual, with minimum pressure on the tummy.

An ideal litter size, with which the mother can comfortably cope, is three to four. Some queens cannot rear five or six kittens unaided.

SIGNS OF PREGNANCY

If mating is successful, the queen does not usually return into oestrus. However, if it is not, oestrus will recur within two to three weeks. Occasionally, a pregnant queen will show some signs of oestrus and mating behaviour at about the 21st and 42nd days – times that would have corresponded to heat periods in the absence of mating.

POINTS TO WATCH FOR

- Reddening nipples – this is known as "pinking-up" and occurs around the third week of pregnancy;
- Gradual weight gain – 1–2 kg (2–4 lb), depending on the litter size;

- A swelling abdomen – do not prod and poke the abdomen to feel the developing kittens, since this could cause serious damage;
- Behavioural changes – the queen tends to become "maternal".

PREDICTING THE BIRTH DATE

If you know the date of mating, estimate nine weeks from then. If you do not know the date of mating, estimate six weeks after the first evidence of pinking-up.

WHAT TO DO BEFORE THE BIRTH

- Discuss the birth with your vet.
- Obtain some safe worming drugs from the vet and give them to the pregnant queen.
- Provide a good, well-balanced diet with some extra vitamins and mineral supplements. Discuss this with your vet.
- In late pregnancy, the presence of growing kittens in the womb can cause constipation. If this occurs, mix a few drops of liquid paraffin oil with the queen's food.
- Prepare a kittening box for the queen in good time. This should be placed in a warm, quiet spot. It should be of wood or cardboard, open at the top and on one side. Line it with newspaper, which is easily changed when soiled and is an efficient insulator. Blankets and sheets quickly become dirty and kittens can get lost in the fabric. Hang an infrared lamp no lower than 1 m (3 ft) above the box. If the queen refuses to use the box you provide and picks her own place, put newspapers down there and hang the infrared lamp above.
- Queens must be kept indoors during at least the last two weeks of pregnancy.

EXPECTANT MUM This pregnant queen shows a very distended abdomen and reddening of the nipples and will probably kitten in the next few days.

The Birth

Pregnancy ends when special hormones, sent out from the pituitary gland, set birth into motion.

Up to one third of all kittens are born tail-end first. This is perfectly normal and these are not breech births. The term "breech birth" signifies a birth position where the kitten's bottom passes first through the vagina with its hindfeet pointing towards its head. So pliable are kittens' bodies that even the occasional true breech birth usually occurs without causing difficulties.

The first stage of labour may last up to six hours. It begins when the cervix of the uterus opens up and a "wedge" of placental membranes enters it. As this happens, the involuntary contractions of the uterine muscles begin to push the kitten towards the outside world. When these contractions begin, the queen will probably make for her kittening bed. She may start breathing rapidly, panting, and purring, but she is not in pain. A clear vaginal discharge may be seen.

The second stage should last around ten to 30 minutes, but no longer than 90 minutes. It begins when the emerging foetus and its membranes stimulate the mother to aid the involuntary contractions with her own voluntary abdominal muscle contractions or straining ("bearing down"). At first, bearing down occurs once every 15 to 30 minutes. Soon, a cloudy grey bubble, the first sign of the membrane that surrounds the kitten, appears at the vulval opening. The interval between bouts of bearing down decreases, until straining occurs once every 15 to 30 seconds. The membrane protrusion increases in size, and part of the kitten may be glimpsed within it. With a few final contractions, the queen pushes out the kitten.

The third stage, following the birth, is the expulsion of the membranes and placenta. Each kitten has its own membranes and placenta, except in the case of identical twins, where the kittens may share one set.

As soon as a kitten is born, the queen starts licking it, and she bites off the umbilical cord 2–4 cm (1–2 in) from its navel. Do not worry if she tries to eat the placenta when it emerges – this is instinctive in many mammals.

When all the kittens have been born, they should be ready to suckle. Make sure that they each latch on to a teat to receive their ration of first milk (colostrum), which contains important antibodies and nutrients.

TENDING A WEAK KITTEN

If a kitten is very cold and weak at birth, dunk it up to its neck in a bowl of water at blood temperature. Hold the kitten by its head and stroke and massage the body gently under the water. After two or three minutes it should become more vigorous. Remove the kitten from the water and dry it with warm towels.

DELAYS DURING DELIVERY

The time between successive kitten births can vary between five minutes and two hours. Sometimes a queen will deliver half a litter and then rest for 12 to 24 hours before delivering the others.

If this happens, should you call the vet? If the first group of kittens were delivered normally and at short intervals, and the queen appears content, suckles her kittens,

The membrane around the kitten begins to appear.

1 *After a period of straining (bearing down) by the queen, a cloudy bubble appears, which is the first sign of the emerging kitten.*

2 *The kitten is now visible within its membrane, and a few more contractions will complete the birth. In about one third of cases, the kitten will be born hindlegs first, but this is rarely a problem.*

The kitten can be seen within its bubble.

3 *The kitten is born. The membranes and placenta will usually be delivered very quickly after this.*

A kitten is born.

and accepts food, there may be no need to worry. However, unfortunately, a delay of this type can be confused with uterine inertia, where the contractions gradually fade and the queen tires of bearing down, eventually giving up. This condition needs veterinary attention. Queens with uterine inertia usually appear more fatigued and

4 *The mother will lick the kitten clean, rupturing the semi-transparent sac, if still intact, and removing the amniotic fluid from its face. This persistent licking stimulates the kitten's breathing reflex.*

By licking her kittens, the mother stimulates their breathing and circulation.

The queen chews through the umbilical cord of a newly born kitten.

5 *Immediately after the kitten is born, the mother, with all the skill of the best obstetrician, will sever the umbilical cord with her teeth approximately 2 cm (1 in) from the kitten's body.*

6 *Almost immediately the kitten will reach out at a nipple and begin to suck. Just as quickly, the mother's maternal instincts will surface and she will begin to make a fuss over her offspring.*

The warmth, attention, and purring vibrations of the queen strongly attract her offspring.

with the umbilical cord. Sterilize a length of cotton and a pair of scissors in an antiseptic solution. Tie the cotton tightly around the umbilical cord about 3 cm (2¼ in) from the navel.
• Put a double knot in the cotton and then cut the umbilical cord 0.5 cm (¼ in) beyond the knot on the placental side of the knot.
• Put the kitten in the kittening box beneath an infrared lamp.

LABOUR PROBLEMS
Labour problems are unusual, but if they do arise, arrange for the vet to make a house call, or take the cat to the surgery. Time is the vital factor. Do not try poking your finger inside the vagina of the queen. Put her into a well-padded box and take her to the vet in a warm car.

CONTACT THE VET
DURING THE BIRTH WHEN…
• A queen has been bearing down for two hours without delivering a kitten;
• No bearing down at all has been seen six hours after blood or any other coloured discharge appeared from the vulva;
• Bearing down has stopped for more than two hours, although the queen is obviously still carrying a kitten or kittens.

CONTACT THE VET
AFTER THE BIRTH IF…
• The queen bleeds significantly from the vagina (more than about two teaspoonfuls);
• You see a coloured, white or foul-smelling vaginal discharge;
• The queen seems lethargic or dull;
• Normal eating is not resumed after the first 12 hours;
• The queen is still straining after the birth of the last kitten and the expulsion of its placenta;
• The queen seems abnormally restless or feverish;
• The queen shows no interest in her new kittens.

---

uninterested than a purely resting cat, but the difference may be difficult to judge. Therefore, if your queen clearly has not finished giving birth two hours after the last kitten was born, contact the vet.

WHEN TO HELP
If an inexperienced queen does not seem to know what to do with the new kittens, and does not break open the membranes

as needed or sever the umbilical cord, you must play the part of the feline midwife.
• If the kitten is still draped in its membranes, simply strip them off with your fingers.
• Dry the kitten in warm towelling and make sure the nostrils and mouth are unobstructed.
• When the kitten is breathing, making faint squeaking noises, and wriggling, deal

Maternal Behaviour

Over the next two to three months, the mother cat gradually teaches her kittens all they need to know in order to look after themselves.

A newborn kitten is 11–15 cm (4–6 in) long and weighs between 70 and 135 g (2–5 oz). It is a fairly helpless creature at this stage, unable to see because of closed eyelids, unable to hear with ears that are folded back, and capable of wiggling and squirming but not walking.

KEEPING WARM Brothers and sisters instinctively bunch together to conserve warmth.

MOTHER'S LICKS Mother's grooming stimulates the breathing, circulation, and muscles of her offspring.

BONDING

In the first few days of life, the queen is absolutely vital to the kittens' survival, not least in protecting them while they are physically so vulnerable. Instinctively, the queen knows what to do, even if it is her first litter. When she decides to carry a kitten, she does it by gently but firmly grasping the scruff of its neck.

A firm bond is established rapidly between mother and infants. Shortly after giving birth, a queen will accept kittens other than her own, but once the bond is forged strange kittens are not easily accepted. The sense of smell plays an important part in this bonding. Queen and litters recognize the "personalized" odour of the secretions of each other's skin glands, especially those on the head. The pleasurable rubbing of heads transfers the characteristic scent.

In the first few days after giving birth, a queen may decide to move her kittens to a new "den". This often occurs with wild cats and is an instinctive act designed to remove the babies from the liquids produced by the birth process, which might attract predators. If your queen moves home like this, simply put her kittening box in a new spot.

SUCKLING

The kittens rely on their mother for their supply of milk. Each kitten adopts its own individual teat, and there is rarely much swapping of teats. By pushing with their forepaws against the mother's body as they suckle, the kittens

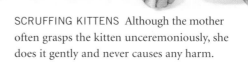

SCRUFFING KITTENS Although the mother often grasps the kitten unceremoniously, she does it gently and never causes any harm.

FOSTERING The foster mother is taking as much care of the kittens as if they had been her own.

USEFUL STIMULATION The mother cleans her kittens' rear ends, thereby encouraging regular bowel movements and urination and keeping a delicate area clean.

trigger a nerve/hormone reflex that initiates the "let-down" of milk. Restless, fretful kittens that cry a lot may indicate that the queen is failing to let down milk or, more rarely, that she simply cannot produce enough milk.

Where the let-down mechanism is faulty, a veterinarian may decide to give a pituitary gland-hormone injection that almost instantly corrects the problem. If the queen simply cannot manufacture the necessary amount of milk, fostering or artificial rearing will be necessary.

Sometimes only one of the kittens appears to be short of milk, and in this case the vet can examine it to see if it has a congenital condition, such as cleft palate, or some other problem.

COMMUNICATION

A mother licks her kittens often. This stimulates their breathing and the circulation of blood and tones their infant muscles. Licking their bottoms encourages and teaches them to defecate and urinate regularly. At first queen and kittens communicate mainly vocally. The mother produces a range of greetings, scolding, soothing, warning, and "come-to-me" sounds. When the kittens are bigger and go on family walks, visual signals come into play. Everyone keeps together as the youngsters follow the "flag" made by the queen holding her tail high with the top bent backwards.

GAINING INDEPENDENCE

Although the kittens learn by watching their mother and other cats, some things are instinctive. Even before their eyes are open, they will react to certain stimuli – spitting or hissing if disturbed, for example.

Kittens tend only to rest when together as a litter. This instinctive habit serves to keep them warm and ensures that they do not become separated as a group. The snugness and the sound of their own heartbeats probably comfort them by reminding them of their life within their mother's womb.

The first major advance in independence is when their eyes begin to open at five to ten days of age. They are fully open at eight to 20 days. At 16 to 20 days, the kittens begin to crawl; at three to four weeks, they start to take solid food; and by two months of age, they are usually fully weaned. When they begin to wean, the bond with their mother gradually weakens until she stops differentiating between her own and other kittens. At this stage the kittens can fend for themselves.

HAPPY LITTER This litter of kittens is obviously well fed, well groomed, and content.

Kitten Development

CURIOUS CAT War games might as well begin with a toy bird.

The transformation of the kitten from its blind and helpless newborn state to full independence takes about six months.

During that time, physical and mental abilities mature steadily. The kitten's instinctive, in-built knowledge is progressively enhanced by a process of learning by observation, imitation, and practice through play. Play is the vehicle of the feline learning process – the life of the specialized natural hunter-killer is rehearsed and perfected in the theatre of the game.

A lone, artificially reared kitten with no role models around to copy and emulate will never learn much of the repertoire of feline hunting skills. What is not learned during the formative first few weeks of life cannot be acquired later. Kittens that watch, and are in a real sense taught, by their mothers, learn more quickly than they would by watching some unrelated adult. It is therefore nothing to worry about when your young kittens indulge in regular rough bouts of fighting. Play "combat" of this kind almost never results in any wounds or the loss of a single drop of blood. As well as refining physical and mental abilities that will serve the cat well in adult life, there is quite obviously lots of sheer fun in kittens' boisterous play. As with a human child, play with its peers increases the social skills and sociability of a kitten. The kitten that is denied the opportunity of

NO HARM DONE Combat is practised without inflicting damage.

play may grow up into a rather antisocial, insular, and perhaps neurotic adult.

Under normal conditions, the kitten packs a lot of learning and physical growth into half a year, equivalent to about ten years in the human lifespan, and, as with humans, a perfect feline upbringing can best be achieved by a family environment (normally a one-parent family in the case of the domestic cat). In raising a strong and sensible cat, there is nothing to equal the natural milk and constant attention of the queen, the endless games and competition with siblings, and the opportunities to learn from and inwardly digest the example of mother and other sophisticated adults.

The same applies to the young cubs of wild cats. I have attended hundreds of young lions, tigers, leopards, and other cat species in captivity that have had to be hand reared by humans without the influence of feline kith and kin. Such animals are never, in my opinion, quite as well adjusted as naturally reared ones. Their reintroduction into a naturally reared pride or group is often difficult.

MUM KNOWS BEST Techniques taught by mother are vital if a kitten is to develop its natural hunting skills.

FIRST DAY

Giving birth to a large litter of kittens can be exhausting for a queen, and she will need to rest for about 12 to 24 hours after her labours. Under normal circumstances the kittens should stay with her.

Newborn kittens are completely helpless.

SECOND DAY

By the second day the queen should be feeling much recovered, be eating and drinking normally, and happily getting down to the business of rearing her kittens.

Blind, two-day-old kittens respond to the touch, warmth, and purring vibrations of the mother.

EIGHTH DAY

The kittens now weigh, depending on their breed and the physical characteristics of their parents, between 110 and 250 g (4–9 oz). The eyes may open at any time between now and 20 days.

Seeing the world for the first time, as the eyes open after the eighth day.

Just over two weeks old, and this kitten is about to become a rather wobbly crawler.

SIXTEENTH DAY

The kitten's weight is now between 180 and 340 g (6–12 oz) and crawling will start within the next four days.

TWENTY-FIRST DAY

The weight is now somewhere between 215 and 420 g (8–15 oz). This is the time that weaning after natural rearing can begin. Give powdered cat-milk substitute, or tinned milk diluted with water as for human babies, but at double strength. Offer the liquid on a teaspoon, four times a day.

Toilet training should also start now. Put a litter tray in a convenient, quiet, and easily reached spot. At the first sign of a kitten even looking as if it might be thinking of defecating or urinating, pop it on it. If you have more than one kitten, make sure the tray is big

Toilet training should begin early, as with these three-week-old kittens.

enough for communal toilet sessions, and if you have a single, nervous kitten provide a covered litter tray.

FOUR WEEKS

A one-month old kitten weighs 250–500 g (9–18 oz) and is now making great strides – literally. It begins to run and play games between four and five weeks old, and at about the same time first washes itself. Toys should be provided, either special cat toys or simple household objects such as empty cotton reels or ping-pong balls; but avoid giving balls of knitting wool to breeds such as Burmese and Siamese. A little baby cereal or puréed, tinned, or bottled baby food (fish, meat, or cheese varieties) can now be added to the milk mixture.

One month old and washing begins.

At around four weeks of age, game-playing begins.

FIVE WEEKS

The weight is between 290 and 620 g (10–22 oz), and it is time for you to register the kitten's pedigree with the breed authorities.

Finely minced best meat, finely chopped tinned cat food, or chopped, boiled, or milk-poached fish should be substituted for one of the four milk feeds. Place the food in a shallow tray or saucer and give the kittens as much as they will eat once a day, but do not put too much down at once.

As kittens grow, their nutritional demands on the mother increase.

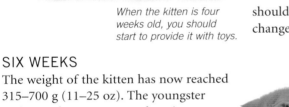

When the kitten is four weeks old, you should start to provide it with toys.

SIX WEEKS

The weight of the kitten has now reached 315–700 g (11–25 oz). The youngster makes its first attempts at hunting practice between six and eight weeks.

Although it is best if a kitten stays with its mother until it is fully weaned at about eight weeks old, it can be separated from six weeks onwards.

Increase the amount of solid minced food in the diet by replacing two more of the milk feeds with a balanced tinned cat food.

EIGHT WEEKS

Weighing 400–900 g (14–31 oz), the kitten is now normally fully weaned and possesses all its milk teeth. Feeding should comprise two or three solid meals a day and a saucer of cow's milk, which can be substituted with fresh water once the kittens are six months old. Milk or water should be available all the time, but change it at least twice a day.

At six weeks, hunting practice normally begins.

NINE WEEKS

At nine weeks old, the kitten will receive its first vaccination against the virus diseases feline influenza, feline infectious enteritis, and feline leukaemia. This is followed by a second shot three to four weeks later. Never neglect to have kittens protected against these potentially lethal diseases – and, when adult, ensure that they receive annual booster vaccinations. Although in special cases, when there is a high risk of infection, your veterinarian may recommend vaccination of a kitten younger than eight to nine weeks, it is not normally done before this age. This is because antibodies transferred by the mother to the kitten will still be circulating in its blood and may neutralize the effect of the vaccine.

THEODORE'S FIRST NINE WEEKS
Theodore is a typical kitten and a number of important occasions in his first nine weeks of life have been recorded.

One minute old.

Five days and increasingly noisy when hungry.

At ten days, Theo's eyes open.

At 15 days old, Theo first tries to crawl.

This group, nine weeks old, have just had their first vaccinations.

POINTS TO REMEMBER

- Vaccination is not dangerous and very rarely produces any side-effects. Should these occur, they are easily countered by the vet.
- Kittens are not protected by the vaccine until about ten days after the first vaccination. Keep them indoors during that period.
- Pregnant cats must be given dead or inactivated vaccines, never the live sort.
- Vaccination should only be given to a healthy kitten.
- Do not forget to return the kitten for its second vaccination on the date advised. Animals vaccinated on veterinary advice earlier than eight weeks will normally receive a second shot at 12 weeks, or repeated doses at three- to four-week intervals until they are 12 weeks of age; the vet will advise you what is best for your particular kitten.
- Make sure you receive a signed veterinary vaccination certificate. Take it with you for endorsing when you go for the annual boosters and also when taking your cat to a breeder or boarding cattery.
- If in doubt as to whether a kitten you acquire has been vaccinated, play safe and have it revaccinated. An "extra" vaccination will not do it any harm at all.

TWELVE WEEKS

About now, the kitten's eye colour changes to its permanent shade, and the permanent teeth begin to push through during the next six weeks. This is the time for your kitten to receive its second influenza, enteritis, and leukaemia vaccination.

SIXTEEN WEEKS

If you are not planning to breed from a queen, make arrangements with your vet to have her spayed. Spaying involves the removal of both ovaries and much of the uterus under general anaesthetic. It is a very safe operation, is irreversible, and has no after-effects. Because a general anaesthetic is used, you must keep the animal off food and drink for 12 hours before admission.

A spayed queen will have either dissolvable or non-dissolvable stitches in her small skin wound. Non-dissolvable stitches will be removed by the vet five to ten days after the operation.

TWENTY-FOUR WEEKS

By now the kitten is totally independent of its mother.

This 16-week-old queen has just been spayed.

THIRTY-SIX WEEKS

This is a good time to have tom kittens castrated. The operation is a safe, simple, and painless one carried out under general anaesthetic. Keep the animal off food and drink for about 12 hours prior to admission. The cat will be ready for collection the same day and will require no nursing other than the provision of rest, warmth, light meals, and affection. There are normally no stitches to be removed.

Twenty-one days and he toddles towards his litter tray.

One month and he is ready to run.

At nine weeks old, Theo is already a handsome cat about town.

Raising and Fostering

There are occasions, such as the death of a queen or when she simply cannot produce a sufficient supply of milk, when you may be faced with the problem of rearing kittens in some other way.

KITTEN FOSTERING If available, a foster mother is preferable to bottle rearing.

When it comes to hand rearing kittens, you have two options – fostering and artificial rearing. (If, on the other hand, you decide to "destroy" the kittens, do not even consider drowning them. Animal euthanasia must always be carried out by a vet or clinic.)

FOSTERING

A veterinarian, pet shop, breeder, or cat club may be able to put you in touch with somebody who has a newly kittened queen with spare teat capacity. Ideally any such adoption should be carried out as soon as possible after birth and before the queen has bonded too strongly to her own offspring.

To transfer a kitten, smear a little butter on it. The fostering queen will lick it off and in the process come to accept the newcomer as her own. To monitor a fostered kitten's progress and check that it really is getting enough warm milk, you should weigh it regularly. It should steadily gain some tens of grams in weight every day.

CHARTING PROGRESS Weighing a kitten to check on its progress is essential.

ARTIFICIAL REARING

It is not difficult to raise kittens on the bottle, but try to ensure they receive at least a few drops of the mother's first milk (colostrum). Try to express a few drops of colostrum from her teats by gently squeezing, and then give it to the babies by dropper. The colostrum gives the kittens some valuable antibodies against disease.

WHAT ARTIFICIAL MILK?

Pure cow's and goat's milk are too weak for kittens, and you should never give cow's milk to very young kittens. Instead you can use one of two alternatives: either a special cat-milk powder, available from the veterinarian or pet shop, made up with water as directed on the container; or human baby milk powder (or evaporated tinned milk) made up to double human-baby strength with water or lime water.

EQUIPMENT

Obviously, standard human-baby equipment is much too big for kittens. Specially designed, curved, kitten-feeding bottles are available, but premature-baby bottles serve just as well. Eye-droppers and 2-ml syringes without needles can also be used. All the equipment must be washed and sterilized between feeds.

ADMINISTERING FOOD
Young or weak kittens
that do not suck well
should be dropper-fed.

MOTHER'S MILK Bottle-fed
kittens do best if they receive
at least a few drops of their
mother's first milk (colostrum).

FEEDING METHODS

The bottle method is the best for most kittens, but with very weak ones or those that at first do not suck and swallow well, the dropper or syringe have advantages. A 2-cm (1-in) length of plastic tube attached to the syringe will deliver milk into the mouth, while a longer, 5-cm (2-in) tube would permit you to introduce milk directly into the stomach by sliding it gently over the back of the tongue and down the gullet. Note: this technique is very efficient, but should only be done after veterinary instruction. If the plastic tube is inserted wrongly and enters the windpipe, choking or a fatal milk-fat pneumonia may be the result. Never rush the feeding process, since it is easy to overwhelm the kitten's rate of sucking.

Whichever method you use, the milk should be at about blood heat, 37° C (98.6° F). Up to seven days of age, give 3–6 ml every two hours. Between seven and 14 days, increase to 6–8 ml every two hours during the day and every

four hours during the night. Between 14 and 21 days the quantity should be raised again to 8–10 ml given every two hours during the day and once at night between 11 pm and 8 am. When a kitten has fed, it should be encouraged to urinate and defecate. To imitate the licking of the queen's tongue, use some cotton wool moistened in warm water to wipe the anal area and gently stroke the tummy with your fingers. When the kitten has responded, clean and dry the area beneath the tail and anoint it very lightly with nappy cream.

Between feeds, keep the kittens warm in a clean box with disposable bedding, a heating pad or infrared lamp, and a mother substitute such as a hot-water bottle wrapped in a woolly cover. The box temperature should be 25–30° C (77–86° F) for the first two weeks, gradually reducing to 20° C (68° F) by the sixth week.

WEANING

Begin weaning bottle-reared kittens when they are three weeks old. Add about half a teaspoonful of the best baby cereal, puréed baby food (meat, fish, or cheese), or calves'-foot jelly to the bottle feed for a few days. Thereafter wean the kittens in exactly the same way as naturally raised kittens.

GENERAL POINTS ON RAISING

- Do not pick up young kittens by the scruff of the neck.
- When kittens are three weeks old, discuss worming with your vet.
- Keep all kittens, and their mothers, indoors if possible until one week after the first vaccination. Do not let the queen meet up with toms until after the kittens have been weaned, since many queens come into oestrus a few days after giving birth.
- If kittens pester their mother for milk after weaning fully she will start becoming thin and debilitated. Throughout the suckling period, and for a while thereafter, make sure that the queen has ad-lib high-quality food. Discourage weaned kittens from suckling by smearing the queen's teats with a mixture of petroleum jelly and quinine, or by using a non-toxic repellent aerosol from the pet shop or a vet.

LITTLE PESTS It is not a
good thing for kittens to
pester their mother for food
after they have been weaned.

Showing

The showing of pedigree cats has played the central role over the past century in creating the rich spectrum of breeds that delight cat lovers today. Through the shows, breeders have produced many new kinds of cats and had them recognized.

It must be said, of course, that the artificial selection carried out by breeders has been confined to the human ideal of a good-looking cat. Nobody bothered to ask a cat what it thought! In fashioning cats to charm the human eye, scant attention has been paid to the possible physical disadvantages. However, it is certainly true that genetic engineering has produced fewer harmful effects with pedigree cats than has been the case in some areas of dog breeding.

Should you decide to make a serious foray into cat shows, you must be prepared to spend a lot of time and money, but it will bring great fascination and excitement.

If you have a pedigree cat, or even if you do not, go along to a cat show or two. You will enjoy yourself immensely, even though nothing there is likely to convince you that your faithful old tom, which you left snoozing by the fireside, is not the most perfect cat on earth!

BEST IN SHOW Anyone who loves cats will adore cat shows. Even if your pet is not show standard or you just are not interested in carting it around the country, a show is a feline beauty parade, a place where folk like us gather to celebrate the cat.

Heredity and Breeding

Breeding cats for showing depends on the workings, be they calculated or accidental, of heredity.

BASIC MECHANISMS OF HEREDITY

Every cell of an animal or plant contains structures called chromosomes. These look like microscopic strings of "beads" called genes. Each gene on a chromosome string carries details of the design of a particular part of the body. Some genes are concerned with eye colour, others with coat colour, and so on. The genes are arranged in a fixed order along the length of the chromosome, so the chromosome contains a "blueprint" of the total make-up of an individual.

Domestic cats carry 38 chromosomes arranged in pairs of 19. Eighteen of these pairs are virtually identical, but one pair differs slightly. This is the pair that decides the kitten's sex. Females carry a pair of so-called XX chromosomes, while males carry an XY pair. A kitten will inherit one of its mother's X chromosomes plus either the X or Y from its father, and thus its own sex will be determined.

Each kitten in a litter inherits genes from both father and mother in equal amounts, but they will be arranged in a slightly different order along the chromosome bead chain. It is this new arrangement that gives each kitten its individuality.

Occasionally outside factors, such as X-rays, can alter the fundamental characters of genes, and the changes they induce are called mutations. Sometimes, though very rarely, a gene mutation occurs spontaneously. Changes such as these result in the sudden popping up of new breeds, colours, and types of cat.

LINKED GENES

Some genes tend to stick together and pass "arm in arm" from one generation to the next. These are "linked genes" and, where they are found on only one of the pair of chromosomes, they are termed "sex-linked" genes. A good example of sex-linked genes in the cat is the fact that tortoiseshells are always female. This is because a tortoiseshell coat is produced by a combination of genes linked to the female chromosome, and a male cannot therefore inherit it.

DOMINANT AND RECESSIVE GENES

Dominant genes are those that tend to get their own way, while recessive genes are shy and retiring types. When two colour-carrying genes meet in a newly fertilized egg, it is the dominant one that dictates the eventual colour of the kitten that will be born. Tabby (agouti) coloured genes, for example, are dominant, whereas solid (non-agouti) genes are recessive.

CAT FAMILY TREE A noble feline lineage showing two generations in the family tree of a typical cat family where the father is ginger and the mother is tortie. Their offspring show the variety of colours that can result according to the rules of genetics.

Ginger

Tortoiseshell

Tortoiseshell

Colourpoint-and-White

Cream

Brown Tabby

Tortoiseshell Tabby

Blue Tabby-and-White

Brown Tabby

Cornish Rex

Devon Rex

MIMIC GENES
Occasionally, quite different genes can produce similar bodily effects. These are said to be "mimic" genes. There are two well-known feline mimic Rex genes – the Cornish and the Devon. These two breeds look similar, but genetically they have developed separately.

CROSS-EYED BEAUTY
The squint of the Siamese is caused by an inherited fault in its vision.

MASKED GENES
This British Cream kitten shows faint tabby markings from a "masked" gene.

UNDESIRABLE GENETIC EFFECTS
A dominant white gene frequently induces wasting away of the inner ear structures. This is why white cats, especially ones with blue eyes, have a tendency to deafness.

The Manx gene, which causes taillessness, is similar to the condition of spina bifida in humans. If Manx genes are passed on by both parents, the kittens die in the uterus. Manx therefore are not true breeding cats. The fact that they survive at all means that they can only be carrying one Manx gene in each pair of chromosomes.

GENETIC TAILLESSNESS The Manx gene carries the inherited deformity of taillessness. Where kittens inherit Manx genes from both parents they usually die before birth.

The Siamese gene may produce a defect in the optic nerve connecting the eye to the brain. This results in reduced binocular vision and a degree of double vision, which the cat tries to correct by squinting.

Other undesirable effects controlled by genes are hairlessness (sometimes allied to red genes), undescended testicles, badly positioned ear flaps, extra toes (polydactyly) and a cleft in the forefeet (splitfoot).

MASKING
A phenomenon known as masking occurs when some genes are so powerful that they swamp the characteristics produced by other genes. The best example of this is where the non-agouti gene masks the effects of the various tabby genes. This explains why a black cat with tabby genes usually has no tabby markings –

POLYDACTYLY
Extra toes are a genetic feature.

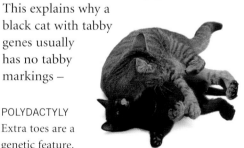

the non-agouti gene has eliminated the agouti ticking of the hairs to produce a solid black appearance. Sometimes partial masking occurs, explaining why a faint tabby pattern is often seen in the coat of young, solid-coloured kittens.

SELECTIVE BREEDING
The breeder of show cats has to operate within the labyrinth of the miraculous natural processes I have just outlined. Little can be done yet by way of genetic engineering, although the day may come when we can actively make cats the way we want them. The breeder must select those characteristics that he wishes to promote, and enhance them by careful breeding plans. He or she can suppress unwanted features (cross-eyed Siamese have been quite successfully bred out) and experiment by crossing cats of different body type, colour, hair length and so on.

Pedigree Birman kittens

Of course, to win prizes at the cat show, the end product of all this considered breeding must resemble the ideal standard currently in vogue for a particular breed.

CATS FOR SHOWING
In cat shows, pedigree cats are judged against a scale of points for their particular breed. The maximum number of points is 100, with marks being deducted for features that do not match the breed standard. If your cat is not up to scratch for showing, then consider buying a good pedigree kitten. Register it with the governing body or, if it is already registered, notify the change of ownership.

In order to breed cats for shows it is best to start with one or two female kittens, rather than to buy an entire male (stud). Remember, however, that if you are going in for a rare breed, suitable studs may be difficult to find.
- Always consult an experienced breeder and join a cat club before you begin.
- Wait until your kitten is one year old before starting to breed.
- Compare the pedigrees of various studs and

select the one most suited to your queen. Your aim should be to improve on her characteristics.
- Go to cat shows in order to study the potential stud's kittens and the judges' opinions of them.

If you have not got a pedigree cat, do not worry. There is a Household Pet Class at many shows in which prizes go to the prettiest or most characterful individuals.

The Show

The first cat show on record was held as part of an English fair in 1598, but serious showing really only began in 1871, with a large show at London's Crystal Palace for British Shorthair and Persian types.

At about the same time as the first British show, the first American cat show was held in New England for the Maine Coon breed. British cat shows are still run on the same lines as the early ones, with judges going to the pens. Later, some shows had a ring class with cats on leads being paraded around a ring by their owners – you can imagine the fracas that often ensued!

HOW SHOWS ARE ORGANIZED

Each country has a controlling authority for all the cat clubs and societies. In Britain this is the Governing Council of the Cat Fancy (GCCF). In Australia there are two registering bodies: the Co-ordinating Cat Council and the Australian Cat Federation. In New Zealand the largest is the New Zealand Cat Fancy Incorporated. These bodies approve breed standards, provide the registration of pedigrees and transfer of ownership, and approve show dates.

When you apply for a show, you will be sent a schedule giving details of the show

FAMED BREEDER Mrs W Eame Colburn, America's most famous cat breeder, with her champion cat called Paris in 1901.

rules and classes, together with an entry form. Show rules are laid down to ensure fairness and to protect the interests of the cats. For example, the use of any colouring matter that could alter a cat's appearance is prohibited. If a cat is unable to be handled, or if it bites or scratches a judge, the veterinary surgeon, or the steward, it will be regarded as fractious. After three reports of such behaviour the cat will be disqualified from future showing. Also, some cat clubs insist that after showing a cat you must wait 14 days before exhibiting it again.

BRITISH SHOWS AND CLASSES

In Britain there are three types of show: Championship, Sanction, and Exemption.
Championship: This is the major show event and attracts the very finest of felines. Probably the largest championship in the world is the National Cat Club Show, held in London, with over 2,000 entries. Challenge certificates are awarded to Open-Class winners if of a high quality. A cat with three certificates is eligible for the Champion of Champions Class. A three-time winner of this class becomes a Grand Champion.
Sanction: These shows follow the same rules as Championship shows but challenge certificates are not awarded.
Exemption: At Exemption shows, regulations are not applied so stringently. Such shows are ideal for beginners.

In British shows there are usually four class categories – the Open, Side, Club, and Household Pet classes.
Open Class: This is the most important class, and is open to all pedigree-registered cats, neuters, and kittens.
Side Class: Exhibits usually have to be entered in at least four classes, and these can include the various Side Classes.
Club Class: Sponsored by particular cat clubs, these classes are for members only.
Household Pet Class: This class is solely for neuters of unknown or unregistered parentage.

AUSTRALIAN SHOWS

There is a number of different types of cat show run by various clubs throughout Australia, and procedures vary from club to club. The usual classes of cat show are: the all-breeds championship, catering for every pedigree breed; all longhair and all shorthair shows run by specialist cat breed clubs, exhibitions at which no challenges are awarded; and shows for one particular breed only. Show standards are extremely high, so study the breed standards carefully before you decide to exhibit. If your cat or kitten is obviously only "pet type" (displaying any of the faults listed in the standard), it is a waste of time and

AN EARLY SHOW This photograph depicts one of the early English cat shows, held in Richmond.

HOW A SHOW CAT IS JUDGED

Pedigree cats are judged against a scale of 100 points given for features matching the breed standard. Here are the marking systems used for champion Blue Longhairs and champion Siamese.

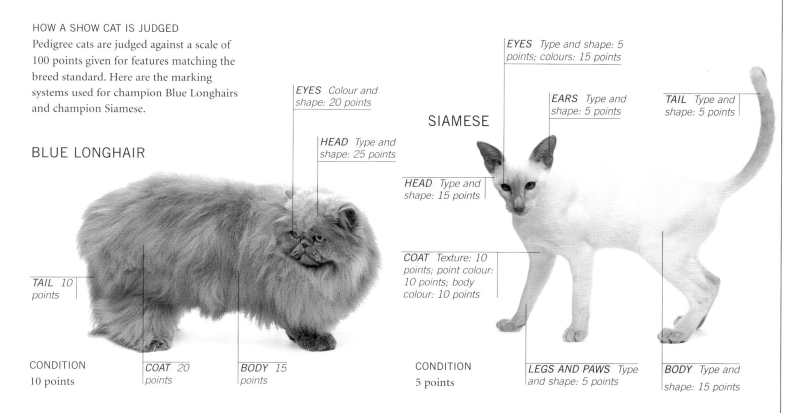

BLUE LONGHAIR

EYES Colour and shape: 20 points

HEAD Type and shape: 25 points

TAIL 10 points

CONDITION 10 points

COAT 20 points

BODY 15 points

SIAMESE

EYES Type and shape: 5 points; colours: 15 points

EARS Type and shape: 5 points

TAIL Type and shape: 5 points

HEAD Type and shape: 15 points

COAT Texture: 10 points; point colour: 10 points; body colour: 10 points

CONDITION 5 points

LEGS AND PAWS Type and shape: 5 points

BODY Type and shape: 15 points

money entering it in a show. However, a novice has to learn, so try your luck if you think you have a fair type of feline.

PREPARING YOUR CAT FOR THE SHOW

- Make sure that your cat is vaccinated in good time before the show. Do not take your cat to a show if it is not in peak condition.
- Accustom your cat to being penned and handled. Put it into a pen for a few minutes a day to begin with and gradually extend the time. Let other members of the family and strangers handle the cat regularly in order to avoid embarrassing displays of aggression or panic when the show judge handles it.
- Accustom your cat to car travel. Car sickness can produce symptoms that mimic those of true illness and may make the cat most unwelcome at the show.
- Give the cat regular grooming sessions and inspections of eyes, ears, mouth, bottom, and feet.

GROOMING

The coat of a longhair should be full and "fluffed up" *(see p.176)*. Do not use grooming powder if the show is less than two days away since traces of powder in the coat will be penalized. If your cat's coat is white or has a lot of white patches in it, you can brush in a chalk-based powder to enhance the whiteness, but make sure you brush it all out. If your cat's coat is black, tortie, or any other dark colour combination, do not use white powder since it is difficult to remove and flattens the colours. If you feel it necessary, use fuller's earth then bay rum conditioner.

Groom shorthaired cats in the usual way *(see p.175)*, using bay rum conditioner instead of powder. To give the coat a final gloss, polish it with velvet or chamois leather.

FEEDING

If you are showing a kitten, you would usually be best advised to feed it before you leave. Otherwise, wait until after the show is over. If you do decide to feed your cat beforehand, give it meat or tinned cat

food, not milky food that may precipitate an upset stomach and spoil the day for both you and your cat.

WHAT TO TAKE

When taking your cat to a show, you will also need to take the following:
- White litter tray
- Newspaper and litter for tray
- White show blanket
- White feeding dish
- White water bowl
- Bottle for carrying water
- Tally (the small white disc with the cat's show entry number)
- White ribbon or elastic for attaching the tally to the cat's neck
- Travelling container
- Blanket for travelling
- Cat food
- Disinfectant and cloth
- Brushes and combs
- Schedule of classes entered
- Entrance ticket and pass-out card
- Vetting-in card

BRITISH AND AUSTRALIAN SHOWS

The first thing that happens at the show is vetting-in, in which the vet gives each cat a thorough health check. If for some reason – such as runny eyes, fleas, or sore gums – the cat fails the examination, you will have to take it home and forfeit your entry fee. You may have to show your vaccination certificate to the vet, so be sure to have it with you.

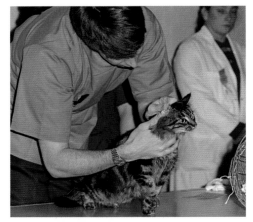

FIRST THINGS FIRST The vetting-in process is generally discontinued in the United States.

Putting your cat in its pen

After vetting-in, you take your cat to its pen – a metal cage displaying the same number as that on the cat's tally. Although the show organizers will have checked that the cages are clean, it is best to play safe by wiping down the bars with some non-toxic disinfectant. Arrange the blanket, litter tray, and filled water bowl in the pen. In Britain and Australia these are the only items allowed in with the cat.

FINAL CHECKS
- Check that the tally is securely tied around your cat's neck.
- Give the cat its final grooming.
- Check the corners of its eyes, and clean them if necessary.
- If you have fed the cat in the pen, remove the bowl and change the litter in the tray.
- Place the cat basket under the bench with the name tag hidden.

Judging

Before the judging, the steward arranges the judge's mobile table, checking that it has a filled disinfectant spray bottle and paper towels. He or she will also check that all the cats are in the right pens.

When judging commences, the steward takes the first cat out of its pen, places it on the table, and allows the judge to make his or her assessment. Before the next cat appears, the table is disinfected.

For each of the pedigree breeds there is a standard of points against which the cat will be assessed *(see p.207)*. In the case of a household pet, where there is no scale of points, the cat will be judged on condition, grooming, colouring, attractive features, and temperament when handled.

After examining each cat, the judge writes his or her comments in a judging book. A judging slip is then placed on the award board. If a slip is marked with "CC", the cat has been awarded a challenge certificate. When all the entries have been assessed, each judge nominates a best cat, neuter, and kitten from the exhibits he or she has judged. Then awards such as Best Cat, Best Neuter, Best Kitten, and Best in Show are decided.

A winning cat has an award card placed on its cage. Prizes may be small amounts of money or rosettes.

BEING JUDGED This handsome entrant at a British cat show is being thoroughly examined.

A GREAT SUCCESS Rosettes decorate the cage of a feline winner in a British show.

AMERICAN SHOWS

While British show organizers remain sticklers for caution, in North American shows vetting-in has generally been discontinued, and the exhibitor is trusted to bring only healthy cats. This is mainly because show organizers have found that the owners of pedigree breeds think far too much of their cats to enter an obviously sick individual. In any case, the vet cannot detect infectious diseases in their early stages. Vaccination is the best safeguard against the spread of infection, although it remains true that wherever there is a high concentration of cats, the transmission of infectious diseases is made easier. If a sick cat is brought, the show manager may tell the owner to leave the show and take the animal to a vet, together with all other entries from the same home. The cats may re-enter the show if the owner can produce a certificate of fitness signed by a vet.

The judges do not visit the cats in their pens, and owners are permitted to furnish and decorate them. Some enthusiasts take the interior design of their cat's show-quarters to extremes. It is possible to buy custom-made sets of pen linings in gold lamé, lace, satin, velvet, and even ostrich feathers, at prices of up to £150 or more.

To protect cats against damage or even fatal injury by jealous competitors, some owners use security cages with built-in ventilation fans and air-filters.

Setting up

When you arrive at the show, the first thing to do is to check in at the table, which is usually set just by the show-hall door. You will receive an envelope with your cat's cage/catalogue number in it and a catalogue. Sometimes the catalogues are free, but there may be a small charge.

On a board you will find a benching chart – a plan showing the layout of the rows of benches with the owners' names inscribed on their positions. (Cats are not benched according to breed because exhibitors may bring more than one breed.) It is a good idea, particularly if you have lots of cat luggage, to move everything to your allotted space on a lightweight wheeled trolley.

The show is usually laid out so that all the shorthairs are in one section and all the longhairs are in another. Chairs are provided for exhibitors.

Judging

Now all you have to do is wait for the judging to start. By referring to the judging schedule, you will be able to calculate roughly when you will be called. Each judge has his or her own ring, with its own cages (often about ten), a table with a formica (or other washable) riser on it to raise the standing cat up to a more convenient level, and a supply of paper towels, disinfectant, and show ribbons. Each judge also has a

EXPLORING HIDDEN DEPTHS An American judge uses a feather to encourage a cat to show off its best points.

"judge's book", which lists the breed, sex, birth date, colour class, colour, and status (Open, Champion, Grand) of the cat.

At the side of the judge's table sits the clerk, often accompanied by an assistant or trainee clerk. It is their job to mark the catalogues, which judges may not see until the show is over, take the appropriate numbers for each cat, and put them on the top of a ring cage in a slot provided, so that they stand up and are visible.

The cats are benched so that male alternates with female, or that a space of at least one empty cage separates adjacent males. The cages are wiped and disinfected between cats by the ring stewards as the classes progress.

There is usually a microphone on each judge's table and the clerk uses this call the cats to the ring. You must listen for your number; if you do not arrive after a third and final call, the number will be taken down and your cat marked "absent". When called you carry your cat to the ring and place it in the cage above which its number is displayed. The judge is not supposed to know whose cat is whose, and owners should not speak to him. If you have something to convey, speak to the clerk or hand him a written note.

The cat is taken from its cage by the judge and placed on the riser on the table for evaluation. The animal will be picked up, turned around, and set down again. US judges do not open the cat's jaws in order to check bite (tooth alignment). Some judges call for the owner to take the cat out of the cage, place it on the table, and put it back, in order to avoid being bitten. Some judges disqualify a cat (from that ring only) if bitten.

THE JUDGE'S CIRCLE At an American show, each cat is taken, when its number is called, to the ring of the judge concerned, and the judging is done in public.

JUDGING ON THE MOVE At the National Cat Club Show in Great Britain the judge moves from pen to pen, using a mobile table to examine each entrant. The results are then displayed on an award board.

The Cat and the Law

It is a great privilege to be owned by a cat, and one that entails a number of legal responsibilities. Although many non-pedigree cats are unwanted, and considered by the uninitiated to be of little value, each and every one is worthy of the esteem due to all sentient living creatures. Although they have less protection under the law than dogs, cats nevertheless do have certain inalienable rights, and we owners take on legal responsibilities when cats share their lives with us.

Neglect, or inflicting suffering on a cat, can result in legal prosecution in the UK (under the Cruelty to Animals Act). Included in the interpretation of "neglect" and "suffering" are failing to provide medical treatment when a cat is ill or injured, not making provision for it when going away on vacation, and keeping it in unsuitable conditions. It is worth reiterating that drowning unwanted newborn kittens is not an acceptable method of humane euthanasia but, rather, constitutes an act of culpable cruelty.

BUYING AND SELLING CATS

In Britain, no licence is at present needed for breeding, selling, or buying cats, but there are some restrictions on the sale of cats. Pedigree cats must be as described on their registration papers and must not have any serious illness at the time of their purchase, otherwise the purchaser may sue the vendor for compensation.

DAMAGE CAUSED BY CATS

You are not liable for acts of trespass by your cat, nor for any damage that it causes as a result of its normal feline inclinations, or if it is provoked. You will not, for instance, be obliged to make reparation if your cat digs up the neighbour's newly planted annuals while constructing an alfresco toilet.

ROAD ACCIDENTS

Under British law, anyone involved in a road accident with a dog must report it to the police, but this is not mandatory in the case of a cat. Nevertheless, if a cat is injured in an accident and is not given first aid, a prosecution for cruelty might ensue.

In Australia, state variations apply to laws regarding cats involved in motor accident injuries. But generally speaking, if someone runs over your cat, they are required by law to stop and make some sort of provision for the animal and to try to find the owner. If the cat is dead, the motorist's only responsibility is to move it off the road. The offence, basically, is in not stopping.

In New Zealand, the driver must try to make provision for the animal and is obliged to inform the police.

TRAVELLING WITH A CAT

In Great Britain, when travelling by road with a cat, it is an offence not to have the animal restrained by another passenger or confined to a carrying container.

Import and export of cats entails observance of strict health and quarantine rules, which are laid down by the particular countries involved. For more information, refer to the section The Travelling Cat *(see pp.170–73)*.

The local regulations allow free exchange between Australia and New Zealand. Any animals coming from the UK and Ireland that are not registered under PETS *(see pp.170–73)* must undergo two months' quarantine in Australia; none in New Zealand. Entry from Hawaii entails four months' quarantine in Australia, six months in New Zealand; from other Pacific countries the quarantine period is nine months in both cases. Animals from all other countries must undergo six months' quarantine in either the UK or Hawaii, and one months' further residence there, followed by two months' quarantine in Australia or New Zealand.

CAT THIEVES

Cat theft and receiving stolen cats (yes, cats are still snatched, not so much for laboratory use as for the value of their skins and even to be sold to unsuspecting butchers, when the carcass has been dressed as wild rabbit!) are criminal offences. However, adopting a cat can also be termed "stealing", so beware if you decide to take in a cat that visits you regularly – it may well be the legal property of someone living nearby. A cat owner can legally reclaim an adopted cat at any time up to six years after it has disappeared. The best way to prove ownership is by having your cat microchipped *(see p.173)*.

Theft is a criminal offence – but ownership of a cat in Australia and New Zealand is difficult to establish. In some states of Australia, cats are regarded as naturally wandering animals and proof of ownership cannot apply for the ordinary pet. Even in the case of pedigree felines with registration papers, it still is not easy. If you are looking after an apparent stray, as a matter of social responsibility you should always try to find out who it belongs to. But once a cat has moved away from its home territory, the owner cannot reclaim it as of right.

Useful Contacts

BREED REGISTRIES

Cat Fanciers' Association (CFA)
www.cfainc.org

Governing Council of the Cat Fancy (GCCF)
Tel: 01278 427 575
http://ourworld.compuserve.com/homepages/
GCCF_cats

The International Cat Association (TICA)
www.tica.org

Traditional Cat Association, Inc. (TCA)
www.traditionalcats.com

The Winn Feline Foundation, Inc.
The health-research arm of the Cat Fanciers' Association
www.winnfelinehealth.org

UK AND IRELAND

Animal Aunts
Britain's largest pet- (and house-) sitting agency
Tel: 01730 821529
www.animalaunts.co.uk

The Association of Pet Behaviour Counsellors
PO Box 46,
Worcester WR8 9YS
Tel: 01386 751151
www.apbc.org.uk

British Small Animal Veterinary Association
Woodrow House, 1 Telford Way,
Waterwells Business Park,
Quedgeley,
Gloucester GL2 4AB
Tel: 01452 726 700
www.bsava.com

Cats Protection
17 Kings Road, Horsham,
West Sussex RH13 5PN
Tel: 08702 099 099; www.cats.org.uk

DEFRA – Department for Environment, Food, and Rural Affairs
For information on the Pet Travel Scheme.
Tel: 0870 241 1710

Feline Advisory Bureau
Tel: 0870 742 2278; www.fabcats.org

Irish Veterinary Association
53 Lansdowne Road, Ballsbridge,
Dublin 4, Ireland
Tel: (353) 1 668 5263

People's Dispensary for Sick Animals (PDSA) (Head Office)
Whitechapel Way, Priorslee,
Telford, Shropshire TF2 9PQ
Tel: 01952 290999
www.pdsa.org.uk

Royal College of Veterinary Surgeons
www.rcvs.org.uk

RSPCA – Royal Society for the Prevention of Cruelty to Animals
Wilberforce Way, Southwater,
Horsham, West Sussex RH13 9RS
Tel: 0870 3335 999
www.rspca.org.uk

ISPCA (Ireland)
300 Lower Rathmines Road,
Dublin 6, Ireland
Tel: (353) 1 497 7874
www.ispca.ie

SSPCA (Scotland)
Braehead Mains,
603 Queensferry Road,
Edinburgh EH4 6EA, Scotland
Tel: 0131 339 0222
www.scottishspca.org

USPCA (Ulster)
PO Box 103, Belfast BT6 8US, Northern Ireland
Animal Helpline: 08000 28 00 10
www.uspca.co.uk

For information on microchips and the Pet Travel Scheme:
www.identichip.co.uk

Petlog – National Microchip Register
PO Box 2037, London W1A 1GP
Tel: 020 7518 1000; www.petlog.org.uk

AUSTRALIA

Australian Vet Association
PO Box 371, Artarmon
NSW 1570
Tel: (61) 2 9411 2733
www.ava.com.au

Australian Cat Federation
PO Box 2151, Rosebud Plaza,
Victoria 3939
Tel: (61) 3 5986 1119
www.acf.asn.au

RSPCA Australia
PO Box 265, Deakin West,
Australian Capital Territory 2600
Tel: (61) 2 6282 8300
www.rspca.org.au

Index

Acknowledgments

AUTHOR'S ACKNOWLEDGMENTS
Many, many thanks are due to my editors at Dorling Kindersley, Deirdre Headon and Simon Tuite, and to the rest of the magnificent staff at DK who must have all things feline engraved on their hearts after the past months' labours. Also to my researchers and typists – Chris, Liz, Nicola, and Penny – and my colleagues in the International Zoo Veterinary Group, to my sister-in-law Niki Levy (and her great cat, Cagney), and my family who put up with me working on the book in the early hours of the morning.

Thanks are also due to all the lovers of cats that I know – and they number many hundreds – for encouraging me in what they insisted was a worthwhile task, and to all the cats I've had the pleasure of working with – from Buck Tooth, who tragically died in a timber-yard fire behind my old surgery in Rochdale, to the tigers of Windsor Safari Park and the Atlas lions of the Zoo de la Casa de Campo, Madrid, Spain.

PUBLISHER'S ACKNOWLEDGMENTS
Dorling Kindersley would like to thank: Daphne Negus, editor/publisher of Cat World ™ International, who provided much expert advice on the US cat scene; Margaret Stephenson, assistant secretary of the Royal Agricultural Society Cat Control, who supplied information on the Australian cat scene; Karen Tanner, of Intellectual Animals, for locating the cats to be photographed in the studio and for her feline expertise; Jan Beaumont; Eileen Fryer; Kim Taylor; Carolyn Woods; Ann and Arabella Grinsted; Georgina Parker and Family; the Covent Garden Pet Centre and P E Hatch for supplying materials; Jan Croot and Anne Lyons for picture research; and Ella Skene for the index.

PACKAGER'S ACKNOWLEDGMENTS
Sands Publishing Solutions would like to thank: Hilary Bird for revising the index; David Roberts at DK Cartography for sourcing the map on p.9.

PHOTOGRAPHIC CREDITS
Key: b = bottom; c = centre; l = left; r = right; t = top
Agence Nature/NHPA: p.13 r
Animals Unlimited/Paddy Cutts: pp.17 t, 18 r, 21 t, 45 br, 52 l, 60 t, 63 br, 64 bl, 67 br, 69 br, 74 t, 75 cr, 93 br, 113 br, 114 tr, 115 tl, 119 tc, 123 tr, 125 t, 171 t, 208 1; Animals Unlimited: p.125 b
Ardea London: pp.164 t, 178 l, 159 t; Ardea London/John Daniels: pp.139 tr, b, 208 tr
By permission of the British Library: p.206
Jane Burton: pp.10 l, t, b, 11 tr, 12, 13 l, b, 14, 15, 17 r, b, 18 t, l, 19 l, 20 bl, br, 21 b, 22 t, 23, 25, 26, 27 t, 156–158, 162, 163 b, 166 t, 168 t, 174 tr, 178 r, 179 b, 180 t, 182, 188–201, 204, 205 b
Chanan Photography: pp.82 t, b, 151 tl, tr, 208 b, 209 bl
Bruce Coleman: pp.8 (except bc), 124 b; Jane Burton/Bruce Coleman: pp.11 tl, 16 t, 24 l, 167 t, 179 t, 184 b, Hans Reinhard/Bruce Coleman: pp.22 b, 24 r, 26 t, 55 tr, 78 cr, t, 90 br, 135 c, 169 br, 183 b, Kim Taylor and Jane Burton/Bruce Coleman: p.16 r
Corbis: Yann Arthus-Bertrand pp.28 tl, tr, bl, br, 29 tl, bl, 86 c, 186; Darrell Gulin pp.35 cr, 202; Jule Habel p.34 c; Lester Lefkowitz p.33; Dan Mason pp.2, 87 tr; Roy Morsch p.5; PBNJ Productions p.6; Dale C Spartas p.35 tl
Geoscience Features Picture Library: p.168 b
Getty Images/Walter Hodges: p.154
Marc Henrie ASC (London): pp.26 l, 49 bl, 51 cr, 66 bl, 67 tr, 68 bl, 78 tr, 85 br, 96 t, 97 br, 101 br, 103 tl, 107 tr, 114 bl, 119 tl, 123 cr, 130 bl, c, 131 tl, 183 t, 184 t, 205 c
Dorothy Holby: pp.109 b, 110 bl, 127 br, 152 tr
Pete Turner/Image Bank: p.27 b
Vicky Jackson: p111 tl
Eric Jenkins: pp.70 bl, br, 122 bl
Larry Johnson: pp.129 bl, 209 t, br
Dave King: pp.1, 8 bc, 16 r, 19 r, 25 tr, 31 t, 32, 36–48, 49 t, l, 50, 51 t, bl, 52 r, 53, 54, 55 l 56–59, 61, 62, 63 tl, 64 r, 65, 66 t, 67 l, 68 t, 69 l, tr, 70 t, 71–73, 74 b, 75 t, b, 76, 77 tl, 79 t, b, 85 l, tr, 88, 89, 90 t, bl, 91, 92, 93 t, 94, 95, 96 b, 97 tr, 99–100, 101 tr, 102, 103 c, r, 104, 105, 106, 107 tl, b, 108, 112, 113 t, bl, 114 cr, 115 tr, 116–118, 119 b, tr, 120, 121 t, br, 122, 123 tl, 126 l, tr, 127 bl, tr, 128, 129, 130 tr, br, 131 tr, cr, br, 132–134, 138, 152 b, 153, 159, 160 tl, bl, 161 tl, 163 t, 165 t, 170 l, 171 b, 174 tc, tl, b, 175 t, l, 176, 177, 205 t, l, 207
Simon Murrell: p.175 br
Robert Pearcy: pp.85 cr, 109 t, 121 bl, 123 br
Spectrum Colour Library: pp.168 l, 170 r
Warren Photographic/Jane Burton pp.30 br, 87 cr, 173 tr
Tetsu Yamazaki: pp.30 bc, 80 bl, 81 tl, 83 b, 110 c, 111 tr, cr, 137 tr, b, 146 b, 147 tl, br, 148 b, 149 tl, c, 150 c
Zefa: pp.20 t, 84 t, 124tr

All other images © Dorling Kindersley
For further information see: www.dkimages.com

STUDIO CATS

p.1
Birman kittens
Litter of Kamasaki Midnight's Child
owned by Karen Tanner

pp.36–7
Black Longhair
Ryshworth Inky Dink
owned by Rose Cook

p.38
White Longhairs
Doleygate Clarino and Doleygate Chaconne
owned by Fred and Freda Greenhill

p.39
Cream Longhair
Downswood Emily
owned by Coral Allam

pp.40–41
Blue Longhair
Grand Premier Doleygate Pacesetter
owned by Fred and Freda Greenhill

p.42
Red Self Longhair
Premier Downswood Red Baron
owned by Fred and Freda Greenhill

p.43
Blue-Cream Longhair

Gablemist Ophelia
owned by Janet Fagg

pp.44–5
Chinchilla Longhair
Ginaliza Eaton Princess
owned by Mrs E Charles

pp.46–7
Cream Cameo Longhair
Premier Jandora Casino Royale
Tortie Cameo Longhair
Jandora Caleidoscope
owned by Mrs Jan Beaumont

p.48 Black Smoke Longhair
Nosredna Excalibur
owned by Mrs P Craven

p.49
Black-and-White Bicolour Longhair
Amilynd Eastend Wicksie
owned by Janet Fagg

pp.50–51
Blue Tabby Longhair
Jindivik Ferniste
owned by Mrs Burgess
Brown Tabby Longhair
Jindivik Cala Manda
owned by Mrs H Howe

pp.52–3
Tortoiseshell Longhair

Llegamos Dixie
owned by Mrs Burgess

pp.54–5
Tortoiseshell-and-White Longhair
Pergoda Lotus Blossom
owned by Rose Cook and Gordon Cady

pp.56–7
Seal-point Colourpoint Longhair
Samoto Louise
owned by Fred and Freda Greenhill
Blue-point Colourpoint Longhair
Grand Premier Omicron Prima Donna
owned by Eileen Fryer
Seal Tabby-point Colourpoint Longhair
Zibaroue Gizzamo
owned by Janet Fagg

pp.58–9
Pewter Longhair
Premier Jandora Silver Crusader
owned by Mrs Anna Lodwig

pp.60–61
Lilac Longhair
Champion Catricat Lilac Limerick
owned by Mrs Carol Noel

pp.62–3
Chinchilla Golden Longhair
Catricat Golden Charm
owned by Mrs Carol Noel

pp.64–5
Blue-point Birman
Gazella Everso Chumley
owned by Karen Tanner
Birman Kittens
Litter of Kamasaki Midnight's Child
owned by Karen Tanner

pp.66–7
Seal-point Ragdoll
Grand Champion Pandapaws Rag Fearless Fred
owned by Mrs Sue Warde-Smith

pp.68–9
Lilac Tabby-point Balinese
Northstar Minkey
owned by Anne Heslop

pp.70–71
Turkish Van
Champion Cheratons Antigone
owned by Mr and Mrs Brett Hassel

p.72
Chocolate Tabby Oriental Longhair (Angora)
Rocques Wotinelizat
owned by Mrs R Beauhill

p.73
Tiffany/Chantilly
Kartush Abeche
owned by Mrs Southwell

pp.74–5
Silver Sorrel Somali
Pandapaws Peach Melba
owned by Mrs Dawn Lingley

pp.76–7
Brown Tabby Maine Coon
Majanco Moshatel
owned by Mr and Mrs Tex Morgan

pp.78–9
Blue Smoke Norwegian Forest Cat
Saqqara Fleur
owned by Mrs Pamela Wallsgrove

pp.84–5
Non-pedigree Tabby Longhair
Suki
owned by Mrs Melanie Munns

pp.88–9
British Black Shorthair
Tapestry Moon Shadow
owned by Mrs Julie Avery

p.90
British White Shorthair
Cherubin Snowberry
owned by Mrs J Avery

p.91
British Cream Shorthair
Millcoombe New Moon Rits
owned by Mrs Pat Richards
Britsh Cream Shorthair kitten
Cherubin Honey
owned by Mrs J Avery

pp.92–3
British Blue Shorthair
Adiuesh Malletts Mallett
owned by Mrs Christine Mainstone

pp.94–5
British Blue-Cream Shorthair
Camille
owned by Mrs J Avery

pp.96–7
British Red Tabby Shorthair
Dubolly Raymor Red
owned by Miss E Button

pp.98–9
British Tortoiseshell Shorthair
Champion and Grand Premier Czarist Cascade
owned by Mrs Joan Walls

pp.100–1
British Silver Spotted Shorthairs
Premier Khaffra Silver Bojangles
Khaffra Burlington Bertie
both owned by Mrs Rosemary Evans

pp.102–3
British Blue-and-White Bicolour Shorthair
Champion Cherubin Arlene
British Cream-and-White Bicolour kitten
Cherubin Sherlock
British Blue-and-White Bicolour kitten
Cherubin Sugarberry
all owned by Mrs J Avery

p.104
British Black Smoke Shorthair
Premier Tolray Phoenix
owned by Mrs Joan Carthy

p.105
British Black-tipped Shorthair
Champion Brocton's Macgowan
owned by Mr and Mrs Tex Morgan

pp.106–7
Tortoiseshell-and-White Manx
Grand Champion Jindivik
Rainbow's End
owned by Mrs Burgess
Manx kitten
Manninagh King
owned by Melinda Rowe

pp.108–9
Van Pattern American Shorthair
Linkret Tequila Sunrise
owned by Mrs Maureen Trompetto

pp.112–13
Blue Tabby Exotic Shorthair
Jindivik Davallia
owned by Mr and Mrs McGuire
Colourpoint Exotic Shorthair
Boadicat Gypsy Love
owned by Mrs J Avery

pp.114–15
Lilac-point Siamese
Tsuchiya Kumo
owned by Sue Roy

pp.116–17
Russian Blue
Mirakhan Afternoon Delight
owned by Karen Tanner

pp.118–19
Abyssinian
Grand Champion Iolas Akhenaten
Abyssinian kitten
Iolas Iolana
owned by Angel and John Wolfenden

p.120
Korats
Keiko Acrabat
Keiko Elvis
owned by Sandra Collicot

p.121
Havana
Khaffra Chocolate Truffle
owned by Mr and Mrs Morris Dean

pp.122–3
Burmese
Grand Champion Rumba Edelweiss
owned by Karen Tanner

pp.126–7
Red-point Tonkinese
Windermere High Noon
owned by Cherry Young

p.128
Bombay
Astabazy Prospero
owned by Billie Davis

p.129
Snowshoe
Linkret Arctic Slippers
owned by Mrs Trompetto

pp.130–31
Foreign Lilac Shorthair
Premier Khaffra Silveroberon
owned by Mrs Caroleen Iremonger
Oriental Chocolate Tabby Shorthair
Chocind Marbled Solitaire
owned by Mrs P Wallsgrove
Oriental Blue Tabby Shorthair
Khaffra Blueberry Pi
owned by P Wallsgrove

pp.132–3
Black-tipped Burmilla
Astahazy Jacynth of Kartush
owned by Karen Tanner
Brown-tipped Burmilla
Kamasaki Nice Nigel
owned by Mrs Nicola Cane

p.134
Chocolate Tortoiseshell Cornish Rex
Lohteyn Swansong
owned by Mrs Leo Heath

p.135
White Devon Rex
Grand Champion Chantrymere Lotus
owned by Mr and Mrs Morris Dean

p.138
Egyptian Mau
Khaffra Con Amore
owned by Mrs P Wallsgrove

pp.152–3
British Non-pedigree Ginger-and-White Shorthair
Baldrick
owned by Mrs Trompetto
British Non-pedigree Tabby Shorthair
Kremlin
owned by Lucy Alexander

p.174
British Blue-Cream Shorthair
Pretty Paws Crystal
owned by Mrs Eileen Fryer

p.176
Blue Longhair
Champion Sapajou Jolee
owned by Mrs Eileen Fryer

p.177
Cream Longhair
Champion Pretty Paws Candy Kisses
owned by Mrs Eileen Fryer